USING GAMES TO ENHANCE LEARNING AND TEACHING

CW01500313

Using Games to Enhance Learning and Teaching provides educators with easy and practical ways of using games to support student engagement and learning. Despite growing interest in digital game-based learning and teaching, until now most teachers have lacked the resources or technical knowledge to create games that meet their needs. The only realistic option for many has been to use existing games which too often are out of step with curriculum goals, difficult to integrate, and require high-end technology.

Using Games to Enhance Learning and Teaching offers a comprehensive solution, presenting five principles for games that can be embedded into traditional or online learning environments to enhance student engagement and interactivity. Extensive case studies explore specific academic perspectives, and featured insights from professional game designers show how educational games can be designed using readily accessible, low-end technologies, providing an explicit link between theory and practice. Practical in nature, the book has a sound theoretical base that draws from a range of international literature and research.

Nicola Whitton is a Research Fellow at Manchester Metropolitan University. She holds a doctorate in the use of educational games for learning and has recently led projects in the use of alternate reality games for student induction and gaming for older adults. More broadly, her research interests encompass learning and teaching innovation and the use of rich media and technology for learning.

Alex Moseley is an Educational Designer and University Teaching Fellow at the University of Leicester, where he has had long experience as both practitioner and researcher of course design and development for higher education. He has particular interests in online and distance education, games-based learning, museum education, student engagement, and provision of effective research skills. He designed a successful games-based approach to teaching historical research skills, and was also part of the team behind the first charity alternate reality game, *Operation: Sleeper Cell.*

USING GAMES TO ENHANCE LEARNING AND TEACHING

A BEGINNER'S GUIDE

EDITED BY
NICOLA WHITTON
AND
ALEX MOSELEY

Routledge
Taylor & Francis Group

NEW YORK AND LONDON

First published 2012
by Routledge
711 Third Avenue, New York, NY 10017

Simultaneously published in the UK
by Routledge
2 Park Square, Milton Park, Abingdon, Oxon OX14 4RN

Routledge is an imprint of the Taylor & Francis Group, an informa business

Library of Congress Cataloging in Publication Data
  Using games to enhance learning and teaching : a beginner's
  guide/[edited by] Nicola Whitton, Alex Moseley.
    p. cm.
  Summary: 'Until now, most teachers have lacked the resources and
  knowledge to create games that meet their needs. This book presents five
  principles that can be embedded into traditional or online learning and
  teaching to enhance engagement and interactivity'—Provided by publisher.
  Includes bibliographical references and index.
  1. Educational games.   2. Computer games.   3. Education—Computer network
  resources.   I. Whitton, Nicola.   II. Moseley, Alex.
  LB1029.G3U75 2012
  371.33'7—dc23
                                                                    2011039472

ISBN: 978-0-415-89771-6 (hbk)
ISBN: 978-0-415-89772-3 (pbk)
ISBN: 978-0-203-12377-5 (ebk)

Typeset in Minion Pro
by RefineCatch Limited, Bungay, Suffolk, UK

Contents

FIGURES

TABLES

Notes on Contributors

Nicola Whitton is a Research Fellow at Manchester Metropolitan University. She holds a doctorate in the use of educational games for learning and has recently led projects in the use of alternate reality games for student induction and gaming for older adults. More broadly, her research interests encompass learning and teaching innovation and the use of rich media and technology for learning.

Alex Moseley is an Educational Designer and University Teaching Fellow at the University of Leicester, where he has had long experience as both practitioner and researcher of course design and development for higher education. He has particular interests in online and distance education, games-based learning, museum education, student engagement, and provision of effective research skills. He designed a successful games-based approach to teaching historical research skills, and was also part of the team behind the first charity alternate reality game, *Operation: Sleeper Cell.*

Danielle Barrios-O'Neill is currently completing a doctoral research study on contemporary literature and interactive media at the University of Ulster. Her research integrates traditional critical methods with creative practice in the arts, with a view to fostering post-textual modes in both, where the boundaries determining genre are fluid. She is especially interested in the emergence of transmediality, hyper-dialogic forms, and integral semiotics in contemporary art works.

Simon Brookes is a Principal Lecturer in Enterprise Education at the University of Portsmouth. His main research interests lie in the use of games-based simulations for the provision of authentic learning contexts as well as in the broader field of games-based learning.

Alan Hook is a Lecturer in Interactive Media and Course Director of Interactive Media Arts at the University of Ulster. His research is primarily practice-lead and focuses on new and emerging digital media gravitating towards a praxis-driven investigation into games and play, with an interest in augmented, pervasive, and alternate reality gaming. His work investigates the dialogues that immersion and play have in shared spaces and how we engage with and through these practices with new technologies.

Michelle A. Hoyle is multi-faculty member at The Open University. As a course presentation chair in the Faculty of Mathematics, Computing and Technology, she authors and oversees a course on Open Source philosophies and development. In the Institute for Educational Technology, she's an associate lecturer on an accessible e-learning postgraduate course. Recently, she has been a critical reader and marker on courses involving virtual worlds and gaming. In her University of Sussex doctoral research, she is utilizing her online community background to investigate how communities form and contribute to persistence, motivation, and learning – key issues in distance education – in the massively multiplayer online game *World of Warcraft*. She plays a variety of traditional and digital games. You can find her on Twitter as @Eingang and as Elsheindra in *World of Warcraft* (EU).

Rosie Jones is the Learning Commons Development Manager at the University of Manchester. She is currently the Treasurer for CILIP's CSG Information Literacy Group and for the Librarians' Information Literacy Annual Conference (LILAC), the UK's biggest Information Literacy conference. In her previous role at Manchester Metropolitan University she was involved in the development of their first alternate reality game, where she was able to provide expertise on the design and implementation of student induction, particularly in the area of library and information literacy. She has also disseminated the outcomes of this project through various conferences and publications. She is particularly interested in investigating new and exciting ways to deliver core learning skills.

Katie Piatt has been working in the field of educational technology for over ten years, with a wealth of experience in development, implementation, and evaluation. Her PhD looked at staff attitudes to learning technologies, and she uses this experience to support and implement changes in academic computing at the University of Brighton. Her research focus is now on methods of student engagement, particularly regarding 'gamification' of undergraduate teaching and support materials. Recent projects include the award of a fellowship grant from the university to investigate the use of alternate reality game formats to support existing mechanisms for introducing new students to university information and services.

Sarah Smith-Robbins has for some time been an international thought leader on the use of multi-user virtual environments for educational purposes. She has published extensively on the subject and is co-author of *Second Life for Dummies* book, as well as being in demand as a public speaker. Her research focuses on the ways digital communities engage with one another via social technologies including social networks and virtual media. Currently, she is a member of the Marketing faculty at the Kelley School of Business and Indiana

University as well as being the Director of Emerging Technologies in Kelley's executive education.

Dave White manages the Technology Assisted Lifelong Learning unit at the University of Oxford. He has worked on many projects funded by the Joint Information's Systems Committee (JISC) assessing how individuals and groups engage with new forms of technology. This led to the development of the 'Visitors and Residents' typology of online engagement (White and Le Cornu, 2011). He was Principal Investigator for the Open Habitat project which explored small groups' use of online virtual worlds such as *Second Life*. The project generated the theory of 'Eventedness' (White and Le Cornu, 2010), which details the compelling nature of presence in immersive online environments and how this relates to notions of belonging. He has also undertaken research into the *World of Warcraft* massively multiplayer online game with a particular focus on how the game's social architecture draws individuals into ever more demanding roles, ultimately encouraging the formation of communities and a 'professional' attitude towards the game.

Peter Whitton has worked in UK Higher Education since 2001. Over this period he has had various roles supporting the use of technology for teaching and learning including time spent in design and development, project management, and academic development. Before working in HE, Peter spent 12 years as a commercial designer working for clients in the retail and financial services sectors. Peter's research interests include the use of multimedia for teaching, collaborative learning, and the potential of game spaces as learning environments. He is currently a Learning Technology Adviser at the University of Salford.

Notes on Guest Expert Contributors

Naomi Alderman is the author of three novels: *Disobedience, The Lessons*, and *Doctor Who: Borrowed Time*. She has won the Orange Award for New Writers and the *Sunday Times* Young Writer of the Year prize. She's also a games writer, was lead writer on puzzle alternate reality game *Perplex City* and has recently completed a language teaching game for the BBC. She writes regularly on games for the *Guardian*.

Richard A. Bartle is Professor of Computer Game Design at the University of Essex. He is best known for having co-written in 1978 the first virtual world, *MUD*, and for his 1996 Player Types model which has seen widespread adoption by the MMO industry. His 2003 book *Designing Virtual Worlds* is the standard text on the subject, and he is an influential writer on all aspects of online design and development. In 2010, he was the first recipient of the prestigious Game Developers Online Choice Award of Online Game Legend.

Jacob Habgood is now a Senior Lecturer in Game Development at Sheffield Hallam University. His games industry career spanned 14 years and includes a dozen published titles for all the major console gaming platforms. He studied his PhD in game-based learning at the University of Nottingham and was awarded his doctorate in 2007. His research interests focus on harnessing the motivational power of games for learning, as well as the affective motivational components of digital games themselves. He is the author of a popular series of books on hobbyist game development, beginning with *The Game Maker's Apprentice*.

Adrian Hon is co-founder and CEO at Six to Start, specializing in creating new forms of storytelling through ARGs, transmedia, or mobile and web-based games. Clients have included Disney, the BBC, Channel 4, and Penguin, and Six to Start has won multiple awards including Best of Show at SXSW. He also writes about technology for the *Daily Telegraph*, is writing a Kickstarter-funded book and blog called *A History of the Future in 100 Objects*, co-organizes the Hive Mind Challenge, and is the founder of Transmedia London. He studied Natural Sciences at Cambridge, specializing in experimental psychology and neuroscience.

Eric Klopfer is Associate Professor and the Director of the MIT Scheller Teacher Education Program (http://education.mit.edu) and the Director of The

Education Arcade (http://educationarcade.org). His research explores simulations and games on desktop computers as well as mobile devices like smartphones and tablets. Klopfer's work combines the construction of new software tools with implementation, research, and development of new pedagogical supports that transition the use of these tools to broader use in formal and informal learning. He is the co-author of the book *Adventures in Modeling: Exploring Complex, Dynamic Systems with StarLogo* and author of *Augmented Learning: Research and Design of Mobile Educational Games*. He is working on a new book about the intersection of academia and private industry around technology enabled classroom innovations. He is also the director of The Education Arcade, which is advancing the development and use of games in K-12 education, as well as co-founder and President of the non-profit Learning Games Network.

Nikki Pugh is an artist whose main area of enquiry is centred around interactions between people and place, often using tools and strategies from areas such as pervasive games and physical computing to set up frameworks and rulesets for exploration. Through the Creative Partnership programme she has spent three years working in primary schools designing and delivering immersive experiences that draw on elements of gaming to develop confidence with problem-solving and collaboration in staff and pupils alike. She co-founded and ran events through the Birmingham-based games network BARG and has also been commissioned by Hide&Seek and igfest. See http://npugh.co.uk/tag/schools/ and http://barg.org.uk/.

Kris Rockwell founded Hybrid Learning Systems in 2003. Prior to starting Hybrid, Kris worked for US Airways developing and implementing computer based training (CBT) and desktop simulation systems for the flight-training department. For the past eight years, Kris has focused on mobile learning content development and delivery and serious games. In addition to his work in the eLearning world, Kris has served as an adjunct teacher in the Multimedia Program at Duquesne University in Pittsburgh, PA. Additionally, he serves as the head of the sub-committee on Emerging Technologies Committee for the Aviation Industry CBT Committee (AICC), and presents his ideas and work internationally.

Jesse Schell is the CEO of Schell Games and a faculty member at the Carnegie Mellon University Entertainment Technology Center as well as the former Creative Director of the Disney Imagineering Virtual Reality Studio. He is the author of *The Art of Game Design: A Book of Lenses*, which *Game Developer* magazine named book of the year in 2008. Upon founding Schell Games he has continued to help design and develop interactive theme park attractions as well as widely recognized massively multiplayer online games and other projects.

Lee Sheldon is Associate Professor and Co-Director of the Games and Simulation Arts program at Rensselaer Polytechnic Institute. He has written and designed over 20 commercial video games and massively multiplayer online games. He has published two books: *The Multiplayer Classroom: Designing Coursework as a Game* and *Character Development and Storytelling for Games* (which is required reading by many game developers and in university game design programs). He is a contributor to several books on video games and regularly lectures and consults on game design and writing in the US and abroad. Before his career in video games he wrote and produced over 200 popular television shows, including *Star Trek: The Next Generation, Charlie's Angels*, and *Cagney and Lacey*. As head writer of the daytime serial *Edge of Night* he received a nomination for best writing from the Writers Guild of America. He has been twice nominated for Edgar Awards by the Mystery Writers of America. His first mystery novel, *Impossible Bliss*, was re-issued in 2004. Lee began his academic career in 2006 at Indiana University where he taught game design and screenwriting; first instituted the practice of designing classes as multiplayer games; worked on the serious games *Quest Atlantis* and *Virtual Congress*; and wrote and designed the alternate reality games *The Skeleton Chase* and *Skeleton Chase 2: The Psychic* funded by the Robert Wood Johnson Foundation; and *Skeleton Chase 3: Warp Speed* funded by Coca-Cola. He continues as creative director of the narrative-driven massively multiplayer online game *Londontown*; and is head of the team working to build the Emergent Reality Lab at Rensselaer. He was design consultant and lead writer on the upcoming casual massively multiplayer online game *Star Trek: Infinite Space*; and is currently writing a new Facebook social game for Zynga.

George Siemens is writer, theorist, speaker, and researcher on learning, networks, technology, analytics and visualization, openness, and organizational effectiveness in digital environments. He is the author of *Knowing Knowledge* and the *Handbook of Emerging Technologies for Learning*. He is currently a researcher and strategist with the Technology Enhanced Knowledge Research Institute at Athabasca University.

ACKNOWLEDGEMENTS

We would like to thank everyone who has provided us with support and advice during the writing of this book; in particular Juliette Culver for her insights and feedback.

We would also like to thank everyone who has kindly helped us to secure permission to use the screen shots and illustrations that feature throughout this book, in particular Kris Rockwell, Cathy Orr, and the nice people at Asymmetric Publications Ltd. Special thanks go also to Peter Whitton for contributing his original artwork to the book.

Grateful thanks also go to David Schaffer, Jane McGonigal, and Katie Salen for their support of this project.

Alex would like to give heartfelt thanks to his girls (Sarah-Ruth, Lizzie, and Katy) for their invaluable support and patience with the long nights of writing; his parents and brother for all the family games we played growing up; and finally special posthumous thanks to Alan McWhirr, who gave him some of the best examples of how to make learning fun.

Nicola would like to thank Peter and Daisy for their support throughout, particularly when she promised that she would never write another book.

Part I

BACKGROUND

1

INTRODUCTION

ALEX MOSELEY AND NICOLA WHITTON

'Games have always had a place in education. Every time a teacher says something like 'Bob has a problem. He needs to measure the height of a telephone pole, but he can't climb it. What should he do?' they have created a game. The entire educational system, with its scores, points, and grade levels is a game system, already. The key is to figure out how to best integrate games into education.'

Jesse Schell

As Jesse Schell nicely foregrounds, there are already countless games in education – from the simplest problem solving described above, to high-end commercially produced simulations which replace whole courses. Which is wonderful.

Until you decide, 'Yes, I'd like to see how games can work for me', and sit down to find out more about them. That's when you'll find that the websites, journal articles, books, and news sites cover an awful lot of the high-end side, and the barest whisper of the simple side. Which means that if you have a big budget and team of designers and programmers at your call, you're fine. But if you're a teacher, trainer, or lecturer who has a couple of hours tomorrow night and some card and felt-tips, you're not so fine. We felt that this needed redressing, which gave birth to the idea of this book.

Another assumption you'll find in much of the existing literature and rhetoric around games use for learning is that games are unequivocally perfect: they motivate learners, and provide all-inclusive action-packed elements which students will love you for. This is also representing just one end of the spectrum; clearly, if you tried to use Super Mario Brothers to teach History to undergraduates, for example, we doubt that much learning would take place, or that all students would find it motivating (many, in fact, might feel that it devalues the course they paid good money for). With this book we also wanted to question some of this perceived wisdom surrounding the use of games for learning, and provide a more measured view (whilst still retaining our enthusiasm for games in general and their use in *appropriate* contexts).

Our book therefore aims to look in detail at *whether* and *how* games can help learning in a variety of contexts, before giving practical advice, ideas, and case studies for their use in practice. We take two approaches: first, examining five of the characteristics of games that make them good for learning, and considering how to embed these within more traditional pedagogic practice; and second, showing how low-cost solutions to game development (in particular traditional games, alternate reality games (ARGs), and virtual worlds) can be used to enable anyone to create their own games for learning.

We place game development within the context of modern education: across most formal and informal education there are reduced budgets (and in some contexts, such as higher education, rising student numbers), an increase in administrative load, a rise in the use of targets or external accreditation, and other pressures. How can games help in this context, with the resources available to us as educators? We also acknowledge that successful games (in the sense of engaging their audience and being fun to play) require creative skill and experience: there is a multi-billion-pound games industry with specialists who are geared to making games fun and engaging. To capture and access some of this expertise, we interviewed a range of experts from the games industry – along with top creative thinkers or researchers in the field – and their tips and perspectives can be found throughout these pages at relevant points. These insightful quotations can be found highlighted in boxes at appropriate places throughout the main text.

In our aim to focus on *appropriate* use and availability of games techniques for educators, you will find we use, learn from and suggest uses for games from traditional board, card, or other genres, through new forms of *transmedia* or mixed-media games, to high-end forms such as simulations, virtual worlds or massively multiplayer online (MMO) games. Our focus throughout is on the elements of these games that are useful or interesting for learning, and how to make use of those elements within learning design and delivery.

We should note at this point that neither of us stay up late every night battling hordes in *World of Warcraft* (though some of our chapter authors and experts do, and we do play the odd board game, adventure game, or a quick *Angry Birds* on the train), nor do we claim to be game designers in a commercial sense. Our experience and expertise comes from our interest in what we can learn from games, and apply to a learning context. We are both researchers in this area, and practitioners who have used our findings to design and run games-based courses and activities within higher education, museum education, and charity contexts. While our work in these contexts is used as a basis for – and case studies within – these chapters, we widen out our scope to cover any form of education: including formal, informal, child, and adult. We have purposefully avoided covering young child development and learning through games, as there is already much literature around the value of play to child development and it would be counter-productive to attempt to cover that here.

Our principal theoretical background is unashamedly constructivist: the work of Piaget, Vygotsky, Bruner, Lave, and Wenger is included or implied in many of the chapters. Gaming can be an individual or shared experience, but always involves construction, synthesis, and application of knowledge (when you play a game you continually develop better or alternative approaches every time you play, lose, and win); and so it is a natural link for us to make between this and a constructivist model for learning. If you are unfamiliar with this approach to learning, games are a good way to begin to explore it – and in its own small way this book could form a useful primer for active and constructivist learning approaches.

There are six themes that recur throughout the book, and link much of the content:

- *Pedagogy* and effective active and collaborative approaches to learning through games is at the heart of much of this book. We believe that the use of games in education must be driven by the pedagogic goals and needs of the learners, rather than by the technology or game itself.
- *Integration* with curriculum is a key challenge. While there is a whole chapter dedicated to dealing with the important practical issues involved in using any games-based approaches within a formal academic structure, all other suggestions and approaches within the book are made with this consideration in mind.
- *Motivation* is a driver and challenge for the use of games and learning. While we, and our fellow chapter authors, share a love for games and believe they have a lot to offer the teacher and learner; we are also very aware that, in reality, not everybody plays games or would find a game within their course a wholesome element. All chapters therefore avoid making assumptions, and question 'universal truths' such as 'games are motivating'. Ideas and recommendations are made with particular contexts in mind, and carry appropriate warnings or workarounds for real teaching and learning environments. We also do not propose that games can be used for everything: there are some situations where games might offer no useful elements at all.
- *Affordability* of pedagogic approaches is a crucial question in the modern age of austerity. Games need to be seen to be value for money rather than simply expensive motivational gimmicks, and this issue is

one that is highlighted throughout, particularly through an emphasis on traditional games, multi-media environments, and virtual worlds.

- *Creativity* is needed to address the fact that learners (and teachers) are unique. Unlike the Henry Ford model, not all people learn in the same way; and as a result not all respond to learning activities in the same way. Games or game approaches in learning are not immune to this fact, and flexibility and variety is therefore an important part of any design process.
- *Technology* (and the lack of it) is also an important consideration. Depending on your own environment, you may have access to high levels of technology, or none; you may have technical, design, or programming teams available to you, may take on some of these roles yourself, or may have no recourse to these. Throughout the book we therefore aim to provide a broad spread of approaches – suggesting technology where appropriate, but providing as many approaches that require little or no technology or technical knowledge. Occupying a useful position in this gamut are new mixed-media approaches such as ARGs, where technology can be used where available or appropriate, but paper and pen could be just as effective.

Book Structure

The book is split into three major parts (which together reflect a logical design sequence) topped and tailed by introductory and concluding parts.

Part I: Background

Following this introduction, Chapter 2 draws from both education theory and game design principles to make a case for the role of games in learning. Our aim is to challenge existing stereotypes and provide a more compelling base from which to work.

Part II: Applying Game Principles to Education

In this first of the major parts, five chapters each take an aspect of games that we feel has particular usefulness in learning environments: challenge, communities, narrative, competition, and use of multiple media. For each, a theoretical background and summary of use within games is followed by practical suggestions about how the elements could be used within learning and teaching, whether as part of a game or in 'standard' teaching.

Part III: Creating Games for Learning

Building on Part II, the four chapters here focus on the development of games within educational environments. Three principal types of game (all low-cost and low in technical needs) are suggested throughout: traditional games, ARGs and virtual worlds; with a number of worked examples demonstrating how to build, and integrate into the curriculum, effective games for learning.

Part IV: Games in Practice

The final major part culminates in three games-based approaches to learning designs, where practitioners and researchers in the field describe how they have integrated the principles from Part II in real-world applications. We hope that these will provide inspiration, and a comforting proof that low-cost, highly-effective games *can* be built for education.

Part V: Conclusions

Bringing together the other parts of the book, the concluding chapter summarizes key themes that became apparent to us, as the book began to take shape, and looks ahead both to your own journey we hope you will now be equipped to make, and to the environment surrounding games and learning and how it might change in the future.

Fuller details of the three major parts, and how they fit together, are provided in short introductions preceding each.

How to Approach this Book

If you have limited awareness either of constructivist approaches to learning, or of the main areas of benefit games provide to education, we strongly suggest you begin by reading on through Chapter 2. This will equip you with the background you need to engage with the main parts of the book.

If, however, you are coming from a strong game design or educational design background, you may prefer to start with Parts II and III – picking particular features of games you would like to use in your learning designs. If you want to use elements from games within traditional teaching and learning, Part II is the one to focus on; whereas if you are interested in creating whole games, turn to Part III.

Our strong recommendation, however, is to treat the book as a linear narrative: if you can take the time to work through each part in order, you will be rewarded with a slowly building knowledge base which gradually feeds more developed ideas until you finish with the real world examples and application of theory in Part IV.

We have, however, designed the chapters in such a way that you can dip into each with very little knowledge of previous chapters – you should therefore, at any point in the future, be able to return to the chapter on, say, assessment to explore a particular problem within your learning environment and look for inspiration.

Expert Tips

In order to bring together our perspectives as researchers and educational practitioners with views from industry and experts in game design, we interviewed a number of experts in the games industry, creative industry, and academia (see Notes on Guest Expert Contributors for details). We have taken key quotes and tips from these interviews and placed them in appropriate contexts within the book, giving rich insights and creative sparks. In this way, we hope that this book will bring insights beyond the academic perspective about what games bring to education and how they can be designed effectively.

> 'In the best games, the designer is trying to say something that they can only say through the medium of the game. Game design is an art form. If you can say what you want to say using some other art form – a novel, a drawing, a movie – then you should do that instead. If you can only say it through a game, that's what makes the game powerful. It's passion and vision that makes a game. Sure, you need mechanics and genre and balance and so on, but it's the heart of the game that makes the difference between a curiosity and a revelation.'
>
> Richard Bartle

Web Resources

A number of extended resources (including links to the various case studies mentioned in the book and the full 'expert' interviews) to support your exploration of the concepts and examples covered are available at the following URL: http://gamesbook.playthinklearn.net/

We hope that this book will provide an easy path for anyone – regardless of existing knowledge, experience, or time – to see the value of game-based approaches for particular learning and teaching needs; and more importantly, to see a way forward which will allow you to develop them within local budgets and means. Building on a solid theoretical and games design base, the numerous suggestions and examples in chapters, as well as the expert tips, should provide all the argument and motivation you need.

From then, it's over to you: we hope that future articles and books will be able to report on many more examples of how games – in all shapes and sizes, from scribbles on paper to complex cross-media courses – have been used in many contexts, but always to improve the experience for learners.

With this book, we hope to have helped douse the old bonfire of rhetoric and uninformed truths around games and learning, re-laid the firewood, and applied a match to the kindling: it's now up to you to build and feed your own fires. Good luck!

2

GOOD GAME DESIGN IS GOOD LEARNING DESIGN

NICOLA WHITTON

Why Use Games for Learning?

In recent years there has been increasing interest in the use of games, and in particular computer games, for learning. There are many examples of their effective use in all stages of formal education. This includes work in primary schools such as the use of mind games to enhance strategic and reasoning skills (Bottino and Ott, 2006) or the use of brain-training software on game consoles (Miller and Robertson, 2010). Examples of effective game-based learning in secondary schools include the use of mobile games to teach history (Huizenga et al., 2009) and alternate reality games (ARGs) for language learning (Connolly et al., 2011). Games have also been used in further and higher education, in subjects as diverse as civil engineering (Ebner and Holzinger, 2007) and marketing theory (Whitton and Hynes, 2006). As well as in formal education, games have also been used successfully for training, work-based learning, and in informal contexts.

The value of games for learning does not stop simply with their use as vehicles for delivering learning. As well as the case where the educational content is within the game itself, games can also be used as a trigger for educational discussion or as a design activity where learning takes place through the design process. When we think of games for learning, it is often the image of high-end computer games that presents itself, but in fact simple digital games or traditional games such as card or board games can be used just as effectively, and at a fraction of the cost (Moseley, 2009a; Charlier and De Fraine, 2010).

We, as educators, can also learn a lot from the way in which games are designed to engage players and move them seamlessly from novice to expert. There is also a lot of potential in the idea of supporting learners themselves as game-builders, learning transferable skills – such as teamwork and collaboration – as well as design and development skills throughout the creation process.

While there are many examples of the use of games in education, a common rationale for their use is simply that learners find them motivational. However, this is often not the case, and there is a growing body of evidence that there are many learners – particularly other learners – who do not play games at all, who do not play the types of game most applicable to formal learning, or who simply do not feel that computer games are an appropriate way in which to learn (e.g. Whitton, 2007a; Bekebrede et al., 2011). In this chapter, I aim to provide a sound pedagogic rationale for the use of games in learning, beyond the notion that games are intrinsically motivational. I do not, however, argue that games are an educational panacea, and that while they can be an effective technique to support active and engaging learning in many situations, they cannot (and should not) replace the techniques that teachers have been using effectively for years.

> 'I certainly think that games have a place in education as another kind of tool available to teachers to stimulate learning, but I would have great reservations about replacing traditional teaching activities with game-based learning.'
>
> Jacob Habgood

First, I will briefly introduce a selection of learning and teaching theories that, I feel, resonate strongly with the potential of games for learning, and provide a far stronger basis for their use in education than the notion that it is what learners expect, or that they are motivating. Second, I will discuss six key advantages of games when applied to learning situations, which help to support and enhance the educational process. I aim to show how games and playful spaces can encapsulate a wide variety of learning theories, and use this as evidence that they can be a successful learning tool in both formal education and informal learning contexts, for children and adult learners alike.

Games and Learning Theory

In this second section, I aim to provide a whistle-stop tour of the key learning and teaching theories that I think are most pertinent to games, and which best provide theoretical evidence as to their appropriateness and efficacy for learning. In a short chapter such as this one, I don't even hope to provide a comprehensive overview of each theoretical stance, but simply to introduce the reader to the key concepts and ideas presented, and to relate them to the potential of games.

Constructivism

The dominant educational paradigm at the present time is the constructivist perspective; prior to this, as late as the 1950s, the behaviourist school of thought was predominant (Cooper, 1993). Constructivism puts forward the idea that learning is active and that learners construct their own knowledge about a subject through active engagement in learning by building on past knowledge and experiences (Bruner, 1966). Three precepts of constructivism are the ideas of: 'situated cognition'; 'cognitive puzzlement'; and 'social collaboration' (Savery and Duffy, 1995).

Situated cognition is the idea that people's understandings are developed through interaction with the environment, and that the context – as well as the content, goal, and nature of an activity – shapes an individual's construction of it. Games provide meaningful contexts for activity, which players can explore and make personal sense of; they allow the player to take part in authentic and purposeful tasks that map on to real world activities. Cognitive puzzlement suggests that perceived inconsistencies or conflicts of understanding provide a stimulus for learning; the key goal of many types of game is problem-solving of this nature, be it strategic planning, lateral thinking, or how to work as a team to defeat a powerful enemy. Social collaboration is the idea that we learn through social negotiation, testing our ideas on others and experiencing new ideas to challenge our own thinking. I believe that it is this social aspect of games that, increasingly, makes them such a powerful learning tool, whether it is by co-located players working together to solve an adventure game, virtual teams in multiplayer role-playing games, or simply the communities that develop around particular games or genres.

An important feature of the constructivist viewpoint is that learners should be empowered to have meta-cognition in the learning process; to understand why and how to learn, and to be aware of the approaches that suit them best. These ideas of learner responsibility for planning and structuring learning, and reflecting on the learning process, are not typically considered in the design of games for entertainment, but are important for educational games. By considering the context in which the game is used, and associated activities, this reflective and self-evaluative process can be supported. This goes against the notion in game-based learning of 'stealth learning' (Prensky, 2001), which suggests that games can be employed to make players learn without realizing it, because they are enjoying the game so much. In my opinion, this undermines the role of the learner, and does not get to the heart of the learning process; knowing that we have learned something is as important as learning it.

Behaviourist thinking is still very common in educational game design today. Behaviourists viewed the mind as a black box that could only be studied by observing changes in behaviour, where learning could be reinforced through rewards or punishments for desirable behaviour. This model forms the basis for many successful educational games: players are rewarded for successfully achieving game tasks, for example by moving up levels or for spelling words correctly. I suspect that there are two main reasons for the predominance of behaviourist learning games: first, they are relatively easy to design and build as they tend to be created using standard patterns; second, because they focus on relatively low-level learning outcomes, they are easy to evaluate (being generally quantitative), and the body of evidence as to their efficacy is larger. However, I believe that while there may be some merit in behaviourist games, simply focusing on this type of game really misses the potential of games for learning. While behaviourist games are effective for learning outcomes such as recognition and recall, it is by harnessing the full constructivist potential of games that we can best enable higher-level learning outcomes – such as analysis, synthesis, evaluation, problem-solving, and critical thinking – to be met.

Experiential Learning

One of the crucial things that games enable is for players to take part in an active experience: not simply to passively receive information, but to explore, try things out, and see the effects of their actions. The Experiential Learning Cycle (Kolb, 1984) puts forward the idea that students learn better by discovering and engaging in experiences for themselves, and eliciting their own meanings and understandings from these experiences. It emphasizes the importance of a cycle of actively undertaking a learning experience, personal reflection on the experience, relation of the new experience to what was previously known or understood (and possible reforming of conceptions), and planning the next experience in the light of what was learned.

This process puts experience at the heart of learning, in contrast to the more traditional model of learning followed by practical experience. Starting with experience allows learners to develop and test their own hypotheses and piece together their own models of the world. Computer games (and computers in general) are ideally suited to support this model of learning because of their ability to provide interaction and feedback, in addition to context and purpose. It is this interaction that is crucial to games; when a player makes an action it has (a usually immediate) effect and the player can then take further actions based on what has happened. Of course, the complexity of outcomes that can be modelled in a game will be no way as rich or varied as in the real world, but games (and simulations) allow learners to engage in and experience microcosms of reality that are both physically and cognitively safe. Chapter 8 covers the topic of designing authentic gaming experiences in much greater detail.

Collaborative Learning

The idea of learners working together, sharing ideas and opinions, and clarifying and reaching shared understandings is very powerful. It not only allows students to learn about the topic of interest, but also to learn key transferable skills such as communication, negotiation, and teamwork. Working collaboratively allows students to work to their strengths while learning from those who are more able in particular areas, to develop critical thinking and analytical skills, to think creatively and problem-solve, to rationalize and validate their ideas, and appreciate a range of learning styles, skills, preferences, and perspectives.

The 'Zone of Proximal Development' (ZPD) (Vygotsky, 1978) is a very useful way for theorizing learning that happens through interaction with others. The ZPD is the difference between what an individual can learn alone, and what he or she can learn when supported or guided by another person, for example a teacher, mentor, or more able student. I think this is a very useful notion when considering the ways in which experienced players support and tutor new players, through, for example, sharing equipment and tips or teaching the game etiquette.

When you think of collaborative gaming, the first image that springs to mind is often of multi-user networked games, but there are many effective ways of collaborating in games beyond the synchronous online play. For example, collaborative gaming would include two people playing on a console (or one person playing and one offering advice), a group working together to solve a puzzle; a family playing Monopoly; or an individual finding hints in an online game community. There is a longer discussion of the benefits and implications of collaborative gaming in Chapter 4.

These communities that develop around certain games or genres are also very interesting from a learning theory perspective. Gee (2003) calls them 'affinity groups', while they can also be considered 'communities of practice' (Lave and Wenger, 1991). Participating in these communities provides a legitimate way for new players to learn from others as part of the wider group through a kind of apprenticeship: not simply learning about the gameplay, but about the social norms and identities of the player group.

Inquiry-based Learning

Inquiry-based learning encompasses a number of approaches, such as problem-based learning, investigations, projects, and research, that are student-led and in which learning is centred around a process of meaningful inquiry. Inquiry-based learning involves students working on rich and multi-faceted real-life, often cross-disciplinary, problems for which there is typically no one correct answer. A key feature of the inquiry-led approach is that students take responsibility and ownership of their own learning goals and trajectories, situated within the context of the original problem.

Computer games have the facility to create real-life problem-solving experiences, and provide context, meaning, and motivation for achieving certain goals. Many games (particularly games such as role playing games or adventure games) are typically composed of a series of smaller puzzles or problems that build up into larger problems and allow the player to achieve the ultimate goal of the game. Many games now, in particular genres like ARGs, which mix the real and online worlds (more about these in Chapters 11 and 12), online quests, and some adventure games, require players to leave the game world and carry out independent research on the internet in order to achieve the game goals. This takes the process of inquiry out of the game domain and supports the development of core digital and information literacy skills.

I believe that games, both computer games and non-digital games, have the potential to be powerful learning tools, when we go beyond the simple arguments that they are motivational when they are used as a reward for learning. Good computer games are rich and interactive, providing context, purpose, authentic activities, meaningful problems to be solved, new experiences, and environments to explore, and a forum for social activity. The learning theories presented in this section provide a far stronger rationale for their use in learning. However, we cannot assume that games in themselves provide the whole story: activities that support collaboration, reflection, meta-cognition, and transfer of learning all come together to create a holistic learning experience. In the section that follows, I am going to highlight, in more detail, some of the attributes of games that particularly support the learning process.

Some of the Benefits of Games for Learning

I've already looked at four theories of learning that I think are particularly relevant to making the case for games and learning. I hope by this point you are at least some way convinced that there is some real value in games themselves as educational vehicles. In this section, I am going to discuss six aspects of games that I think particularly support and enhance the processes around learning.

Playfulness

Games provide access to another world, one that is typically safe from the consequences of the real world. In games the player can experiment, explore and try out new things without risk of negative outcomes outside of the games. Players can try things out that they wouldn't dream of trying in the real world. (I realize that this is a bit of an over-generalization as there may be social consequences, and this often does not apply when games are played for money or other external rewards.) The playful state that games can engender can spark creativity, innovation, and new ideas, as well as allowing players to engage with fictional narratives, characters, and plots. They allow players freedom and control to create new identities and interact with both the environment and other people in novel and surprising ways. They can also create a sense of fun and enjoyment, removing some of the stresses and pressures that are often associated with formal education, and allowing learners to engage with the game activities in a relaxed and light-hearted manner.

'I think there's huge scope for more playfulness in education and by play-fulness I basically mean not-being-afraid-to-be-wrong-ness.'

Nikki Pugh

Practice

Making mistakes in games is not only seen as an intrinsic part of the gameplay for many games, but also as an inevitable part of the progress from novice to expert player. In this respect, they provide an ideal forum for practice and reflection on progress; if a player is unable to beat an opponent or complete a level there is ample opportunity to keep attempting the same task and refining the playing strategy each time until the goal has been achieved. Games also provide many built-in mechanisms for encouraging reflection on the gaming process itself. These include video replay of levels or areas, the ability to pause (and possibly save the game) to think about the next stages of action, or 'rewind' and replay in real time within the game. In-game statistics can show progress, points of weakness, summaries of activity after the game has finished (such as time taken or resources gathered); working with other players or online communities to share hints, tips, and strategies.

Engagement

While games may not be universally motivating, they do contain a variety of elements that support ongoing engagement while the learner is playing. Levels of engagement in games can be influenced by a number of factors, including the appropriateness of the level of difficulty, motivation to play the game in the first place, belief that a winning outcome is achievable, a feeling of control, choice and agency over the game, a feeling of immersion in the game, and intrinsic interest in the game subject matter. In the case of games for learning, an appreciation of the purpose and value of the game is also important. Intrinsic to the design of games are several elements that can increase engagement (although not for all games or all people: this is very much a generalization). This includes the use of challenge, which stretches the player with ongoing goals, gradually increasing in difficulty, coupled with uncertain outcomes and rewards, and the use of overt competition (both individual and group) through leader boards and high score tables. Engagement can also be enhanced through mystery and stimulating curiosity, uncovering secrets, or journeying with a character through a story to discover what happens at the end. Another tech-nique used commonly in games to keep players 'hooked' is the collection moti-vation: the human desire to complete sets, be it cards, tokens, or levels. Each of these elements engage different people to different degrees, but well-designed games can strike a balance that overall enhances gameplay and engagement.

It has also been argued that games are, in themselves, motivating and while I believe that this is true for *some* people, for *some* types of games, in *some* circumstances, this is such a sweeping generalization that it really can't be viewed as absolute fact. However, games offer a different way in which to approach learning and teaching, and use of a variety of methods that support a variety of different learning styles can be motivational in itself.

> 'You cannot motivate someone to learn by your game alone. But you can make the experience delightful. Think about things that will make your player grin, and about how you can emphasize how these skills will be *useful*.'
>
> Naomi Alderman

Scaffolding

Games are particularly good at guiding players – in an enjoyable way – as they make the journey from novice to expert. Many games are designed so that new players can make big gains early on, increasing their confidence and 'buy-in' to the game in the early stages, before they tackle the more difficult challenges or levels later on. Goals start small and gradually increase in difficulty as the player becomes more accustomed to the game dynamics, and in the case of computer games, the interaction design. As gameplay progresses, the support or scaffolding decreases so that clues become less obvious, hints are more cryptic, rewards or power-ups are less frequent, so that as the game becomes harder, in parallel, the player becomes more independent. For many games, the process of learning the game, uncovering the hidden secrets or pushing the boundaries of the games, is part of the gameplay process itself.

Feedback

Feedback on actions is essential to be able to reflect on their effectiveness and modify them for future occasions, and games – computer games in particular – are very good at providing appropriate and timely feedback. A key advantage of feedback in many games is that it is intrinsic, that is directly related to the activity undertaken. For example if you want to open a door in a game, you don't write a list of possible ways to open a door and receive a mark for your list (extrinsic feedback), you try turning the handle, and if that doesn't work the door won't open, so you can try breaking it down, or finding a key. Each action you try will receive immediate feedback on whether or not it was successful in achieving your objective. It is this link between action and immediate, relevant feedback that is one of the reasons that games can be so powerful for learning. Feedback can also be tailored to provide hints or clues, so for example if you tried to break the door down you might hear a crack, indicating that the door was about to give way and another mighty shove was all that is required. Computer games also offer a variety of ways to provide feedback; written such as reading a note or a sign, verbal when a character speaks, visual such as a change in the environment or an object, or auditory such as the splintering door mentioned previously (mobile devices and console handsets now offer tactile feedback in the form of vibrations too). This variety in feedback types again caters for a wider variety of learning styles.

Digital Literacy

As well as having a number of attributes that support learning in general, computer games of all sorts have the additional advantage that they can build digital literacy and support confidence with computer interaction. At a very basic level, skills like using the mouse and keyboard to interact with a game can be built up for inexperienced computer users. In fact, some of the early games distributed with operating systems, such as solitaire or minesweeper, were designed as a way for new users to practice their mouse skills. Games allow players to experience visual and aural media simultaneously, and to manage data gathering and extraction from multiple competing sources. This skill of identifying, evaluating, and focusing on important information, in a mass of competing information streams, is a key skill for the information age, as is the ability to manipulate interface objects. The ability to participate in the online communities that exist around games in a safe and responsible way is also an essential skill for anyone communicating online. It is important also for new computer users (and we cannot assume that all young people are 'digital natives' or completely happy with technology, even if we are only focusing on the young) to gain confidence in safe and purposeful environments.

In this section, I've tried to highlight the key areas in which, I believe, games (and computer games) can benefit learning. In a short chapter such as this I can't hope to give a comprehensive analysis, but I hope what I have done here is provide more evidence that games, when used thoughtfully and critically, can have a range of important benefits for learning.

A Final Caveat

While I hope that after reading this chapter you are convinced of the potential of games for learning, it would be wrong of me not to point out that games also have their drawbacks, both pedagogic and practical. Games are great for encouraging active learning, but they are less effective for supporting reflection and meta-cognitive thinking about the process of playing (or learning) itself and, while some games are designed to be collaborative and support co-operative learning, others can be stand-alone or encourage negative behaviours. Developing reflective and meaningful collaborative activities – either within the games themselves, or as an associated activity, is crucial to creating a holistic learning activity, and some of the later chapters in this book suggest ways that this can be achieved. Playing a game should not be seen as the whole learning activity, as discussion and critical reflection around it can be equally important. Even if a game is good for learning, there is no guarantee that what is being learned will be retained for any significant period of time, or transferred to other situations or real life. Again the use of supplementary and supportive activities around a game can promote this.

> 'They must remain true to the design principles of non-educational games. Too many educational games begin with curriculum, then try to slap a game on top of that. They are too literal. Abstraction and fun are essential. I've yet to discover a subject that cannot be taught with greater engagement and retention using games.'
>
> Lee Sheldon

There are also many practical problems associated with using games for learning, including the difficulty of finding (or developing) games that map exactly to a particular curriculum, that can be played in a specific time frame, that will work on a particular system, that are affordable and will appeal to the students concerned. In my experience, games can be a very effective pedagogic tool, but they are not a magic bullet, and the difficulty in designing an effective games-based learning experience should not be ignored. I would never advocate using games in every learning situation (just as I would never advocate using *any* single teaching model) but they can offer advantages on some occasions, as I hope I have argued in this chapter. What is most important for me, however, is that good game design is, by its very nature, good learning design; learning is an intrinsic by-product of games. It is when we, as educators, try and dictate exactly what is learned from a game that everything gets difficult. This is not to say that it can't be done, but we must recognize that it isn't an easy task we set ourselves.

Part II
APPLYING GAME PRINCIPLES TO EDUCATION

While there are many advantages to using games for learning, a major drawback is the availability of appropriate games and the ability of teachers and course designers to create their own digital games. This means that a typical educator can find it extremely difficult to obtain games that meet their exact pedagogic needs, and cover the required curricular goals in a manner appropriate to their learners, without first acquiring technical skills and being prepared to invest a lot of time to develop games for themselves.

So does this mean that games for learning are an unrealistic option for most educational situations? We believe not, although we also think that there is a need to move beyond the typical model of high-end computer games for learning. In Part II of this book, we look at one solution to this issue by presenting five principles of computer games; things that games do well that, we believe, can be applied to or embedded into traditional or online learning and teaching situations to enhance engagement and interactivity.

In each of the five chapters in this part, we have highlighted key areas where we think that education can learn from computer games. Each chapter takes an individual area in depth, providing a theoretical background and suggesting ways in which teaching and learning practice could be enhanced by adopting game-based principles – without necessarily having to use a complete game-based format, or a complex technological solution. This makes the ideas presented in this part accessible to even the most technology-phobic teacher.

The topics covered in this section are:

- Ways in which to create appropriate levels of *challenge* through techniques such as goals, outcomes, reward structures, scaffolding, intrinsic feedback, and gradual introduction of complexity (Chapter 3).
- How to utilize the benefits of the types of *communities* that often develop around multiplayer online games, and the advantages of these community groups for supporting learning (Chapter 4).

- The role of *narrative* in games, the different forms that it might take, and ways in which to apply narrative structures and devices to learning situations (Chapter 5).
- The use of *competition* in games, its drawbacks as well as advantages, and how these techniques can be applied to education in appropriate ways to engage learners (Chapter 6).
- How to make the most of the benefits afforded by the use of *multiple media*, which is intrinsic to computer games, but often under-utilized in educational settings (Chapter 7).

We hope that reading this section will convince you that there is more to the potential of computer games in learning than simply using them as a tool to teach; that an understanding of what we, as educators, can learn from games more generally can offer new insights and ideas of how to improve teaching and learning practice.

3
CHALLENGE
Levelling Up

NICOLA WHITTON

The Importance of Challenge in Game Design

The notion of challenge is fundamental to the design of games that people want to play, and want to keep on playing. Challenge provides a reason for taking part, it allows players to see improvement as they progress through the game, and it is a core part of gaming engagement. Of course, while appropriate challenge can create a fantastic game, it is just as easy to create a boring game with challenges that are too easy or obvious. Getting the type and level of challenge right is key to creating a playable game, whether this is a game for fun or a game for learning.

> '[a really good computer game] manages to be both hard and fun. That means it can't be too hard, or too easy. And it can't be "just fun". I think the notion of giving people badges as rewards for various activities isn't what it is about. That just focuses on fun without connecting that deeply to the hard challenges of games.'
>
> Eric Klopfer

Inherent in the design of practically all games are features such as goals, measurable outcomes, reward structures, scaffolding, and gradual introduction of complexity, which create challenge, as well as support learning. In this chapter I aim to highlight the importance of appropriate challenge – both for learning and engagement – and show how this can be brought about using a variety of game mechanisms. In the latter half of the chapter I will discuss four different types of challenge – puzzles, creative, physical, and social – with examples of each, and I finish by considering ways in which challenge can be used to enhance teaching and learning.

So what exactly do I mean by challenge? For me, it's the idea of an activity that is difficult to do, that takes thought and effort, and for which there is a feeling of satisfaction when a challenge has been achieved. An activity can be a challenge without being a game, but a game will have a very limited appeal if it is not challenging. Take, for example, snakes and ladders, which has little challenge because the outcome is entirely dependent upon the throw of a die – popular with younger children, virtually unplayed by adults.

Different types of challenge will appeal to different types of people and different learning styles. Some people prefer sports and others crossword puzzles, some like team games while others like to play alone. As people have different backgrounds and abilities, appropriate levels of challenge will naturally differ between individuals; a game of chess that would challenge a novice is unlikely to challenge a Grand Master. For this reason it is important that we – as game designers and learning designers – provide both variety and flexibility in challenge, so that players and learners can have greater choice and control in order to approach challenges that cater for their preferences and are most effective for them.

Challenge and Learning

Some of the original and seminal work on gaming and engagement was produced by Malone (1980), who investigated the elements that make computer games motivating. He initially presented three aspects of games that positively influence motivation: 'challenge', 'fantasy', and 'curiosity' (he later added a fourth aspect, 'control', to this list (Malone and Lepper, 1987)). In the context of this chapter I am going to focus on his work with challenge. He says that 'in order for a computer game to be challenging it must provide a goal whose attainment is uncertain' (p. 162), so fundamental to his ideas about challenge are the notions of goals and uncertain outcomes.

Goals are aims or targets in the game, things that need to be achieved to progress. They can be critical to the completion of the game, or optional; they can be immediate or long-term; they can be simple, or complex and multi-faceted. Malone suggests that goals should be obvious and compelling, with which the players can identify (although how you make a goal universally compelling is less clear), and they should be practical and intrinsic to the game rather than based around learning outcomes: such as firing a rocket at a target rather than simply calculating an angle. Players must also be able to tell whether they are getting closer to a goal, for example by seeing progress on a meter or by using a score; and in an environment where no explicit goals exist (such as simulation or virtual world) it should be structured so that users can easily generate their own goals of appropriate difficulty.

Uncertain outcomes is the idea that the player does not know at the start of the game whether they are going to win or lose. If they are certain to win the game will be boring; if they are certain to lose it will be pointless. Malone suggests four ways to ensure that the outcome of a game is uncertain for players over a wide range of abilities: variable difficulty levels; multiple-level goals; hidden information; and randomness. Good games, which engage users at different ability levels, should be able to be played at variable difficulty levels, which can either be determined by the game, by the user, or determined by a (virtual or real life) opponent's skill. Difficulty levels can also be progressive, supporting players through a chain of events or levels, or adjust dynamically to a player's current skill. Multiple-level goals encompasses the idea of having short-term and longer-term goals, which may be in conflict; for example a long-term goal – or meta-goal – might be to save a lost civilization, but in order to do this they might have short-term goals (or sub-goals) to find a torch, to enter a cave, to gain access to a secret coded message, and so on: the conflict comes from having to decide whether to spend time on the short-term goals, or progress with the long-term goal above all else. Malone suggests that score-keeping or time limits can be good ways of balancing the different levels of goal within a game, but I would suggest that with modern computer games this can be done in much more sophisticated ways such as integrating information or objects from sub-goals that support (or contradict) the long-term goal. Hidden information, such as secrets and mysteries, and an element of chance also provide ways in which the outcome of a game can be made more uncertain.

As well as goals being clear, meaningful to the player, and of an appropriate level of difficulty, it is important that the player believes themselves capable of achieving them; perhaps not on the first try, but within a reasonable time. The level of challenge needs to be mapped to the player's skill level so that they are not too easy or too hard. Csikszentmihalyi (1992) presents a model of challenge level mapped against skill level (see Figure 3.1). When the level of challenge is appropriate for the level of skill the state called 'flow' can be achieved. Flow is described as the state of optimal experience, 'in which people are so involved in an activity that nothing else seems to matter; the experience itself is so enjoyable that people will do it even at great cost, for the sheer sake of doing it' (p. 4). Of course, the flow experience is not unique to games, but can be seen in all types of leisure, work, and learning activities; it's just that games are particularly good at developing the optimal balance between challenge and skills.

Games also allow users to undertake progressively more difficult challenges as they move through the game or levels in the game. Novice players are typically supported with various types of 'scaffolding' such as hints and clues or more obvious or easier challenges that enable them to pick up the skills needed for later in the game, when the support decreases and the challenges get more demanding. Often games will start simply, allowing players to make swift and steady progress in early levels, and 'buy-in' to the game as they gain a feeling of satisfaction at their success; later levels will swiftly increase the degree of challenge once the players' skills and confidence have grown.

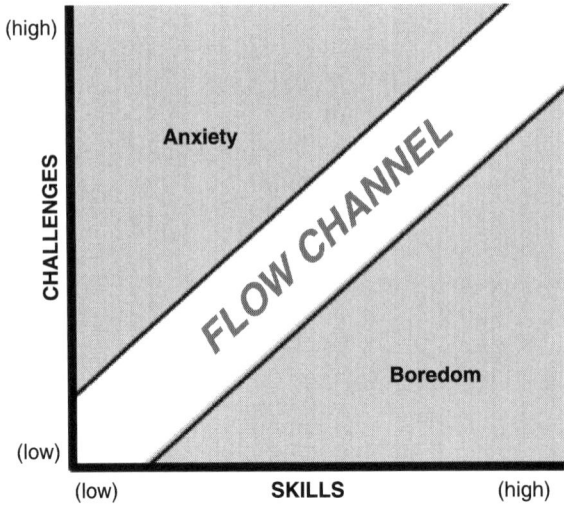

Figure 3.1 Challenge versus skill level
Source: adapted from Csíkszentmihályi, 1992, p. 74

Use of tools such as progression meters, scores, timers, and levels allow players to gauge their progress throughout a game. Measurable outcomes are not just important for players to be able to evaluate their own progress, but also to compare themselves with others; tools such as high-score tables and leader boards also facilitate this. Overt competition against others (rather than against oneself or the game system) can be motivating for some people, but equally can demotivate others, particularly players with lower skill or confidence levels, so should be used with caution. The way in which games allow outcomes to be measured is important because it allows players to be rewarded, either with artifacts that are useful in the game, such as receiving a sword for completing a quest, by finding out a mystery or secret, by being able to personalize a character or avatar; or by recognition from other players, such as being top of a high-score table.

The combination of balanced goals with outcomes and rewards is a very powerful motivational driver, but it is not always an easy balance to achieve. In the following section I explore four different types of challenge that are commonly used in games, and consider how these might be used to support teaching and learning.

Different Types of Challenge

A huge variety of different types of challenge are used in games and other activities, and this chapter cannot possibly hope to discuss them all. Instead, I will look at what I consider to be the five main types of challenge as they apply to learning: knowledge and recall, puzzles, creative problems, physical tasks, and social challenges. For each of these areas I will briefly describe what I mean by that type of challenge, provide examples of different sub-types, and finally consider how they might be applied to teaching and learning contexts.

Knowledge and Recall

Challenges that involve knowledge and recall are some of the most basic challenges, and players usually either know the answer or they don't (there is no 'working out'). This type of challenge is associated with the lower levels of learning, such as remembering and recalling facts, and is commonly used in educational 'games' because the question–answer format is easy to design, test, and provide simple feedback for. It is also a useful format in areas where facts simply do have to be learned: language vocabulary for example.

Knowledge and recall challenges, which often take the form of quizzes, can also be used in an educational context to test basic knowledge about or understanding of topics, or can provide a fun activity for groups – hence the popularity of pub quizzes. For example, a quick quiz could be used at the start of a lecture to refresh learners' knowledge and orientate them to the session. A more sophisticated model of the knowledge and recall challenges in education is the web quest or treasure hunt idea, which does not assume that the player knows all the answers at the start of the challenges, but provides hints and clues to where the information can be found. As well as supporting the learning of facts, this model also supports information literacy and evaluation skills, for example by asking students to find the answers to specific questions through web research.

Puzzles

Puzzles are problems for which there is typically only one solution (although this is not always the case for more complex puzzles) that can be solved by applying rules or systems to the problem. They are used in many types of computer game: for games that are puzzles in themselves (such as *Tetris* where players have to navigate falling bricks into lines), games that use puzzles extrinsically to progress a storyline (such as the *Professor Layton* series for the Nintendo DS, which reward players for solving puzzles), or those for which puzzles are intrinsic to the gameplay, such as the majority of adventure games (where, for example, the player needs to work out the combination to unlock a safe).

A wide variety of puzzle types are used in games and in learning and teaching. There follows a list of some of the most common.

- Cryptic – using codes or ciphers, or conventions as in the case of cryptic crosswords.
- Lateral thinking – need to be solved by thinking in an unconventional manner, or seeing things from a different perspective.
- Logic – the solver must use reasoning and deduction to work out the solution.
- Memory – such as repeating a pattern, or recognizing objects that have been moved or removed.
- Musical – puzzles based on note forms, pitch, or keys.
- Numeric – puzzles based around arithmetic or algebra, where the solver has to manipulate numbers in some way to arrive at a solution.
- Spatial – puzzles based around the movement or comparison of objects or moving around an environment, such as mazes.
- Tactile – using actual physical objects, such as puzzles that involve separating objects.
- Verbal – using language, letters or words as the basis for the puzzle, such as crosswords or anagrams.
- Visual – analysing pictures, such as spot-the-difference or finding a hidden object.

Of course, different puzzle types can be combined and there may also be puzzles that share elements of two or more puzzles types described here, such as *Sudoku*, which is both a numeric and logic problem.

Puzzles can be used to support teaching and learning in two ways: intrinsic and extrinsic. The former is more powerful but it may be difficult to map many curricula with appropriate puzzles; areas such as basic numeracy, literacy and language learning may lend themselves more than other areas. They can also be used extrinsically as a way to start a topic or to take a break and provide a motivational activity to learners.

Creative Challenges

Creative challenges are, I believe, one of the most powerful ways in which to stimulate and motivate learners. They provide a meaningful and achievable challenge and also lead to all sorts of incidental learning, as students have to master new concepts and ways of thinking, software packages, or transferable skills such as information literacy. For example, playing *NotPron* (see www.deathball.net/notpron/), described as 'the hardest puzzle on the internet', actually provides an excellent problem-based tutorial to the internet. In early levels players have to learn simple concepts such as how the address bar works, and viewing page code, but the challenge difficulty soon increases so that they are quickly unpacking animated images and decoding sound files.

There are two key ways in which creative challenges can be used in teaching and learning: through creative problem-solving, and through the development of artifacts, such as graphics, videos, songs, stories, animations, and so on. Creative challenges differ from puzzles in that there may be more than one correct solution; in fact, the development of creative solutions is at the heart of the challenge. Presenting players (or learners) with engaging non-trivial problems, which they are motivated to solve, provides an ideal basis for learning. Games, such as adventure or role-playing games, where players take part in a narrative and have to solve a variety of problems to progress, are great examples of inquiry-based learning (discussed in more detail in Chapter 1). The problem provides the stimulus for learning (and progressing in the game) and it is then up to players to find and use the necessary resources. Of course, in games, this may not always be straightforward: clues may be cryptic, objects may be hidden, and lateral or creative thinking is often required, but if the problems are logical, hard-to-crack, and internally consistent, then there is likely to be a feeling of satisfaction on finding a solution. One of the big complaints of adventure game players is when a problem can't be solved through logic and thought alone, but requires guesswork or facts that simply couldn't be known; this is viewed as very unfair.

Problem-solving creative challenges typically provide some initial information, and the learner has to use that to come up with a solution. They may have to find more information, talk to people and try things out before coming to an elegant solution. Creative challenges that involve the development of artifacts, are typically still trying to solve a problem but require the learners to develop or design something that meets the terms of the brief. This can involve using technology to develop things such as videos, digital graphics, animation, or digital music, or can use offline technologies, for example writing a story or creating a physical object. Here is an example of a physical challenge from the *ViolaQuest* ARG (see Chapter 11 for more details):

1. I need to create a new Manchester A–Z.
2. Please can you take a photograph here that clearly represents one of the letters of the alphabet.
3. It must clearly be an original photograph (e.g. include yourself or the letter you intend to represent).

In this example, players have to select an object and create an original photograph, which may also involve learning additional digital literacy skills such as uploading to a collaborative photo site. Creative challenges can be used effectively throughout most aspects of teaching and learning as a way of giving learners control over what and how they learn, and enabling them to see real value and tangible outputs of their work.

'From an academic perspective, the psychology of creating absorbing game-mechanics really interests me. How you create something which creates fun from a small set of interactions, rules and goals is a fascinating art which is still poorly understood. I really relish the challenge of applying the motivation created by games to learning goals, which is the main focus of my research.'

Jacob Habgood

Physical Challenges

Physical challenges involve actually doing something with your body, as opposed to the primarily mental challenges of puzzles, knowledge and recall, and creative challenges. They can involve challenges such as sports activities, crafts such as clay-pot throwing, or 'twitch' and reaction time skills in computer games. Modern computer-game consoles, such as the Nintendo Wii, Sony Move, or Microsoft Kinect, offer great potential for movement-based challenges, and it has been suggested (Johnson et al., 2011) that gesture-based learning will become big in the next three to five years. Physical challenges may appeal to those students with tactile or kinesthetic learning styles, but they can also provide a break or change of scene for all learners, and as a way of using energy and relaxation, but might also be strong demotivators for learners who find physical activities or sports difficult or alienating.

Social Challenges

Social challenges are ones that involve working with, or against, other people. They can involve skills such as teamwork, negotiation, discussion, and diplomacy. These types of challenge can help to build skills such as social literacy, interpersonal skills, communication skills, and group interaction skills. Social challenges are also key to collaborative learning (more detail on this is provided in Chapter 2 and Chapter 4).

Of course, each of the types of challenge described in this section are not mutually exclusive. A challenge can be a puzzle as well as a social challenge, such as a team-building task, or a physical and creative challenge, such as designing a dress. The five different types are presented here to provide an overview and as a basis to start you thinking about the whole range of different types of challenge that can be used in learning and teaching. It can be useful to use this typology when designing activities to think about the different ways they can be combined to engage students, for example by developing a group treasure hunt in a library (knowledge and recall, social, and physical) or by asking learners to develop puzzles for one another to test and evaluate (creative, puzzle, and social).

Using Challenge in Teaching and Learning

There are a variety of ways in which challenge can be used in learning and teaching, and there are some specific examples at the end of this section. One key way, however, is the adoption of an inquiry-based or problem-based curriculum, which uses meaningful problems – or challenges – as the basis for learning. However, challenges can be integrated into all types of curriculum models, but it is important to remember that different people will prefer different types of challenge, so it is good to try and design learning so that there is a good mixture of different types.

There are several other aspects that need to be considered. The level of difficulty of challenges for the target students may be tricky, so that higher ability students are still engaged while those of lower ability are not put off. Making a large number of relatively easy challenges available at the beginning will help players to make quick initial gains, see themselves progressing, and hopefully help them to become immersed. However, it is also important that a range of challenges are available at different levels so that players of all abilities can be kept engaged. Balancing types of challenge can also be problematic but it is important to provide a balance of types of challenges that require different skills and previous knowledge, take place online or in the real world, and are individual or collaborative.

Three easy ways in which to introduce the idea of challenge to teaching and learning is through scaffolding, leader boards or use of progress levels. Each of these ideas is described in more detail below.

Scaffolding involves the provision of a large amount of support in the early stages of learning a new subject or topic, which gradually decreases as the learner gains skills and confidence. It can take the form of hints or clues, additional information, or the ability to seek expert advice. Scaffolding allows learners to move quickly through the foundations of an area and learn the basics, while gaining buy-in and a perception that they are achieving. As the subject or challenges within the subject become more difficult, the scaffolding can be slowly withdrawn until the student can tackle harder challenges without additional support. This can also be an excellent way to help learners know where and how to find resources and support for themselves.

Leader boards allow learners to see how they are progressing compared to others in their peer group. As with all forms of competition, it can be motivating for some but may put others off (particularly the poorer performers) so is best used in team or group situations or as a fun element of a course. An excellent use of leader boards is the University of Brighton's *Never Ending Uni Quiz*, which used a quiz format as part of the induction and was so motivating for some students that they completed the question sets several times in order to stay at the top of the leader board (see Chapter 10 for a more detailed discussion).

Progress levels provide a concrete way for students to see how far they have come in their learning journey and where they need to reach. They can also be motivational if the learner knows that he or she is near to moving up a level. There are a variety of ways of implementing progress levels, such as (automated) formative assessment at the end of each level (or topic), self-evaluation tests, or peer voting on whether it is time for a learner to move up a level. Progress levels can be used in conjunction with leader boards so that learners can evaluate their progress through the course in relation to others, which can be particularly useful for less structured or self-study courses.

This chapter has provided an overview of how challenge – a core component of games – can be used to enhance learning and motivation. The examples provided here are really only the tip of the iceberg of how challenge can be applied, as it is so fundamental to effective learning. The challenge now is for the reader to use these principles to create deep and engaging learning experiences that are meaningful and motivating for students.

4

COMMUNITY
The Wisdom of Crowds

MICHELLE A. HOYLE AND ALEX MOSELEY

The Scene

Dragons, dilemmas, and death. These recently bound together a pool of thirteen intrepid explorers in Blizzard Entertainment Inc.'s massively successful multi-player online game *World of Warcraft* (*WoW*). The thirteen players met two evenings a week to defeat two of the game's hardest dragons: Onyxia and her big brother Nefarian. The dragons were the final challenge after a series of other challenges, all to be overcome before the team could stare down into the dragons' lair. The group had heard rumours this was a difficult fight. Nefarian had been taunting them for weeks as they successfully challenged his minions. Other groups had avoided this fight, going for easier pickings. Before just blindly running in, the group examined the situation. Some had researched the fight in *WoW*-related, user-maintained encyclopedias. Others had watched YouTube movies of successful encounters with explanatory narration. Their leader had an initial plan. However, reading about it or seeing it done is not the same thing as doing it yourself. Despite their plans and preparation, they died – a lot.

The encounter is complex, broken into three phases, each requiring a different strategy. While guides exist, success really depends on the group's composition, character skills, character equipment, and each player's skill and knowledge in playing their character effectively. It goes beyond having good reflexes and a good environmental awareness, although those help. The group had to learn through experience how far apart the two dragons must be kept. They had to develop skills in jumping on top of pillars with an overhang that made straight jumping up impossible, not helped by a heavily damaging, rising pool of lava. There were many mechanics that would cause players to be stunned or take massive damage. A stunned healer at an inopportune moment meant the group's death. Every person was crucial with a critical role to play. Each person brought their own expertise and, when the attempt failed, offered suggestions and reflection on what they thought had gone wrong. Together, they built a mental model of what was happening, when, and why.

In a three-month period, this team tried ninety-two times to kill Nefarian. While initially most attempts were short – a minute or two – the group did improve. Later attempts were as many as seven or eight minutes, with the group usually reaching the last phase of the fight before dying. Unfortunately, time was not on their side. While they had killed Onyxia many times during the first phase, they only managed to get Nefarian down to 10 per cent of his total health on their best attempts. Blizzard then tweaked the encounter, making it substantially easier. After the 'tweak', the group easily annihilated Nefarian on their first attempt, disappointing after trying so hard for so long. Still, they had some pride. Even though they 'failed' to kill Nefarian before, they had managed on their own to get him down to 10 per cent through persistence, analysis, teamwork, communication, reflection, and a willingness to fail.

Communities and Learning

The value of communities in the epic struggle outlined above is clear (and we'll unpack some of the elements touched on later in this chapter). But communities are not unique to games, of course: we're all used to the value (and hazards) of communities in our everyday lives. Indeed, as humans we've been aware of the benefits of working together since our first early hominid days – whilst the early fossil record can't reveal much in the way of collaboration or communal work, archaeologists have inferred communal food gathering, sharing, and division of labor from the concentrations of bones and tools at East African prehistory sites (Toth and Schick, 1986, p. 72), and certainly by the Upper Paleolithic the use of communal-hunting methods (such as multiple hunters using nets) rather than solo hunting or setting of traps or snares marked an 'increased efficiency of food procurement and intensification of production' (Lupo and Schmitt 2002, p. 149): using communities for a distinct advantage.

In learning terms, modern humans depend on social and communal inter-action for their development from childhood onwards. Many theorists (Bowlby (1958), Bandura and Walters (1963), Piaget (1977), and Vygotsky (1978) in particular) argue that the social relationships with parents, carers, peers, and wider culture shapes child development, and further that 'communal play' or activity is essential for the development of higher order functions. Vygotsky (1978) takes this further, through formal education and into work-based learning, to suggest that active learning (solving real or simulated problems) in collaboration with more capable peers or experienced guides provides the best and most rapid learner development. Those versed in modern educational practice will be familiar with these concepts as 'social constructivism' (described in more detail in Chapter 2): an approach that puts social collaborative learning to the fore (and is often evidenced by discussion groups, problem solving, case-based approaches, and inquiry-based learning).

Vygotsky's 'more capable peers' or 'experienced guides' have particular relevance to the way that players in massive multiplayer online (MMO) games learn how to succeed in the early phases of the games. The existing wide game community is almost always eager to help and support new players; but more importantly, by joining together with other new and more experienced players, newcomers will soon be solving quests and fighting foes, learning from the more experienced players or those newcomers who develop more quickly. These supportive groups are an example of what Lave and Wenger (1991) termed 'communities of practice', where members are engaged in similar activities using the same tools and practices, and set up a continual process of learning and co-creating new knowledge: extremely high levels of engagement with the (often subconscious) learning process ensue.

How long does it take to form a community? Communities do not form immediately and spontaneously. They take time to grow and evolve. This is the situation when a new school year starts and students are thrown together with new peers and surroundings, or when a new permanent group – a guild – forms in massively multiplayer games. Gee's (2007a) work on 'affinity spaces' can be useful for thinking about promoting learning in these emerging communities. In affinity spaces, the initial focus is on the bonds created around a shared interest and not between the people. Gee enumerates eleven characteristics in total, but it is important to realize these are neither prescriptive nor binary: they can be present or encouraged in degrees. Affinity spaces share some common characteristics with communities of practice. For example, both experienced and inexperienced participants share the same space; tacit knowledge is shared and used; there are many different routes to participation and to status. In addition, affinity spaces promote knowledge dispersion, intensive and extensive knowledge, and both individual and distributed knowledge. If we incorporate these ideas into educational environments, we can forge more cohesiveness, autonomy, and higher levels of learning.

As a group evolves a culture and ethos over time, it can become a community of practice. Even if it remains an affinity space rather than a community with its implied ideas of belonging and membership (Gee, 2007a), autonomy is forged by individual knowledge and content organization transformed by interactions between individuals. This bears a striking resemblance to Downes' (2007) and Siemens's (2008) ideas about 'connectivism'. Connectivism, which shares some of the same roots as constructivism, is a model of the learning behaviours seen in an increasingly digital world where myriad tools connect us together. The learning is in the network and the ability to traverse that network

(Downes, 2007). That ability includes what some call 'digital literacies': how to find information, how to evaluate information, how to create content, how to participate, and the facilitating tools. What and where knowledge exists is perhaps more obvious. It exists in the network's human resources, on their forums, in their wikis, in their videos, and in their interactions. It is the technology, the context, the people, and their interactions (e.g. Siemens, 2008). Knowledge is a creation process, not just consumption; and knowledge does not reside in just one location. It is distributed, as suggested by Gee's affinity spaces, but the abundance of it requires guides ('sensemakers') to help 'filter and make sense of the chaos' (Siemens, 2008).

> 'Connectivism is the exploration of complex, rapidly adapting knowledge in information settings, which is really a direct parallel to what's happening in game settings, especially looking at *World of Warcraft* instead of just an Xbox shooter game. You're creating together. You're making sense together. You're finding a way together. It's fundamentally applying this connection-based model to developing competence and solving complex problems.'
>
> George Siemens

However we might choose to describe or make sense of these groups, when they become more mature, even more interesting learning starts to occur – something we return to later in this chapter.

Traditional and Emerging Game Theories

Traditional gaming covers a wide range, including family Monopoly squabbles, competitive two-player chess games, single-player Solitaire, party games like Twister, card games like bridge, or classic children's games like tag. While single-player games can be engrossing, as social beings we also enjoy games where we play with others. How we play together influences our learning and our working. Hoyle (2011) differentiates between 'Multiplayer' and 'multiplayer' games. What is the difference? While both are collective play, 'Multiplayer' is playing actively together whereas 'multiplayer' is just playing in the same space. For example, children playing tag are playing the game in the same physical space, but they cannot play the game independently of one another. That is a 'Multiplayer' game. Traditional games are often quite good at this. In the digital game world, however, we have many social games where people play in the same space, but it does not involve any (or much) joint interaction or impact on others in that space, e.g. *FarmVille* where you grow crops in real-time beside your virtual neighbors. Ducheneaut and colleagues (2006) describe this type of game as being 'alone together', where you play surrounded by others and not with them (p. 410).

While we are interested in *WoW*'s 'Multiplayer' aspects, Ducheneaut and colleagues' (2006) study of *WoW* playing and grouping patterns revealed that most players did not start grouping together until near the game's end levels, where problems were too difficult to overcome by solo effort. That is typified by the Nefarian encounter and similar to complex problems in the real world where we form project groups or task forces. Working together and developing relevant expertise in a changing world are key working skills. Being able to discuss a topic with others is a powerful learning tool. Brown and Adler (2008) call this 'social learning': where understanding is socially constructed through conversations or through grounded interactions, particularly with others, around problems; in other words by talking and doing together. Brown and Adler found evidence for this in a study showing that the strongest determinant of a student's success in higher education was their participation in study groups and not in the pedagogical approach or the instructor.

Thomas and Brown (2011) explore how peer-to-peer learning results in the emergence of collectives: a collection of people, skills and talents, where the whole is greater than the sum of its parts. They differentiate between communities and collectives. In collectives, people belong to learn; the reverse is true for communities. 'Multiplayer' game guilds are not collectives, but like collectives have participation and knowledge scaling in an almost unlimited way, due to increasing access to digital resources. In Cormier's (2008) notion of 'rhizomatic education', the community is seen as the curriculum. Rhizomatic plants have no centers, being composed of semi-independent nodes that grow and spread on their own. What these 'Multiplayer' groups need to or want to know is what determines the learning. The Nefarian group's healers needed to model what kind of damage would happen to whom and when. The group's *tanks* (characters who focus the brunt of the enemy's damage on them) needed to learn to anticipate additional enemy characters appearing and heading for the healers, so they could intercept those enemies. How did they do that? It was partially through trial-and-error, and their internal models shared through conversation. Each person was a rhizomatic node. Knowledge was negotiated and the learning process was contextual and collaborative.

Part of the learning process is the development and use of 'collective intelligence'. In the Nefarian encounter, this was demonstrated by the group watching YouTube videos, reading top gaming guild forums, and consulting player-constructed wikis. The creation of these artifacts also engenders 'social capital' (Bourdieu, 2002), whether by sharing objects like swords or sharing dragon slaying knowledge (White, 2007a). White (2007b) describes an entire 'ecology of services' for guild communities and those communities often have communities within themselves, using services within the game and without to create and share social capital. Even if it is only with other players around them, it creates a self-perpetuating cycle: what goes around comes around. Artifact creation and in-game work is hard, but hard work makes us happy and doing satisfying work is an intrinsic reward (White, 2007b; McGonigal, 2011). The Nefarian players were doing both. Doesn't doing hard work sound a lot like learning?

The average adult *WoW* player spends between 21 and 23 hours per week playing the game (Yee, 2006a; Hagel and Brown 2009). What else could be done with that time? McGonigal (2011) estimates that, if the 65,000 registered contributors of WoWWiki spent their usual *WoW* playing time contributing articles, they could collectively create a Wikipedia-sized resource in two months versus the eight years it has taken Wikipedia. Her key thesis is this voluntary effort could be harnessed for social good. Ours is we can take aspects of the group learning activities emerging in these games – activities that involve voluntarily writing, reading, and thinking critically – and channel them into productive, student-led learning, where students go beyond their immediate group to crowdsource additional ideas to incorporate into their joint knowledge.

Types of Communal Games

Communal play is already deeply embedded within a vast array of traditional and commercial games (both physical and online), and most can provide ideas and insights into methods for communal learning (or the value of communities in learning). Indeed, one of the best pieces of advice we can give to anyone interested in using games to improve or encourage learning is to dust off your old board games, gather friends or family around a console, or (if you already play regularly online or offline) adopt a critical or reflective eye next time you play, and assess the value of the community you are playing with: what are its chief benefits to you and which aspects do you find irritating?

Existing communal games (or games with a communal aspect) each lie somewhere within three independent axes: player numbers, location, and interaction mode. These are shown in Table 4.1. Any particular game will occupy a particular position on each of these axes (some examples are given below, but you should be able to place other games you are aware of). Some types of games, though, may move along one or more of the axes at any given time. *WoW*, for example, might include elements of co-operation and competition, but the most obvious example is in *pervasive* or *transmedia* games (a growing genre in which gameplay is played out across multiple media, and pervades in some way into players' own reality: a fictional character, for example, might call a player in response to something they post online, and arrange to meet them in a cafe) which are often co-located and distributed, co-operative and competitive, and have pockets of 'Multiplayer' within an overall 'multiplayer' community.

Table 4.1 *Types of communal games: three axes*

Player numbers	*'Multiplayer'* Games involve a set number of players, all of whom are playing the same game and interacting with each other. Examples: most board games (Monopoly, dominoes, Carcassonne, etc.) and online equivalents (e.g., Scrabble in Facebook or on mobile devices); some console games (Wii sports, etc.); party games; outdoor games.	*'Multiplayer'* Games involve an indefinite number of players, some of whom may be playing and interacting around the same game element; but others will be in the same game space and may or may not interact over time. Examples: massively multiplayer online games (WoW, Minecraft, LOTR Online, etc.), FarmVille in Facebook.
Location	*Co-located* Games are played in one physical location; players playing the game at any one time will form a local community and be able to use all five senses to interact with each other. Examples: most board games; party games; outdoor games (hide and seek, capture the flag, etc.); may include some pervasive games (where people co-locate for a particular game or part of a game).	*Distributed* Games are hosted online or offline in one location, but players are physically distributed. Interaction between players takes place through communication channels; and players can normally only use a limited number of senses to interact. Examples: all multiplayer games; online multiplayer games; traditional play-by-mail or play-by-phone games.
Interaction mode	*Co-operative* Two or more players are working together in the game, to achieve a common aim or a mutually beneficial purpose. Examples: Lego Star Wars (various platforms), Super Mario Bros. (various platforms).	*Competitive* Two or more players or sub-groups within the game are working against each other, in order to obtain an advantage in the game. Examples: chess, Monopoly, Scrabble, Rock Band (various platforms).

'What's exciting me are games which are truly collaborative and multiplayer – for example, in a first person shooter, people offer to help you out or collaborate – not just in chat but in voice and real time.'

Adrian Hon

Which aspects lead to a greater sense of community, or to affinity groups, or a maturing community of practice? Whilst some might lend themselves to particular types (pervasive 'Multiplayer' games where groups are together and sharing experience and knowledge over long timescales would naturally develop into strong communities of practice, whereas a group of new students brought together to play a board game over two hours would start as an affinity group and might develop some sense of community, but not develop further if they never played or worked collaboratively again), other games are more complex, and might develop a strong community over a number of co-located and distributed activities. These generalizations can easily be overlaid onto learning design: whilst many courses might choose a particular type of activity and stick with it, others might adopt a mixed approach to learning, with activities involving student groups in different ways – yet both can produce a strong community of practice with good design.

These three axes, and the location of certain games or activities within them, are a useful starting point for considering how the communal aspects of games can help in a learning environment; and the kind of games you might look to for inspiration in those aspects. We'll unpick some of these in the next section, but you may find it useful to refer back and use the axes to help position the elements as you read.

Benefits for Education

We have identified particular skills and attributes which the playing of communal games could offer to educational contexts, describing their mapping to known educational benefits, and illustrated by techniques used in games to achieve them. These are shown in Table 4.2. In the final section of this chapter, we present advice and approaches for utilizing these skills and attributes within real educational settings.

Using Communal Games within Education: Practical Advice

Taking the skills and attributes identified in Table 4.2 and applying them to real educational uses, we finish this chapter by presenting ten key guidelines for anyone wishing to use the power of (game) communities within their teaching, drawn from Gee (2007a, 2007b), White (2007a, 2007b), Hagel and Brown (2009), McGonigal (2011), Thomas and Brown (2011), and our own

Table 4.2 *Skills and attributes from communal games*

Skills or attributes	Educational benefits	Techniques from games
Co-operative skills Collective intelligence Collective work	Shows the value of specialization, and of combining people and skills to solve a problem. Diverse knowledge acquisition channels demonstrate multiple destination routes or multiple 'right' answers.	Problems that require skills beyond an individual (i.e. need greater number or variety of specialists or skills, for example to build a bridge over a river), or need distributed effort over time or distance (e.g. cracking complex ciphers).
Critical thinking	Alternative explanations of data; use of data/evidence to support assertions or to disprove assertions; use of appropriate references or resources (Steinkuehler & Duncan, 2008).	Player performance metrics available; built-in comparison mechanisms for items and/or players; support for 'add-ons' or 'mods' to collect or present data; complex game mechanics; game item information readily accessible; third-party knowledge aggregation and discussion sites allowed.
Digital literacy	Creativity; multimodal learning (Gardner, 1993); computing skills; lateral thinking.	Screenshot/movie capture built in; personal artwork use permitted; visually appealing environments; tasks which involve the use of social or other media.
Leadership skills	Diplomacy, mediation, resource allocation, and strategy creation are some of useful real-world skills game leaders acquire (Brown & Thomas, 2006). Sensemaking, inventing (organizing tasks, problem solving, implementing new ideas), relating (listening to others and building relationships), and visioning (inspiring people) are common leadership qualities exhibited (Barnet & Coulson, 2010).	Same as collective intelligence; long-term groups (guilds); easy for people to leave or join groups.

Continued overleaf

Table 4.2 *Continued*

Skills or attributes	Educational benefits	Techniques from games
Motivation	Increases desire to learn (and effectiveness of learning), particularly if maintained over longer time periods.	Competitive elements such as leader boards, levels, and prizes (at an appropriate level for the player); involvement in a story or narrative; delivery of regular new challenges (Moseley et al., 2009).
Peer mentoring	With reciprocal apprenticeship anyone can be a teacher (Steinkuehler & King, 2009). Sharing knowledge gains social capital, increases confidence, converts tacit knowledge to explicit, and improves everyone's understanding.	Equipment and player characteristics inspection possible; very large knowledge domain; shared encounter perspective.
Persistence	Complete difficult learning tasks, even with low motivation. Failure acts as immediate feedback. Insight into how pain now leads to a later gain (planning), leading to an ability to complete boring, but necessary, tasks (Yee, 2006b).	'Grinding' quests to do something repeatedly; multiple attempts but at a cost in time and resources; existence of ongoing groups to which members feel an allegiance (peer pressure); dying due to inadequate planning or poor performance; hints when learning new skills; complex, lengthy tasks broken into chunks.
Scientific habits of mind	Systematic approach to problem solving involving research, hypothesis generation, hypothesis testing, and reflection. May involve modelling mentally or with tools like spreadsheets, diagrams, or computer programs; building on the work of others; and systems-based reasoning (Steinkuehler & Duncan, 2008).	Same as critical thinking.

| Shared experience | Failure is more socially acceptable, as an individual or as a group. 'Misery shared is misery halved.' Reinforces shared history and group's identity, increasing social bonds, thereby contributing to motivation and persistence. Attaches emotion to learning events, contributing to memory retention. The past provides strategies for later problems (Voida et al., 2009). | Group achievement tracking; group communication channels; shared 'kill' or experience counters where whole group credited for work by any member(s); ability to name and customize groups somewhat via logos/slogans. |

experiences. Many of these are visible in the Nefarian group example. Following these, we describe some existing learning game case studies illustrating particular communal aspects well. The ten guidelines are as follows:

1. *Encourage groups to connect here, there, and everywhere.* The group's thinking, problem solving, meaning, and knowledge should be distributed across an ecology of services. The services should allow opportunities for the group to generate and share artifacts with themselves and with the larger world. Encourage them to think for themselves but also to apply the collective intelligence available in the world to their problems.

2. *It is better to be frustrated than bored, but make it easy to start.* Structure the problem environment such that a challenge will seem possible to the group but is actually on the outer edges of their abilities. This works best in conjunction with a group working through a series of challenges, starting with something not trivial but easily done and then those of increasing difficulty. Ideally, the challenges should be related, so what the group has learned before can be built on and practised. The end challenge should seem initially epic but increasingly attainable as the group progresses and their domain mastery increases. Honestly earned success reinforces intrinsic motivation.

3. *Encourage affinity group bonding through common goals and shared endeavours.* Common goals and shared problems create bonds between people. Increased social bonds lead to stronger social connectivity and reinforce the affinity group, leading towards a community over time if the group continues. You may find it is better initially to create groups, aiming for a distribution of different types of learners, expertise, and roles.

4. *Encourage development of experts within groups and specialist roles.* Everyone needs to contribute to solving the problem, but no one person needs to do it alone. In real-world and game teams, participants have specific roles or expertise. Each bit of expertise is needed. Encourage learners to take ownership of some domain expertise within the problem space. This works particularly well in a large knowledge space, where someone can become the expert on, for example, Roman army hats and someone else on Grecian swords. Build on existing digital literacy strengths within groups by having someone be the illustrator and another the movie editor or music director for the group's artifacts. Encourage learners to take turns directing the group.

5. *Foster an acceptance of everyone as learner.* There is no master or one person who knows it all. Everyone, regardless of expertise level, shares a common space. While there might be 'leaders' (like you, perhaps), they are just another resource. Everyone is constantly learning something new, building on their existing competencies to adapt to changing or new conditions. Everyone can be a teacher. Learners do not just 'consume' knowledge but actively create and share it with others. Encourage students to thrive on change – knowledge, roles, methods – and own their learning.

6. *Encourage self-discovery and a reflective cycle.* Groups learn more when they discover things for themselves through trial and error. Demonstrate and guide groups through the process of trying something in their problem domain, reflecting on the outcome, and then proposing a new hypothesis that can be tested. Provide explicit information on demand or just in time when the information can best be applied. The key is to get the tension right between encouraging self-discovery and scaffolding just enough. If a solution has been found, encourage reflection on other (better or worse) paths to accomplish the same thing.

7. *Accept and encourage multiple approaches.* This works well in discursive domains where there often is no 'right' answer, but it can be applied in math and sciences as well. The creativity can be in how the solution is presented or in how the solution is obtained. Be flexible. People learn in a variety of ways. This allows the group to create a curriculum in the space that works for them but still accomplishes the end goal: demonstrate understanding. Allow different types of participation (see #4) and perhaps different exploratory activities, some structured and some free (see #6).

8. *Encourage and honor tacit understanding.* We often reward explicit understanding, but there is an immense amount of tacit knowledge

in the world. This is often built up through intuition gained by practice. Affinity groups are particularly good about developing group working tacit skills. Encourage this skill development and help the groups make it more explicit by reflecting on what they are unconsciously doing and why. Even if they cannot articulate or recognize they have achieved something, make sure you do.

9. *Make failure a 'good thing'.* Part of learning is not succeeding. We often learn more from our failures than we do from our successes. Failure can be incredibly motivating, provided the problem seems surmountable (see #2). Provide opportunities to fail in a safe fashion by, for example, giving feedback on early attempts rather than grading them. React in a positive way when something goes wrong and help the group analyse why it is wrong or how it is wrong. Encourage learners to see it as part of the reflective cycle (see #6) so that a new plan or hypothesis is formulated and then tried.

10. *Provide clear metrics to assess performance.* Games encourage frequent and rigorous feedback. You do not stop to take a test. The act of doing is the test. If that is possible to design into your problem environment, then do so. For many, that will be difficult, so concentrate on providing techniques that help groups assess how they are doing, encouraging reflection on what they have accomplished on the journey, even if they have not yet finished. If their work will be assessed, provide the assessment criteria and encourage them to apply it to their own work (or that of another group) and then improve their artifacts before submission. Learners and gamers are often bottom-line oriented. Take advantage of that.

This is not prescriptive; you can mix and match as appropriate. You should not try to incorporate all of these guidelines into every learning activity you design, especially not right off. Try an iterative approach where you introduce one or two elements and then some more another time. Remember that any features should be considered as part of an overall educational design, taking on board student, staff and institutional needs.

To finish, we provide some practical examples of approaches that have already harnessed the power of game communities within educational environments. You may find it useful to explore these for yourself, noting the ways that communities are encouraged and utilized within each. They also prove, much like communities, that this is not a lonely path you are setting out on.

QuestAtlantis was initially developed in 2003 by Sasha Barab and colleagues at Indiana University as a safe online game for 9–12-year-olds based around sound social and academic principles. *Quest Atlantis* is now used in hundreds of schools across several continents. A 3D virtual environment, the game is modular and uses what Barab calls 'transformational play' to immerse the students in realistic situations where they can learn particular subjects in context. What is interesting from a community point of view is the variety of ways that students, teachers and game moderators ('Atlantians') can interact within the game. Students, for example, can work through quests on their own or can 'co-quest' with other students (resulting in shared experience and co-operative skills); they can also communicate in the game (synchronously and asynchronously) with other students in their class, with teachers, and with the Atlantians, in order to solve problems and find out more about the game environment (developing collective intelligence skills). The game's use of standard email, chat, and other communication tools to contact both peers and authority figures also helps students to develop digital literacy skills which have wider benefits.

WoWinSchools was originally developed by Lucas Gillespie as an after-school club for at-risk kids where *WoW* would drive a curriculum exploring math, digital citizenship, online safety, writing, and literacy. Using the narrative of the hero's journey, the student is the hero and the teacher is the wise 'lorekeeper'. Students undertake quests, gain experience points rather than grades, and can incorporate their own real-life experiences. Sample quests have included groups tweeting a story from a particular *WoW* character's viewpoint, creating propaganda posters, designing game quests, and making videos to document learning.

The project recently expanded into a full-featured grade 8 (ages 13–14) language arts curriculum aligned to state standards. Gillespie and co-lorekeeper Craig Lawson produced a source book with rubrics, modular activities, and activity notes (Gillespie and Lawson, 2011). Note how a wide variety of tools and sites are used, including Twitter, Animoto, Audacity, blogs, SlideShare, Machinima, and Google Docs, promoting digital literacy and connective sharing. Even if your learners are not this young, the weaving of course content with in-game content, formation of guild groups, incorporation of cooperative group activities focused on learning and doing, and the use of real-world tools is likely to prove inspirational.

BiblioBouts (Weider, 2011) at the University of Michigan uses *Zotero* (an online reference manager/sharer) to encourage students to find new online resources for a research theme, and then invite other students to rate them for academic suitability/relevance. Points are awarded for both rating/commenting on other students' resources, and for scores given to their own resources. Forming effectively a small research group, there is potential for students to develop as a community of practice together, gradually increasing their knowledge and skills within an authentic research context. They are likely to gain motivation through the awarding of ratings and comments by peers, and develop group analysis skills to find and analyse more applicable resources speedily over time.

5
NARRATIVE
Let Me Tell You a Story

NICOLA WHITTON AND DAVE WHITE

Storytelling and Games

Telling stories is fundamental to the design of many types of digital game, such as adventure and role-playing games, where the characters and plot drive much of the action and puzzles. Use of narrative has also long been used to support learning, through the telling of traditional stories through generations, to the use of allegories and scenarios. In this chapter we look at the ways in which narrative is used in computer games, and consider how these principles might be applied to other learning and teaching situations.

> 'Writing is the biggest challenge in game development. Wedding player agency to meaningful story involves interactivity, logic and sleight of hand. If writing and game design are collaborative and simultaneous wonderful things can happen.'
>
> Lee Sheldon

A narrative, as used throughout this chapter, encompasses the idea of a story, which can be true or fictional (and is most likely to contain at least some elements of fiction) and the way in which games are used to tell that story. Carr (2006) describes narrative as consisting of more than simply the story (the 'what') but also the way in which it is presented or represented (the 'how'), for example the perspective of the character telling the story. Krawczyk and Novak (2006) make a similar distinction between 'story' and 'plot', suggesting that a story is a causal sequence of events and it is the plot that serves to reveal the story so that 'the plot is the structure on which you hang the story' (p. 73). A story is more than simply a sequence of events, because a story involves the idea of progression or change (or in some cases trying to avoid an inevitable change to keep things the same). It has a beginning, middle, and an end; typically journeying with a character as they overcome obstacles and become a different person because of their experiences. A story is set in a consistent narrative world, based around a situation in an environment, with characters experiencing events, and interacting through dialogue. Game narrative, which also uses gameplay to engage the player, has the luxury of being able to employ more simple narrative forms than a pure story, such as the search for an object (or a person), and the description of narrative given here can be seen as being at the sophisticated end of the scale in gaming terms.

So what is the rationale for looking at narrative in games, as opposed to say narrative in books or films? Why is game narrative different from story narrative? For us, there are three fundamental differences: *interaction, agency*, and *immersion*. Traditional stories tend to follow a grand narrative, but within this there may be many sub-plots, and while those reading (or watching) the story may be able to guess what is coming up next, they will not be able to influence it in any way. The ability for the game player to interact with the narrative and shape how the story develops and its outcomes (albeit in a typically limited number of ways) is very powerful. Players are no longer passive observers of the story, but they are agents within it; able to take control of characters and events. There is a difference, however, between the game techniques of embodying a character (where a player takes on the mantel of a specific character; often viewed in first person through the eyes of the character) and situations where they are expected to feel empathy for a character who is separate from themselves (typically shown in third-person view). Both techniques, however, allow players to control the actions and – to some extent – the personalities of the characters.

It is this interaction and agency to engage with and direct the story (or at least have a perception of directing the story) that leads to greater immersion in the narrative and game environment, and association with the characters. However, real narrative agency in games is rare as there are normally a set of fixed routes that the player can follow, even if the order can change or certain tasks or scenes are optional – giving the player the feeling of choice and control can be more important than complete agency. Schell (2008) argues compellingly that readers of non-interactive stories are not passive, saying that 'the idea that the mechanics of traditional storytelling, which are innate to the human ability to communicate, are somehow nullified by interactivity are absurd' (p. 263) but highlighting the participant's ability to take action in an interactive narrative.

A long-running debate in games theory is one that places 'narratology' in opposition to 'ludology', that is the relative importance of story or gameplay. This chapter is not really the place to go into this debate in detail, but it is our view that both of these concepts have their place and are not necessarily mutually exclusive. Different types of game may rely more heavily on one concept rather than another; for example the story may be at the heart of an adventure game while the gameplay may be more crucial to a first person shooter. However, this is really a crass generalization, and both elements can play a part in most games. What is important is that narrative is not seen as being at the expense of gameplay, or vice versa, but that the two can work together to create a wide variety of engaging games. Dansky (2007) suggests that there are three reasons for narrative in games, saying that 'at its best narrative pulls the player forward through the experience, creating the desire to achieve the hero's goals and, more importantly, see what happens next' (p. 5). This is achieved through immersion through the provision of context for game events, using narrative as reward for in-game goals, and providing a sense of identification and kinship with the central character as well as a rationale for action.

In this chapter we will first examine the nature of narrative in computer games, presenting the different forms, ways of delivering them, and examples of narrative-driven games. We will then go on to discuss how narrative can be designed and ways in which to make narrative engaging and compelling. In the final section, lessons learned from the sphere of games that can be applied to more general teaching and learning contexts will be presented, with examples of the possible use of narrative in learning and teaching contexts.

Narrative in Computer Games

The vast majority of computer games use narrative in some respect, even if it is just to provide an overall goal for the action, but for some types of game, the narrative is a crucial aspect. Of course, some gamers aren't interested in narrative and it can be seen as 'too slow' or 'detracting from the action', so complex narrative is certainly not an essential element for an effective game. Adventure games are one example of this. In an adventure game players typically solve a series of problems or puzzles in order to resolve an overarching mystery; the story provides a rationale for action and a context for problem-solving. Role-playing games, including multi-user role-playing games, are also strongly narrative-driven, so that players undertake a series of quests (alone or as part of a group) in order to achieve the narrative goal of the game. The original interactive fiction (text adventure games) of the 1970s and 1980s are another good example of games where narrative is critical. Interactive fiction uses a computer program that can input and generate text, produce narrative, simulate an environment, and present a structure of rules (Montfort, 2005). While this form of computer game is seen as 'retro' by game players (although still has a hard core following of fans), it is very sophisticated in terms of narrative. More recently, alternate reality games (ARGs), which mix online and real life collaborative problem solving, are another example of a game genre driven by a strong narrative.

In many books of films, narrative (even ones that twist and turn, or make extensive use of flashbacks or multiple perspectives) is often linear, in that it starts at the beginning and progresses in a set sequence until it reaches the end. There are exceptions to this in examples such as *Memento*, which is told in reverse order through a series of flashbacks, or *Pulp Fiction*, which presents a number of intersecting storylines each with their own chronology. Narratives in games offer the writer or designer many more choices in terms of the different forms of narrative available. The examples that follow are not intended to be a complete analysis, but are given to provide the reader with an idea of how game narratives differ from other forms, and to spark ideas of the different ways in which they might be used in your own teaching and learning context.

Narrative Structures in Games

Here we are going to introduce four basic narrative structures: linear, branching, open, and key points. Of course, each of these are not mutually exclusive but can also be used in conjunction with one another within the same narrative line. A *linear* narrative essentially starts at the beginning and continues until the end, with one route through it. It is common in many adventure games, so while the player may have to solve puzzles there may be little choice in the order in which they are solved or input into the route of the story. A *branching* narrative offers the player much more choice in decision-making, because decisions made at various points in the game can lead to differing routes through the game, and can ultimately affect the overall outcome. Branching narratives are often used in role-playing games, where progress or outcomes of actions can also depend on the status of a character and decisions previously taken. An *open* narrative is used in what are called 'sandbox' games, where players can progress in any direction they like, and the narrative develops depending on the actions they have taken. However, narratives are rarely truly open, as good stories need to be crafted rather than just a series of events, so this type of narrative will often be used in conjunction with *key points*, where the narrative may branch, loop, or be open in sections, but will always return to linear key points as it progresses, and it is these key points that form the backbone of the storyline. These different types of narrative structure can be seen in Figure 5.1. When a story has optional paths, rather than being linear, the reader can help to shape the outcome, so it is possible for narrative in games to have multiple endings, which can increase the re-play value of a game, but can also leave players feeling that they have 'missed out' on some of the action. Often games that use the key points model will have a single 'end-game' that can be achieved or not. In older computer games such as the text adventures of the 1980s, it was very easy to 'die' and drop out of the narrative completely; this was frustrating for the player and meant that it could be very difficult to re-engage with a storyline. More recent computer games are typically less frustrating for

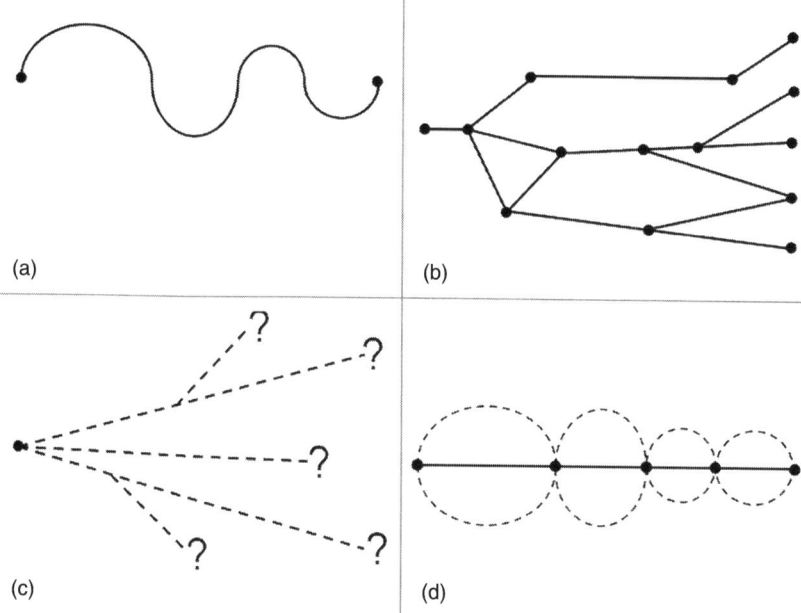

Figure 5.1 Narrative structures: a) linear; b) branching; c) open; d) key points

the player and are very good at providing players with ways to stop this happening: adventure games often do not allow a player to die, while action games may provide opportunities to save or to repeat sections that have been 'failed'. This leads to greater consistency of narrative, and in turn engagement with the story.

As game narrative is, to a greater extent, under the control of the player, as well as core plots, it is possible to have numerous sub-plots, which can also be optional and not affect the overall storyline. This is a common technique used in role-playing games, where side quests may be available that allow players to gain more resources, but do not directly affect the overall outcome. Egenfeldt-Nielsen and colleagues (2008) say that 'the key to successful mechanics is to make players feel that they are contributing to creating a plot' (p. 183). The key word here being *feel* – current technical limitations mean that a genuinely open narrative, in which a player can do or say anything, is a long way off; but providing the feeling of being able to do so is just as important. The emergence of 'sandbox' games, such as the *Grand Theft Auto* series, in which players have a vast virtual world to explore and interact with in seemingly infinite ways, go a long way to achieving this feeling of agency. In some cases the narrative may be planned out in detail by the game designer in advance (such as in the case of adventure games), but in other games types (such as simulations) it will be generated as the game progresses, allowing players to generate their own mythology around the game and create their own narratives. Other game forms, such as ARGs and massively multiplayer online (MMO) games often generate folklore-type narrative in the communities that surround the game, related to or inspired by the original game, extending the overall narrative outside of its original boundaries and putting the power of the narrative into the hands of the players. The game provides a coherent world, through which many different narratives can run – some hard-wired into the game by the designers and others generated by players in the style of fan-fiction.

Having said that we feel that the narratology vs. ludology debate is a bit of a red herring, one or other aspect will still tend to be at the forefront of the game design: either the narrative leading the gameplay with the game story at the forefront, and uncovering the narrative mystery or finding out what happens to the characters one of the core motivations; or with the gameplay at the forefront, where the narrative may be almost incidental but it provides the 'glue' that holds the action together and creates a goal and purpose for playing the game.

Delivering Narrative in Games

'[A really good game is about the] stories; I think a lot of it is about the stories. Not only the ones that drive the game, but also the ones that are generated through participating in it – the ones you are compelled to share afterwards. If it takes me ten minutes to walk across the playground at break-time because children from different year-groups are desperate to share their ideas and experiences with me, then I know I'm doing something right. If I'm running an event in the city centre and shoppers stop to ask questions, share thoughts, or to take part, then that's also a good sign!'

Nikki Pugh

There are a variety of different and creative ways in which a storyline can be communicated to game players; unlike a novel, game writers are not restricted by a single continuous text. In fact, many of the methods of delivering story in games have much more in common with the film industry, such as live action, dialogue or narration. Live action – what actually happens during the game as it unfolds (such as the places visited and people spoken with) – is how characters in the story behave, and how what they do shapes the story; observation can show a lot about a person, but it does not tell the player what they are thinking. This can be achieved through dialogue – what characters say to the player or, less commonly, dialogue overheard between characters – or through narration, where a character explicitly states what is happening against the backdrop of action.

As well as in-game action, where the player has control, narrative can also be delivered through cut-scenes, which are simply short action clips that can be watched by the players but with which they cannot interact. It can also be progressed through the use of artifacts in the game, such as letters, diaries, or newspaper articles, which the player can read in order to further their understanding of the plot.

The way in which narrative is used in games can be similar to traditional media, but it can also be profoundly different. In this section we have tried to give the reader a quick overview of some of the differences, and the creative ways in which game narrative can be used to engage and stimulate the player. In the section that follows, we will look in more detail at how to design narratives that are compelling for those who follow them.

Creating Narrative

'I don't think the hard problems around storytelling in games have been solved yet! In novels, we know how to do free indirect voice and various other tricks; they've been around for hundreds of years. But games are still carving out their storytelling methods and tropes. It's exciting to be part of that.'

Naomi Alderman

Creating effective narrative is not easy; it is an art as much as a science. In this section, we hope to provide some guidelines and tips on how to design a narrative, but it is important to remember that they are not set in stone. Designing a good narrative depends as much on the creativity of the writer as following a set list of structures and techniques. Having said that, for a novice narrative designer, some background into the basics of the craft may be useful. There follows a number of suggestions for ways in which to make narrative more compelling.

Plot

Having a strong plot to drive the story is key. A plot is the series of events that make up the story, and interesting and meaningful events that make sense as a sequence is very important. A good narrative is more than just a sequence of events; the order in which they happen, how they happen, and why they happen is also crucial (more about this in *narrative arcs*), but having an interesting series of events is a great starting point. As well as a main plot, any number of sub-plots can be developed to add colour, texture, and complexity to the narrative; although it is important that all sub-plots head in the same general direction and do not distract from the overall direction of the text. Also important is the backstory (or what happened before the action in the narrative): the events that lead up to the initial starting point for the story.

Conflict

Stories are boring without any conflict or challenges for the protagonists. If a character simply gets on with daily life unimpeded there isn't really much of a story to tell. Compelling narratives generally are based around a character overcoming a hurdle or challenge in order to achieve some goal; without that there is little purpose to the story. A conflict that readers or players can relate to and care about the outcome, that isn't too trivial or easy, is a good starting point for a narrative design.

Tension

Once a conflict has been established, readers should be uncertain as to how it will be resolved. Again, a story where the ending is obvious will generally be less compelling than one where there is an element of mystery. The ability to build up dramatic tension throughout a story, to a climax, while keeping the reader interested is crucial – but very difficult. Challenges should not be too easy, nor should they be resolved in the most obvious way. A feeling of jeopardy or peril can also be built up throughout the story, as readers become attached to main characters and, hopefully, care about what happens to them.

Pace

Pace is all to do with the rate in which events unfold in the story, and their timing. A story that ambles along at a slow pace may not be sufficiently exciting for the reader, while one that hurtles along without a break may not give the reader space for breath or reflection, or time to wonder what happens next. A story that speeds up and slows down at crucial points helps to establish the mood of the action; whether it is a fast chase, or a slower investigation of a haunted house.

Character Arcs

Interesting and rounded characters are essential: those who the reader takes a liking to, or at least can relate to in some respect. A story can have exciting events, perfect pacing, and tension, but if no one cares that the characters are in peril or conflict, then the story will have no impact. Characters need to be well rounded, not perfect, to have flaws as well as positive attributes – just like real people. Characters need to change as the narrative progresses, learn something, become better – or simply different – people as a result of the events that have unfolded. This is the idea of a character arc.

Narrative Arcs

A narrative arc is the way in which a series of events are presented so that they are not simply one event taking place after another, but elements like conflict, tension, and pace are considered. Events are purposeful in narrative, rather than just being *things that happen*, they lead in a certain direction, and influence how characters change and grow. Every event has a reason for taking place, be it to move the plot forward, or simply to show another side of a character.

The Hero's Journey (Campbell, 1993) provides an archetypical narrative arc, on which stories throughout history, such as myths and legends, fairy tales, epic novels, and films have been based. Vogler (1998) further developed this narrative structure into a practical framework of twelve steps and shows how classic stories, such as *The Wizard of Oz* and *Star Wars*, adhere to this format. This need not be strictly adhered to, and provides a very good starting point for designing a narrative arc. In summary, the twelve steps of the Hero's Journey narrative arc (Vogler, 1998) are as follows:

- *The ordinary world*. The hero in his or her normal setting (this is used to contrast with the extraordinary world of the main story).
- *Call to adventure*. The hero is presented with a challenge or problem that takes him or her out of the comfort of the ordinary world (into the extraordinary world).
- *Refusal of the call*. The hero is reluctant to take the call; an event such as a change in circumstances, or the influence of a mentor, changes his or her mind.
- *Meeting the mentor*. The idea of a guide, support, or mentor is common to many stories; it is the function of the mentor to prepare the hero for his or her adventure.
- *Crossing the first threshold*. This is the point of no return in which the hero makes a decision to act and the adventure truly begins.
- *Tests, allies, and enemies*. The hero encounters a series of tests and begins to understand the rules of the extraordinary world. He or she makes allies, and enemies are introduced.
- *Approach to the inmost cave*. The hero prepares and approaches the most dangerous place in the extraordinary world.
- *The ordeal*. A crisis for the hero in which he or she directly faces the greatest fear and the possibility of death (actual or metaphorical).

- *Reward*. Having survived 'death', the hero receives a reward, such as an object or knowledge; there is cause for celebration.
- *The road back*. The hero deals with the consequences of the ordeal and decides to return to the ordinary world, pursued by enemies.
- *Resurrection*. A final ordeal or second life-or-death moment during which the hero is transformed.
- *Return with the elixir*. The hero returns to the ordinary world with some sort of treasure or lesson learned.

While it is certainly true that not every story adheres to the framework of the Hero's Journey, if you think about your favourite books or films it's certainly surprising the number that do. While it might not exactly fit the plot you have in mind, it works as a great starting point for thinking about narrative arcs and the elements within them.

Krawczyk and Novak (2006) suggest three other plot devices or techniques for engaging the reader: 'red herrings', 'reversals' and 'line of action'. Red herrings are story elements that are used to throw the reader off track towards a misleading conclusion. Reversals occur when the story suddenly goes in the opposite direction to that which is expected, for example a shift in perspective such as discovering that a male character is actually female. Line of action involves building the plot around events in which the character can take action or make a choice, rather than the direct causal sequence of events; they argue that forcing the action in this way leads to a build up of dramatic tension.

In this section, we have examined the typical narrative elements used to engage people; although much of the work in this area stems from books or films, it is still very relevant to computer games. In the section that follows, we will examine the use of narrative in the context of learning and teaching, looking at the pedagogic advantages of the approach and suggesting examples of ways in which it might be used.

Using Narrative in Teaching and Learning

Narrative and stories have been used to support learning since the dawn of time: passing mythologies, folk tales, and personal histories by word-of-mouth through generations; making lessons stick in the mind through the use of allegory, exciting events, and memorable characters. There are several pedagogic advantages to the use of narrative in teaching and learning, which we will discuss in the sections that follow.

Narrative allows learners to identify with characters and situations, putting themselves in the shoes of other people and thinking through problems from alternative perspectives. It provides a personal element, taking learning from abstract situations into contexts that have purpose and meaning; this can be very motivational and lead to greater immersion with the story. Narratives are designed, so that the reader is rewarded at the end, either by discovering a secret or mystery or by having the satisfaction of seeing the story reach a neat resolution. By contextualizing learning within a narrative, this provides the learner with a reason for engaging, but also can support transferability to other learning contexts.

'I suggest we look at wonderful educational TV from the past – like the *Look and Read* programs, which use a great story as a motivator to get kids interested in reading. Similarly, a wonderful game can inspire interest in a whole range of subjects. For me, playing the game *Assassin's Creed* has inspired me to learn about the Italian Renaissance. It's not just about testing and badges: games provide an immersive environment, where you find you want to learn more because the world is enticing. I'd like to see educational games use this ability more. Put your player in an exciting, fascinating position, where learning and thinking is the only way to proceed and watch them blast through your learning tools!'

Naomi Alderman

So how might narrative elements be used in teaching and learning in practice? Here we provide three examples of how stories might be used to support learning. These are simply examples, and much potential exists, limited only by the creativity of the learning designer.

Scenarios provide a way of presenting learners with context and backstory to a problem rather than just providing it in the abstract. They can be simple, providing the bare bones of a situation, or more complex, giving detail of characters, background, and interactions. Scenarios can be used on a single level ('This is the situation – what would you do?') or make use of multiple levels, where the scenario branches depending on decisions made by the learners (although the design of more complex scenarios of this type can be much more time consuming and difficult to get right). They can be very effective for students working in groups, as discussion of the content of the scenarios can be as important as the decision-making process itself.

Sparks are ways of introducing learners to a topic, generating ideas, or highlighting issues for further discussion. Again, rather than doing this in the abstract, using narrative devices such as cutscenes – short video clips or pieces of text – can draw a learner's attention to important points while making problems more personal and immediate. Thomson and colleagues (2007) describe three different types of cut scene used in games: video; real-time, rendered in the same way as the main game; and scripted (developed using the actual game engine). What is important is that the cutscene does not have to be in the same format as the main activity. Another way of providing a spark is through the use of commercial computer games to present ideas and stimulate discussion among learners around a topic. A good example of this is Rylands (2011), who used the adventure game *Myst* with primary school classes in order to inspire children's creative confidence.

Creative storytelling moves beyond the idea of the teacher as narrative creator, empowering learners to use narratives to present their own ideas and thoughts. Techniques such as digital storytelling (using tools such as video, animation or still photography) allow learners to engage with learning and assessment in more creative ways than simply writing traditional essays. Another example is through the use of digital tools such as comic strip creators, which allow users to easily develop visual stories to get their points across.

In this chapter we have aimed to provide you with a brief introduction to the way in which narrative is used in computer games, how to effectively design narrative, and possible ways in which it might be used in learning and teaching contexts. We hope that you see this as a starting point, and that it has inspired you to explore the potential of narrative in your own context.

6

COMPETITION
Playing to Win?

ALEX MOSELEY

Is there a Place for Competition in Education?

Competition has played a huge role in our short time on the planet – and is core to our modern understanding of evolution for all plant and animal life. Coming from a basic need to survive and prosper in new or increasingly crowded spaces, competition over time has repeatedly seen one species overtake or outlast another. This is usually linked with 'winning' the competition to adapt first and best to new environmental conditions (human species who emerged from Africa and adapted best to the cold climes and scavenger-type diet needed in northern parts of Europe, for example, were the ones who went on to prosper and eventually become the only human species on the planet).

Competition in shorter timescales has also been at the heart of another aspect of human life: warfare and conflict. The competition for space, or prestige, or religious or moral superiority, has reshaped the modern human world over and over again, and continues to do so.

These two brief summaries of the way competition is wired into the very fabric of being human exemplify the dichotomy modern students, parents, and institutions struggle with whenever the phrase is used. To some, competition and competitive play or behaviour is the best thing for them, their child, or their institution to succeed and prosper; but to others it is at the root of all evil – the aspect that brings out the worst in people and organizations (force, destruction, humiliation).

In both work and play this dichotomy can be seen all too clearly. At work we have sales targets, employees of the month, winners of industry, and professional prizes; and yet we have many employees who want to 'get out of the rat race', 'avoid conflict', or fail at interviews or in promotion because the competition is too fierce or too high. In play, some people dedicate their spare time to individual competitive sports, enjoy competitive board or digital games, enter countless magazine competitions; whereas others prefer non-competitive games, communal activities like book clubs or knitting circles, non-competitive sport or healthy activities.

(Squire (2011, p. 175) warns that 'having only one way to win is not enjoyable if you lose' and that students will 'opt out' of competitive schemes if they don't find them motivating. An interesting side effect of these varying preferences has been the development of ways to combine both competition and collaboration: team sports, for example, where there is a sense of communal effort in the local group, but clear competition with the opposing team(s); team games, where two or more play together but against other teams (such as the card game *whist*, traditionally solo-competitive games like Scrabble or Monopoly played with small teams, and physical games like paintball or laser quest). These 'mixes' create compelling activities, and seem to dull some people's dislike of competition now that it is 'tempered' with co-operation. In a review of these elements in educational settings, Johnson and Johnson (1989) found that co-operation is generally preferable to competition or individual effort, although when used in conjunction with group work, competition could support learning and motivate students. Salen and Zimmerman (2004) considered the forms of competition present in a number of commercial games, and whilst they describe points of conflict, they also note that 'the root of the word "compete" is the Latin *con petire* [or] "to seek together"' (p. 256) and that even when in direct competition, players are also sharing or co-operating from the simple act of playing or discussing the same game together.

In formal education, competition has had an equally troubled existence. The very set-up of our education systems are competitive at their heart: marks, exams, school and university admissions, and qualifications are all competitive: pitting students against each other with smaller numbers emerging as victors at each stage. And yet, over the last few decades in the UK (and over similar timescales and in different ways internationally) competition outside of formal testing or grading (which, paradoxically, has increased over the same timescale) has been seen in its negative form: something which is bad for the children and promotes bullish/violent or otherwise poor behaviour and values; and subsequently reduced: the removal of competitive sports in favor of team or individual pursuits at primary level is a prime example.

Dunlop (1976) noted that 'the arguments of the "anti-competition" lobby in education typically go somewhat like this: "Competitors by definition compete . . . the intention is clearly to win, and this logically entails trying to stop the other competitors from winning . . . we will expect the children to grow up thoroughly selfish"' (p. 127); a decade on, Rich (1988) agrees with the idea that 'selfishness' is at the heart of the anti-competition argument and adds that it is 'a threat to cooperation, incites cheating and other dishonest activities, causes considerable stress . . . stimulates rivalry, engenders shame in defeat, and is a source of envy, despair, selfishness and callousness' (p. 183). You can see why many schools and parents started to question the role of competition within education. Even amongst game designers and researchers, there is an awareness that competition is as demotivating to some, as it is motivating to others:

Whitton (2010a) from her own experience found that competition could 'act as a demotivational factor for some students who feel that they cannot compete' (p. 32) and that there may be gender differences, with men being more likely to be highly competitive. This difference in gender attitudes is supported by Trew and colleagues (1999) who found that boys were much more likely to choose competitive sports, whereas girls tend to engage in those which are non-competitive or recreational, in a review of research around the take-up of sports by primary and secondary pupils.

If, however, you remove the visible signs of competition from education (ignoring, for the moment, the inherent competitive nature of formal education itself), does it disappear? Will children be protected from its negative sides? Well, no, in a word. Internally, we are all constantly involved in small personal competitions of both a positive and negative nature. For one child, in school, their personal competition might be to get through the day without receiving a warning; or to perform better in a team sport and score a goal; or be the first to the front of the dinner queue. All these competitive actions are taking place all the time, regardless of whether competition is designed in or not; although the way they manifest themselves in particular individuals may vary in both prevalence and attitude (some learners may be genuinely non-competitive, even internally; although even they will encounter, and have to deal with, competitive behaviour from peers).

Within this chapter, therefore, I suggest that by utilizing our internal/wired-in competitive natures, and augmenting them with clever design and co-operative elements, we can create games and activities within formal education that promote many of the positive aspects of competition, but guard against some of the negative or exclusion elements.

Lessons from the Games Industry

Game designers deal with competition on a daily basis, with the fine balance between positive and negative competition – or between competition and co-operation – key to whether a game is successful and pervasive for a broad section of the playing community. In his bestselling book for games designers, Schell (2008) notes that 'the psychological forces that drive us to enjoy competition and cooperation have not changed – the better you can understand and balance these forces, the stronger your game will become' (p. 187).

'Remember that the player is not your opponent, and that the job of a game designer is to show the player how to succeed at your game rather than defeat them. It's a very common mistake made by novice game designers and one which can completely ruin a game.'

Jacob Habgood

Just like the wider societal responses to competition I outlined in the opening section, game players are split in their enjoyment of competitive aspects. To some, battling wave after wave of increasingly meaner alien hordes is the peak of enjoyment; whereas others will find this boring and would much prefer to spend their time solving a complex puzzle. There are some aspects though – both tangible and intangible – which have almost universal appeal.

Points and Leader Boards (Intangible)

Obtaining points for actions within a game, seeing those points rise, and (either at the end of a game, or during the game itself) seeing your points appear in a leader board against other known or unknown players (including their earlier scores) is an almost universal source of interest and pleasure ('You got the new high score' is virtually guaranteed to raise a smile). It is also tied very closely to motivation: the wish to play again to better your score, or to rise above your friends or peers on a leader board, is one of the simplest to bank on when designing a game.

Prizes and Rewards (Tangible)

Often linked to leader boards, but can be awarded for a variety of competitive activities, prizes are almost always positively received, and a great many people will partake in a competitive activity if they think they have a chance (even a slim one) of winning a prize. Getting the element of 'chance' right is tricky: if someone thinks that they stand no chance of winning (because the competition is too hard, or conversely because it is too easy and they assume large numbers will therefore compete) they won't be interested in competing; equally, if they have no interest in the prize itself, they may not want to compete. Although popular, it is interesting to note that leader boards are often more engaging to more people than prizes themselves, particularly over longer periods of time; although smaller prizes at regular stages or very large final prizes can be more motivating still. Research in games design (Malone, 1980), and, more recently, marketing (see, for instance, Kivetz, 2003), has found that people are more motivated by large uncertain rewards. In my study of the most motivating elements for players of the commercial alternate reality game *Perplex City*, players found the regular in-game rewards and grand prize more motivating than the leader boards (Moseley, 2008); whereas in the educational game *The Great History Conundrum* at the University of Leicester, I found that students found the leader boards more motivating than the small single grand prize (Moseley, 2009b). Rewards are a special form of prize which might be given during a game for a particular achievement, or for getting a certain score; and may vary from in-game items (new clothes/weapons, badges shown next to your name, etc.) to actual physical items (badges, toys, etc. sent through the post, or given out at stages during face-to-face games). These tend to be more motivating over longer periods than single prizes at the end of a game or which denote the end of a competition.

> 'Never forget they are there. Take them places they have never been. Empower them to acts greater than they can perform in real life. Reward them for their efforts.'
>
> Lee Sheldon

Visible Comparisons (Intangible)

Being able to track yourself against another player or players during a game provides a high level of excitement and interest (a combination of competition and community aspects – see Chapter 4). Some digital games adopt a split-screen approach, showing players racing or moving against each other (*Mario Kart*, on the Nintendo Wii or *DS*, is a popular example); others display opponents' scores or actions in on-screen displays. Many family board games include this aspect: in Monopoly, for example, you can see how much property and money your opponents own compared with your own at all times; in card games, you can often see how other players are doing by piles of tokens, number of cards in their hand, or the numbers of pairs or tricks on the table next to them. In sports, the *Nike+* system combines both personal and communal visible comparisons, allowing you to track each run against a previous one, and either track yourself against a group of friends or have them track and encourage you as you run (mixing both communal and competition aspects).

The Perfectly Matched Opponent (Intangible)

When playing a game or sport against family or friends, there is often a mismatch of skill levels. Either one of you wins all the time, or one of you has to lower your level of gameplay to ensure that the other player(s) don't get bored or give you an easy win. When you find a person, or computer opponent, who is *just* above your level of ability (or around about the same) you get the best possible game experience – you may only win once every 2–4 times, but your opponent challenges you just enough to make the competition perfect. If this can continue to happen as you yourself develop your gameplay, and your opponent remains matched just above, or develops alongside you, then you continue to get a challenging and engaging game. This is known in game design circles as *negative feedback*, or the '*elastic band*' effect: keeping an opponent's ability the same distance away from you as you progress. Computer chess games have developed to the point where they can offer you a perfectly matched opponent in this way;

other games let you choose an opponent from a variety of skill levels so that you can find your own 'perfect opponent'; in some sports – golf being an obvious example – there are handicap systems which remove the need to find a perfectly matched opponent, yet create a pseudo-perfect-partner by effectively adjusting the starting level of each player.

There are many other subtle tricks that game designers use to make competition compelling, but many are based around these core aspects – and these are certainly the best for educators new to game design to focus on. To extend your ideas, reflect on the games you play or have played, and think about what makes the competitive aspects compelling: what do you like about the way you play against opponents; do you get rewards as you play as well as at the end; do the levels of competition get harder or easier over time or in stages, etc. You might also at this point want to reflect on your own attitude to competition: do you fit into some of the player types described earlier, do you find particular types of competition awkward or offputting, does this change how you play games, or reflect the choice of games you play, etc. Through these reflections, you should start to see how even one person's preferences for competitive and collaborative play are nuanced and complex.

Overcoming Doubts

Before designing competitive activities for education, or adding a competitive element to traditional activities, there are a number of doubts or issues you might have to overcome in yourself or in others. Many of these centre around the tried and tested arguments I outlined in the first section, and I offered some counter-reasoning there; but here are some further suggestions for common issues.

'Not everyone likes competition'

This is true: for every student who enjoys competitive elements, there may be another who doesn't or would be disengaged by them. The good news is that by using light competitive elements, by designing activities that mix competition with cooperative or collaborative activity, or by making the competitive aspects optional, you can ensure that both types of student are catered for. It is likely that most people will respond well to light, intangible, competitive elements if they accompany other useful activity.

'My institution frowns upon any kind of competition'

This attitude can still be encountered in many primary and secondary schools; and pressure is likely to be as much from parents as the school itself. It is useful to link activities to the types of competition already used within the school subconsciously – for example, the use of tests or exams, good/bad behaviour charts or rewards, team sports, voting for house captains, etc. By extending these existing activities or modelling new activities on similar competitive methods, games with competitive elements can usually be introduced with positive, rather than negative, responses.

'Games/competitions are not "serious" enough for academic work'

This is a common complaint in further or higher education, where any non-traditional academic activity is seen as wasting staff or student time (by both of those groups). Two approaches can help here. First, tie the competitive elements closely into traditional academic activity: scoring on standard assessment scales, making any prizes/rewards 'academic' (book tokens, certificate from the head of department, etc.); or launch the game as a 'fun side activity for anyone interested' alongside more traditional teaching in the first instance, then move it into the curriculum when it becomes popular. Second, choose a problem area which needs a solution – maybe a failing research skills course, or induction module, or a particular subject area which students always struggle with; by devising a solution to a problem no-one else wants to touch, you will have more of a free reign to try new approaches, and will benefit from having a low motivation platform to work up from.

'Learners will focus on the competition rather than the learning'

This can be a danger when the competitive elements and learning are not designed together; but if carefully designed as described in the paragraph above, competitive items will be linked so closely to learning activity that any focus on the competition will also be a focus on learning (the competition will then serve its purpose as a motivating addition to the core learning).

'I don't want fights to break out in the classroom'

Where there is direct conflict between individuals or small groups, or a sense of unfairness with an activity or reward, emotions may ride high. You can mitigate against this somewhat by using larger collaborative groups, and by ensuring that all points, rewards or prizes are described in detail and awarded by a central authority. Bearing in mind earlier discussions about gender differences, and indi-vidual variations, in relation to competition, the inclusion of tasks and activities which attract points or rewards for non-competitive thought or actions – along-side those of a competitive nature – can help to diffuse focused competitiveness, and include more members of the group in a common aim. For example, whilst one prize might be awarded for doing something the fastest, another prize might be available for drawing the best poster or writing the best report.

Building in Competition

There are countless ways in which competition could be added to an existing, or built into a new, academic course. To help you to start to picture some of these ways, however, I've picked four possible approaches which you might choose (or mix) to base your course on.

'Light' competition: – points, leader boards, and prizes

As described in *Lessons from the Game Industry* above, the use of points, leader boards, rewards and prizes provides the most acceptable (and engaging) face of competition to most people. Assigning points and creating a leader board for an existing activity gives an easy way to introduce some competition, and some raised motivation, to an existing course. This 'layer' of points/rewards is becoming common in a number of other fields, and has come to be known as *gamification* (or, more correctly, *pointsification* – see Chapter 10); and whilst it has its problems, as a way to test the water for some competitive approaches in an existing course it is ideal. Points can easily be allocated to existing academic features such as multiple choice questions, discussion posts, and oral presentations; or you could assign points for particular effort, finding new resources, etc.. Leader boards can simply be charts on the wall or whiteboard, or could be created and manually updated in tables or spreadsheets within a course website; if they become more popular or more embedded over time, automated leader boards could be arranged to provide fast updates for students (more motivating, easier administration). It is important to make sure that students know what they will receive points for, how many points, and what (if any) the rewards or prizes are for positions on the leader board; also ensure that students who don't want to engage with the competitive elements will not be unduly disadvantaged.

A good example of an application of light competitive elements is *The Neverending Uni Quiz* designed by Katie Piatt at the University of Brighton: first-year undergraduates answer a series of simple multiple choice questions about facilities and services at the university, but in turn gain points on a visible leader board – both as individuals and as 'house' teams. Piatt notes (in Moseley et al., 2009) 'this added element of competition – between teams and also between individual players – has been identified as the key to the strong engagement observed. Initial analysis of players' behaviour, and feedback, shows bursts of intense activity – often playing for over an hour in a session until a target (e.g. top of the leader board for their team) is achieved'.

'Heavy' competition – head to head, winner takes all

The design and introduction of full competitive games into the curriculum needs careful thought. If too much emphasis is placed on the competitive aspects, some students might feel bored, alienated or complain. The best games, and certainly the best academic games, will provide competitive elements which are unobtrusive, and yet obvious to those who like them; most importantly, they will be designed with a good mix of game elements such as a strong story, challenge, communal aspects, etc. alongside competitive elements.

Direct student-to-student competition needs particular care, as it carries the potential for conflict or alienation. Use can be made of similar situations within traditional learning to aid the design of head-to-head competition though: debates, for example, pit one student against another but in a controlled, time-limited environment; campaigns for house captain or similar are often public, but the votes are cast anonymously to avoid any personal animosities.

Building in *perfectly matched opponents*, or *negative feedback*, is tricky/impossible to do technically in a computer game without a team of game designers and developers; but in non-digital games, this can be achieved quite easily. In medium-sized groups, you as facilitator can pair up particular students who you think are either at the same level, or would form a mentor/mentee relationship; in smaller or larger groups you might decide to monitor student activity during a game and adjust the level of difficult for individuals or the group according to their performance. At the simplest level, this could be issuing a problem to the group, and seeing how easy they find it. The next problem you issue will then be proportionally harder or easier (or require different skills) to match your group; you can repeat this for each subsequent problem – always aiming to stay a little bit higher than the group to push them *just enough*.

Competition as a Driver to Learning

Squire (2011) describes how, in a class game of *Civilization* (a commercial digital game in which you create and manage your own country and try to win by taking over the world by force or through advances in science or economy), where students played in groups against staff, one of the student groups arranged a secret sleep-over and spent the night researching and planning various strategies to try to beat the staff. Using a problem-solving challenge, you could create a team-based competition to see who can solve a particular problem (or win a particular activity), designing problems that need research or innovative ideas to win, which in turn might encourage students to work on them in their spare time. Even if the problems and the private research isn't 'on topic' (like Squire's student group) you can use it as a driver or catalyst to spark interest in related, 'academic' topics. For example, you might run a modified version of Cluedo with a group of chemistry students, and arrange it so that the clues contain particular chemical traces; students might decide to spend time privately looking into forensics or crime issues, which you could then link to the chemical aspects needed for your core subject.

Use Tension

'While competition and cooperation are polar opposites, they can be quite conveniently combined into a situation where you get the best of both' (Schell, 2008, p. 186). The best way to 'disguise' competitive play from those who don't like it, and yet promote it to those who do, is to mix it with co-operative or collaborative play. This is most easily achieved by pitting groups of students against each other (much like team sports), but you can also adopt more complex arrangements which mix co-operation and competition together in surprising ways (Schell uses the example of the computer game *Joust*, in which two players have individual scores, but also a combined score. The game provides situations where it is clearly beneficial to work together, and others where it is not; and players must decide whether to boost their personal score or work together for the team score at all times). *Marketplace*, a game used at Napier University to teach the application of marketing skills within a real-world context, included a competitive element between class groups, yet the course was assessed on individual academic performance: allowing students to aim for academic achievement without having to worry about the competitive side if they found it demotivational (Whitton and Hynes, 2006). Educationally, these situations provide a valuable source of in-game or post-game reflective discussion: Why did student X behave in that way? Should they have worked with student Y? Why were this team more successful? There are opportunities for creating highly inclusive games, which utilize a wide variety of skills from different students: designing a game in which individual students can only 'win' by using a mixture of skills from their fellow students at various times, for example (you might choose to allocate 'skills' or information arbitrarily to each student, or use their existing knowledge and experience).

Over to You

I hope that this chapter has, at the very least, helped you to either overcome your own personal issues with competition, or provided you with ways to overcome others' issues in your institution. The examples and ideas given are just starting points, and by starting simply or using familiar concepts, and gradually mixing in more complex forms of competition with other game elements, I hope that you'll have the confidence to introduce competitive elements where you think they are appropriate and be able to justify them. Note that competition is in no way a cure-all, and is unlikely to engage all students in all situations, but when applied in a careful and respectful manner, it can stimulate learning and increase motivation.

7
MULTIPLE MEDIA
A Picture is Worth a Thousand Words

PETER WHITTON

The Multi-sensory World of Computer Games

Commercial video game companies have long been aware of the importance of creating a rich multimedia experience. They put a great deal of development effort into producing games designed to please a player's senses of sight, hearing, and increasingly touch, as he or she interacts with the game. In this chapter, I will look at the different ways in which these types of multimedia are used in games and consider the importance of different media types in relation to learning.

The visual, audio, and haptic (touch-based) aspects of game environments are often referred to as 'game aesthetics'. Niedenthal (2009) defines game aesthetics as 'the sensory phenomena that the player encounters in the game' (p. 2) and I use this definition as the starting point of this chapter, before concentrating on the way in which aesthetics are used to represent the world of the video game to the player. Game aesthetics are often unfairly dismissed as mere 'eye-candy' or surface detail by commercial game designers (Schell, 2008) and educational game theorists (Egenfeldt-Nielsen et al., 2008; Squire, 2011) alike. I believe that game aesthetics cannot simply be dismissed in this way, although I do appreciate that other considerations such as gameplay and – in the case of educational games – alignment of gaming objectives with learning objectives may carry greater importance. A disregard for the effect that games have on the senses and the techniques used to appeal to them seems irrational. Surely creating attractive, captivating, and believable learning environments is desirable in both entertainment and education?

Video games employ a number of *aesthetic devices,* including animation, still pictures, video, music, narration, and sound effects. In the case of console games, an additional aesthetic dimension can be introduced by additional hardware that allows the gamer to interact with the game by touch or movement such as a joystick, a Wii controller or a Dance Mat.

It is difficult to detach any discussion of game aesthetics from the concepts of 'immersion', 'engagement', and 'presence', and much research has been published about the nature of these within gaming environments and virtual worlds (Douglas and Haragdon, 2000; Gee, 2003; Brown and Cairns, 2004). There are many definitions of these terms, so I will briefly describe what I mean by each in the context of this chapter. *Immersion* is the positive feeling that we all get when we are deeply engrossed in an activity or event. You may have noticed periods when time seems to fly by, when you are involved in a favorite activity, like reading a book, working on a crossword puzzle, playing music or taking part in sport. The concept of *engagement* is often closely associated with immersion and can be thought of as the emotional commitment or involvement that someone has with a given task: in the literature on both gaming and education it is often considered in relation to depth of interaction with the subject regardless of whether this is in a play or learning context. Immersive and engaging games can make players feel at one with or have a *presence* in the game world – or at least be willing to suspend their disbelief as they play.

Creating feelings of immersion, engagement, and presence can be desirable in both gaming and educational contexts; and aesthetic devices (used in games, such as graphics, audio, and haptic feedback) when used well can help create an environment that facilitates this. Commercial game manufacturers know that creating these feelings is important for customer satisfaction, playability, re-playability, and ultimately sales and, as a result, invest large sums of money in their development. This chapter considers the potential of multiple media and the importance of aesthetics for learning, and looks at what educators can learn from computer games. First, I will discuss the current games market, and the audio, visual, and haptic techniques that game companies use to create exciting entertainment products, before discussing the challenges involved in applying these techniques to learning settings, and finally providing some examples of the potential use of these techniques.

Producing Commercial Games

Research suggests (Boyer, 2008; Meloni, 2010) that the average cost of creating a single platform game runs at $US10 million, and $US18–30 million per title for multi-platform console games. Game development company Ubisoft have stated that 'games for the next-generation (of consoles) may exceed $60 million' (Ivan, 2009). Big budget console games often employ teams of hundreds of dedicated staff working full time for years on a single title. Teams include employees with specialist skills in the aesthetic aspects of the design, which may include visual artists specializing in character development, environments, level design, or texture design and audio specialists concerned with sound engineering or music composition. In addition to high development costs there is also an acceptance of failure within the commercial games industry, with around nine out of ten commercial video games failing to make a profit.

Not all commercial games cost these astronomical sums or require large development teams to produce. Casual and social games development costs can range from $US30,000 to $US300,000 with mobile and smartphone games having much smaller production costs ranging from $US5,000 to $US20,000 per title (Meloni, 2010). There are also innovative shareware games where the developers give away a version of their game in the hope of a donation, or limit its functionality in hope that players will pay for extensions. Casual games are often created at low-cost using tools such as Macromedia Flash and are designed to be played through a web browser. In addition, there are active open-source and hobbyist games scenes where games are often created by keen amateurs using freely available code libraries – sometimes for niche or obsolete playback devices and consoles. Budgets can be small to non-existent for these ventures and often rely more on enthusiasm and goodwill rather than sound financial models, which enable development costs to be kept to a minimum. Aesthetic design is not always at the forefront in these types of game; see for example the donation-financed *Kingdom of Loathing* (see Figure 7.1), whose hand-drawn stick figure graphic style is a good match for its surreal sense of humour.

It is clear that educational game production cannot hope to command the high sums given to commercial game development, as the potential markets are simply not there to make the same types of profit. Therefore, it is unlikely that we will ever reach the situation where educational games have as much emphasis on aesthetics as commercial games. However, this shouldn't mean that we should overlook the importance of multi-modality and aesthetics in educational games – and other learning activities – but focus more on what we can learn from games, and how we can apply these techniques cost-effectively

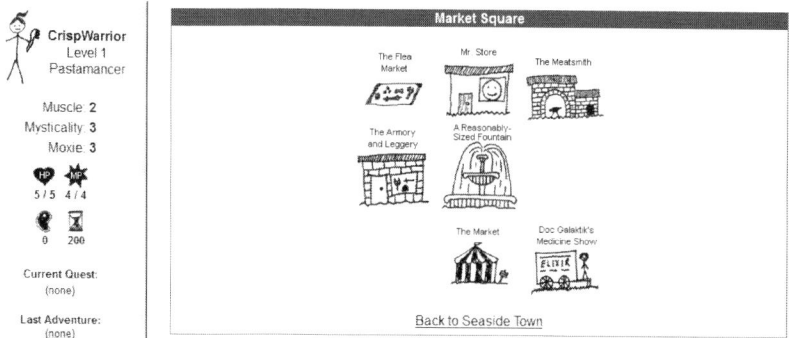

Figure 7.1 *Kingdom of Loathing*

Reproduced with permission of Aysmmetic Publications

to learning. In the next section I examine the graphical, video, auditory, and haptic techniques used in video game design in a little more detail, defining what I mean by each term and giving examples of how and why they are used.

Aesthetic Devices Used in Game Design

This section considers some of the aesthetic devices that are used in game design in greater detail. In each of the following three sections – visual design, audio design, and haptic design – I will present a variety of techniques and discuss the way in which each technique is used in computer games.

Visual Design

By visual design I mean all of the presentational aspects of a game that are seen by the player, including those within the game and those sometimes considered 'outside' the game – such as the user interface. The 'look and feel' of a game has a profound effect on the overall gaming experience and mood of a video game; Egenfeldt-Nielsen and colleagues (2008) go so far as to say that 'graphic types have different properties and afford different gameplay styles' (p. 105) and without a doubt certain game genres have traditionally lent themselves to particular aesthetics. For instance, first person shooters, action adventure, and sports games have traditionally pushed the development of 3D animation, whereas adventure, puzzle games, and strategy games have relied less on graphic fidelity and more on gameplay. There is considerable stylistic variety in the rendering and presentation of current computer games, and Hayward (2005) gives an insightful overview of the diversity of visual aesthetics used in the games market, showcasing examples of different graphics types used such as realistic, abstract, cartoon, and iconographic.

Schell (2008) describes three ways that strong visual design can contribute to the success of a game. He suggests that it can attract players to a game, make the game environment feel concrete, and make players more likely to tolerate gameplay flaws. The graphic style of a game also defines to some extent how it is perceived and marketed to potential players. The rest of this section looks briefly at some of the predominant stylistic or aesthetic trends in gaming and considers the range of visual techniques used by game designers.

Still images were once widely used in video games especially in adventure, role play and strategy genres such as *Civilization*, where the top portion of the screen was a static picture and the bottom half of the screen allowed the player to interact with the game using text. Stills are now rarely seen as part of gameplay in console games but are still used in mobile and phone games, because of the more limited processing capacity. Still images continue to be used to create artifacts such as maps, notes, and clues that a player may find or receive as part of the game and the static interface around the border of some games. They also play an important part in creating the backgrounds and textures used in many games to create atmosphere and realism.

Live action (interactive animation) is the main visual technique used in video game design to represent the game environment to the player. It is often used to depict character movement and transformations from one state to another, perhaps as a player interacts with an object on the screen, or even to draw the player's eye to something that they could interact with. Live action animation can be a simple two-dimensional game-world representation – as used on the early arcade games such as *Space Invaders*, which display the game environment as an elevation, games that use a plan view, such as *Pac Man*, or games that employ a scrolling side view, as is typical in platform games (see Figure 7.2 below).

This two-dimensional type of representation is no longer common in arcade or console games, but is still used today in simple puzzle or casual games that can be downloaded to modern mobile phones and purposefully designed to have 'retro' aesthetics (see Figure 7.3).

The dominant live action animation aesthetic in mainstream console gaming is 3D photorealism, and realism appears to be the benchmark against which many games are measured, and to which many game designers aspire. This push towards sophisticated visual realism is inextricably linked in the mind of the games industry to a desire to continuously improve player immersion and meet increasingly exacting player expectations. The current zenith of the 3D animators' art is exemplified by highly realistic sports games, first-person shooters and action adventure games. These powerful 3D graphics are especially evident in the highly cinematic cutscenes used to move the games from one plot point to another or provide a backstory.

> 'Don't confuse graphical quality with realism. I think aesthetics is extremely important to the experience. But that doesn't mean realistic high polygon 3D graphics. There are many ways of capturing an aesthetic from anime to 3D to cartoons, etc. Thinking about the aesthetic and its match for the audience and game are important.'
>
> Eric Klopfer

Animation is also the main way in which the game designer can convey the complexity, form, and player's point-of-view of the gaming environment to the player. The player's point-of-view has a huge effect on the way that play occurs and also the way in which he or she interacts with the game. Common visual devices used by animators to describe the game environment include: first person, where the game is seen through the eyes of the player; third person,

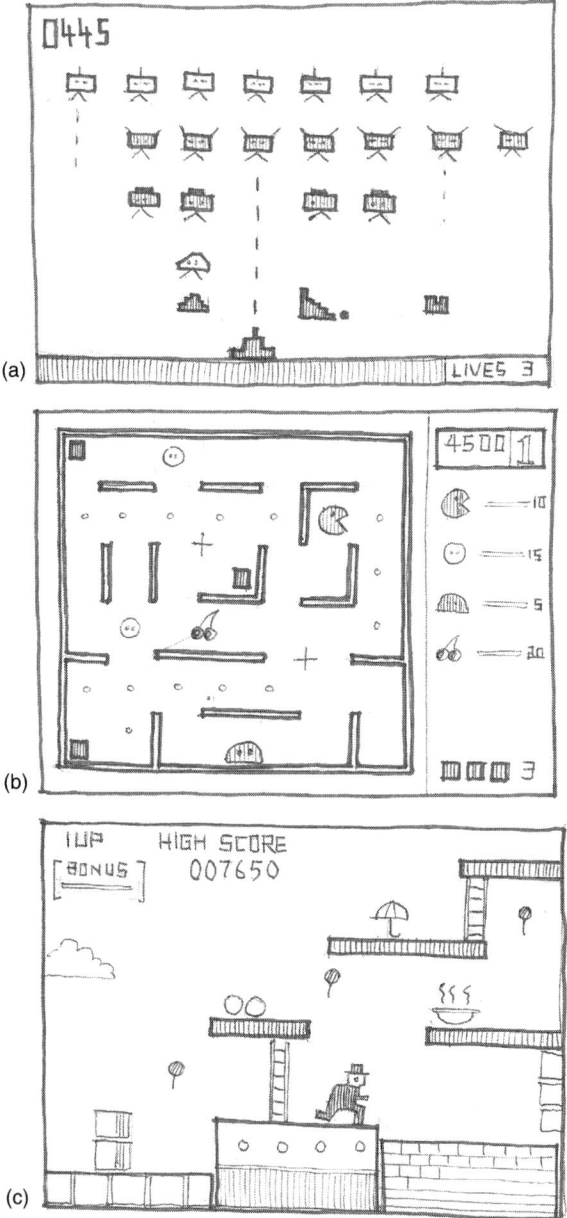

Figure 7.2 Two-dimensional game views: a) elevation; b) plan; c) scrolling

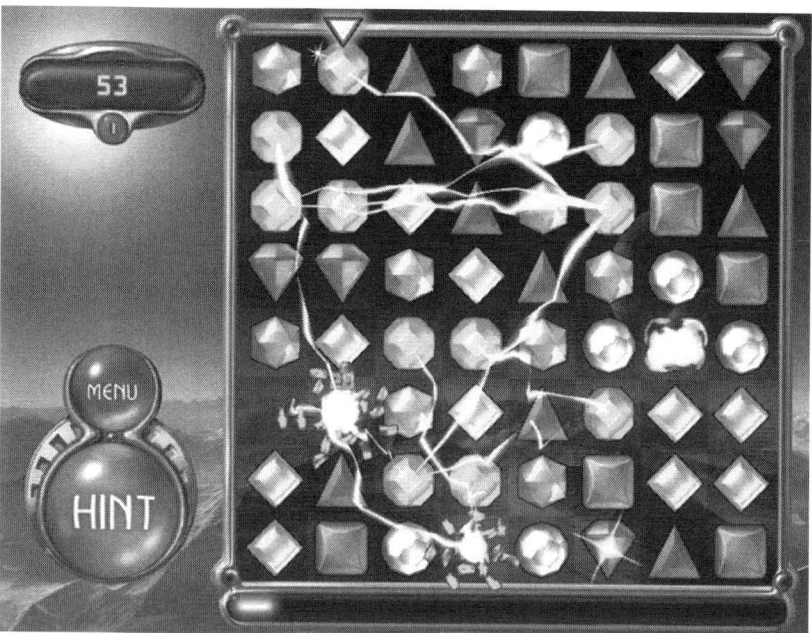

Figure 7.3 *Bejewelled*

Reproduced with permission of PopCap Games

where the player's avatar (or representation) appears in the foreground of the screen; and omniscient view (also called 'gods' eye' or 'ariel'), which are often rendered as if the player was hovering over the game-world. The differences between these views are shown in Figure 7.4.

Comics strips or sequential stills are used to show the progression of action without the need for animation. They are not common in modern games, but are occasionally used in casual games as an alternative to cutscenes between levels to progress the narrative.

Video is also not widely used in modern commercial video games, although full motion video games (FMV) were popular in the 1990s but have lost favor in mainstream gaming as a result of the improved realism in modern 3D animation techniques. More recently, FMV has found favor in the popular *I Am Playr,* an interactive football management game on Facebook that combines video footage and 3D gaming. Although less prevalent now, live-action video sequences, where actors are used in place of the in-game characters, are sometimes used as game cut scenes. Many game players dislike this because of the non-interactive nature of cut-scenes and these sequences are often criticized by gamers for interrupting the 'flow' of play.

Figure 7.4 Three-dimensional game views: a) first person; b) third person; c) omniscient

Audio Design

In this section I use the terms *sound* and *audio* interchangeably, although technically audio should be used for noise that is within the human hearing range, whereas sound could include ultra high and low frequency sound outside this range. Sound is used in games in a number of ways, to transmit information, to create ambience, to dictate or convey the tempo of play, and to communicate the storyline.

Most computer games focus on the graphical display as the primary way that the player interacts with the game. Even with advances in in-game sound, games that explore audio as the main method of interaction are either niche – such as the audio adventure game *Real Sound: Kaze no Regret* originally created for the *Sega Saturn* in 1997 or *Papa Sangre*, a more recent audio-based first-person thriller – or have been designed as 'assistive' games for visually impaired players and others who have difficulties using conventional visual displays, for example *Shades of Doom,* an audio-only first person shooter.

Much of the language and many of the techniques used in video game sound were originally developed by the film industry and, as a result, there is still a great deal of overlap between the two disciplines in the taxonomies used to describe audio. Game audio, like that of film, is sometimes described by its position in the overall soundtrack – or perhaps the amount of attention that it demands of the player – as foreground, mid-ground, and background. Jorgenson (2010) describes the work of audio theorists such as Axel Stockburger who classify games sounds as either 'diegetic' – sound that emanates from inside the game world (footsteps, thunderstorms, engines revving) – or 'non-diegetic' – sound that emanates from outside the game world (feedback elements, status bars). Perhaps a more useful way of classifying and thinking about game audio is that of Folmann (2004) who defines four main categories – vocalization, sound effects, ambient effects, and music; in the rest of this section I will consider each in more detail.

Vocalization can mean any sound that is speech-like, for example the voice of a narrator used to progress the storyline or the dialogue of in-game characters. In modern commercial video games, speech is usually pre-recorded by voice-actors and is triggered by events and interactions in, and with, the game. Some early video games experimented with synthesized speech but this seems to have fallen out of favour as it was difficult to convey emotional nuance, sometimes difficult to understand, and became annoying when overused.

Sound effects used in games are very much like those used in films, and play an important part of creating ambience and describing the gaming environment to the player. Examples of sound effects include a creak when a door opens, the slam when it closes, or the noise of feet running down a corridor, or a gun being fired. Sound effects provide feedback to players on the consequences of their actions and can help to increase dramatic tension.

Ambient effects are the sounds that play in the background that a player may not even be consciously aware of. In addition to providing atmosphere, these background effects can be effective in giving the game world a sense of place. Sound designers often use ambient effects to convey a sense of background activity, the idea that something is going on even when the game is not being played. This could be through the constant pulsing hum of a spacecraft's life support system or the gentle splash of waves and creaking of timber on a pirate ship.

Music is another background effect that is commonly used in most game types, from music with a loud pulsing beat in a game that requires fast reactions, to a gentle background melody in a slower-paced adventure game. Music can be used to convey mood, as well as give an impression of place and space. Background sound and music often convey the amount of activity that is taking place, either through tempo or volume. It is when background music steps out of the background into the foreground that it can become obtrusive and annoying, but this technique can also be used to good effect, for example when a character goes into a busy bar.

Haptic Design

Devices such as joysticks and game controllers have a long tradition in arcade and home video gaming for controlling on-screen characters and providing a means of interacting with the game through touch. Early controllers only allowed one-way communication with the gaming environment, responding to the players' movements but giving no information back to the player. More recent devices employ *force feedback* technology, enabling the player to sense reactions to movements on screen and receive cues from the game in the form of vibrations and pressure, for instance steering wheels that allow the player to feel the bumps in the road or the car slipping out of control.

Advances in motion-sensing technology have seen a renewed interest in haptic interaction design. We can see evidence of this most notably in motion-control devices for game consoles such as the Nintendo Wii, Sony Playstation Move, and Microsoft Kinect which enable players to interact with games through their physical movements, either by locating their position and plotting this in relation to the game environment on screen or by using hand-held interaction devices that are motion-sensitive. There are also a wide range of haptic interaction devices available such as musical instruments, bongos, dance mats, and balance boards, which provide new opportunities for haptic interaction in different ways.

In addition to motion control gaming, touch-screen technology is improving and becoming more responsive and is now commonly used in smart phones and other devices such as the Nintendo DS and Apple iPad, which rely on the users' touch as the main mode of interaction, such as *Guitar Hero* on the

Nintendo DS. This has given mobile-gaming a haptic dimension and allows users to quickly and accurately interact with games on their phones/handheld devices using a range of touch-based commands. Console and games manufacturers are constantly developing new peripheral devices to allow players to interact in new ways with games through touch and movement. These haptic devices offer players another form of feedback and potentially a greater feeling of immersion in the game as more senses are brought into play.

Game Aesthetics in a Teaching and Learning Context

So far in this chapter I have looked at some of the aesthetic devices that the games industry uses to create imaginative and immersive environments for gameplay; and I will now consider the challenge of how best to exploit these techniques for learning. One of the traps that some educational game designers fall into is to try and emulate the aesthetics of high-end console video games too closely – trying to compete on an uneven playing field, in terms both of the financial resources available and pool of artistic and technical talent on hand.

The task of creating appropriate teaching and learning materials that incorporate high-quality graphics and audio may create a number of potential obstacles – lack of technical skills, lack of time available, and lack of institutional support – and also poses a number of questions. Do production values matter to students? What techniques are appropriate to learning in what context? What can we learn from game aesthetics that can be realistically reused in our classrooms and online learning spaces? And what tools can we use to achieve this?

'In my school projects I was never aiming for something realistic; never trying to fool the children into believing something was real. What I wanted was for them to buy into the story we were weaving and to go along with it themselves, recognizing that it was a massive game of 'Let's Pretend' and that that meant that anything was possible.'

Nikki Pugh

Do Production Values Matter to Students?

Some educators worry that because students are exposed to sophisticated production values in television, film, games, and other media they will naturally expect a similar level of quality and fidelity from technologies and media used in teaching, whether this is an educational game, a virtual learning environment, lecture slides or other course materials.

Surprisingly little has been written in this area, and views on whether students expect professional production values in learning media are inconclusive in both the academic and anecdotal evidence. Rieber and colleagues (2001) undertook a study with children critiquing games designed by other children and found that 'although they like the high-quality graphics and sound of commercial video games, the amateur-like quality of these children-designed games was not a problem nor an important factor in their critiques' (p. 8). On the other hand, Elliot and colleagues (2002) were disappointed with the evaluation of their AquaMOOOSE 3D graphical environment for math exploration, stating that 'student expectations for the software were high due to the production values seen in commercial video games' (p. 1).

These examples from educational games research, although dated, illustrate the difference of opinion about production quality and highlight that this argument is really about fitness for purpose and expectation management. Recent debates about production values in video lecture capture and podcasting highlight the choices that educators must make. Do they capture the moment and produce 'quick and dirty' media, which may have flaws, and requires minimal editing, but can quickly respond to student needs? The alternative is to create broadcast-quality productions that rely on the skills, equipment and timescales of others, but which may have greater longevity and conform to notions of professionalism.

Squire (2011) believes that educational designers should attempt to emulate the aesthetics, art, and design skills of the entertainment industry in order to create material that appeals to students. I disagree; I believe that students are willing to forgive flaws in the aesthetics of games and other material created for learning providing that the educational purpose of the game is apparent, and that it is fit for this purpose. I think that learners, particularly at university, do not expect educational games to be of commercial graphical quality; and that they use educational materials as a basis for comparison, not commercial games. We must also remember that not all students (even children) play high end console games – the Wii is the biggest-selling console worldwide, and casual and handheld mobile games with poorer graphic and audio fidelity are growing in popularity.

'Graphical quality is extremely important for selling games, and has a big effect on success in the market place. Nonetheless the perpetual arms race for better graphical quality takes development time and money away from other aspects of a game. Realism can add to the immersive experience created by a game in some contexts, but if the gameplay is good enough then I think players will always willingly suspend their disbelief.'

Jacob Habgood

Game Aesthetics and Multimedia Learning

The previous sections have discussed the use of aesthetic devices (audio, visual, and haptic) by video game manufacturers to create a sense of engagement and immersion in their titles, but how does this relate to learning? This section focuses on the trade-off between emulating or using aesthetically pleasing game environments and their suitability for learning.

Games can use complex interactive interfaces that exploit the potential of multimedia technology, in that they routinely combine and overlay audio, visuals, words, and pictures. With this in mind, this section considers some of the research into multimedia learning and compares the techniques used to enhance entertainment games with research on good practice in a multimedia learning context.

It would be impractical to consider what makes effective multimedia learning without some discussion of the work of psychologist Richard E. Mayer and his colleagues at the University of California, Santa Barbara, who have worked in this area since the late 1980s. Mayer's work on multimedia and learning asks the central question of whether using words and pictures – auditory and visual means to present material – has advantages for the learner. Mayer's 2001 book *Multimedia Learning* distils this work into the seven principles for the design of multimedia learning presented in Table 7.1, in which I have also linked the principles of multimedia learning to the use of games.

The table shows that while there is evidence for the effective use of multimedia in learning, this does not necessarily translate neatly into principles for the effective use of multimedia in game-based learning. It is dangerous to uncritically view commercial video games as learning environments, and educational game designers are likely to face problems if they emulate a commercial game blueprint too closely. Commercial entertainment game designers are not concerned with effective or efficient learning; in fact they purposely place barriers to mastery in the players' way to confuse and impede progress and prolong gameplay. They are, quite rightly, unconcerned with these principles – especially those related to coherence and redundancy. Irrelevant words, pictures and sounds are added in abundance to video games to add atmosphere and interest. Many game genres flood payers' sensory channels with a surplus of information in what Sweller (1999) describes as 'cognitive overloading'. In addition, many commercial games are rich with extraneous, often interesting, information and detail – which may be necessary to enrich the narrative or game environment, but, from a multimedia learning point of view would be considered 'seductive detail damage' (Harp and Mayer, 1998). In other words, material that distracts, disrupts or diverts by activating prior knowledge, which is unnecessary for the learning task at hand. However, in the context of game-based learning, extraneous material can be used to develop a

Table 7.1 *Principles of multimedia learning and their relevance to games*

Principle	The idea that . . .	Relevance to games
Multimedia principle	Students learn better from words and pictures than from pictures alone	Games routinely blend audio dialogue and compelling visuals. Often audio dialogue is shown simultaneously with textual dialogue (or at least this is provided as an option).
Spatial contiguity principle	Students learn better when corresponding words and pictures are presented close to each other on page or screen.	The proximity of words and pictures are not always close in games (for example, character actions in a role playing game might be shown centre-screen, but descriptions or speech appear at the base).
Temporal contiguity principle	Students learn better when corresponding words and pictures are presented simultaneously rather than successively.	The proximity of words and pictures are not always simultaneous in games. In many games, piecing together clues provided in different media formats is part of the game design.
Coherence Principle	Student learning is hurt when interesting but irrelevant words, pictures and sounds are added. It is improved when unneeded material is removed.	Games routinely use irrelevant but interesting multimedia to enhance and add colour to narrative and plot.
Modality principle	Animation and narration is better than animation and on screen text.	Both techniques are used in games, according to the technology and genre.
Redundancy principle	Animation and narration is better than animation, narration and on-screen text.	Options are often available in games to allow players to make choices.
Individual differences principle	Effects are stronger for low-knowledge learners and for high-spatial learners (rather than low).	No research into parallels in games.

Source: adapted from Mayer, 2001

context for learning (see Chapter 8) providing colour and authenticity and greater parallels to real life (where disruptive and diverting material is part of any learning situation).

It is important for educators to be wary of – or at least aware of – the effects that audio and visual media can have on learning when used individually and in combination, but also to recognize that lessons learned from multimedia learning theory may not apply to educational game design.

How can Game Multimedia be Applied to Education?

Some educationalists (Gardener, 2003) argue that each of us has a preferred modality for receiving information and by delivering learning using the correct mode or modes – whether this is using pictures and sound or through touch and physical activity – we can tap into a student's preferred 'learning style' and improve their chances of retaining and understanding information. I believe this idea – although superficially attractive – is simplistic and that the route toward deeper learning is more complex than finding the correct mix of delivery modes.

The previous section looked at the differences between multimedia design for learning and games for entertainment. While games may not offer us all the answers in terms of presentation of learning material, used appropriately, techniques commonly found in video games can enhance the way we make learning available to our students, improve the way that information is presented, and increase the chances of immersion in the learning process.

In this section we will have a look at some activities that modern educators engage in, and consider how visual, auditory, and haptic techniques (applied from a gaming perspective) can enhance the presentation of educational material and the learning process itself. This section will also discuss some of the free tools available to lecturers and students for creating media rich material.

Image Techniques in Education: The Educator as Presenter

Although many are critical of the lecture as a method of teaching, they are still – for many educators – a main method of interaction with students. The usual format for these events is that of the lecturer stood at the front of a large teaching space talking to – or sometimes at – rows of students. The lecture is usually accompanied by slides – often created in PowerPoint – projected on a screen behind the presenter.

The phrase 'death by PowerPoint' is often used to describe turgid, over-long, overcrowded, text-based slides that have more chance of sending the audience to sleep than educating. This doesn't need to be the case: PowerPoint has underused visual and audio tools, and it is only through convenience and an unwillingness to experiment that educators have tended towards using the bullet list by default.

We should be thinking more critically about our presentations. Minimize the amount of text on screen – the written content of the presentation, and more, can always be made available to the student through PowerPoint notes or separate handouts. So much more can be achieved by making full use of the power of the visual through emotive and thought-provoking images. You can consider embedding audio and video or creating simple animations where appropriate, but if these are overused they can make presentations look very unprofessional.

Creating visual material used to require access to expensive software, but there are now many powerful open source and online graphics tools (such as the Aivary and Fatpaint) for producing bitmapped (see Gimp and Paint.net) and vector-based (see Inkscape and Alchemy) artwork, which can be down-loaded or used on the web for free. There are also considerable free picture and graphic resources made available under creative commons licensing through sites such as Wikimedia Commons (http://commons.wikimedia.org/) and Flickr creative commons (www.flickr.com/creativecommons/) that contains photographs, icon sets, illustrations, and diagrams for use, re-use or re-working under a variety of open licenses.

3D models can be created without having to invest in professional tools; using tools such as Google Sketch Up users can also reuse models (mainly architectural and engineering subjects) that have already been created by browsing the Sketch Up Warehouse (http://sketchup.google.com/3dware-house/). Many games now (particularly online games or those for mobile devices) use low-fidelity graphics effectively; these techniques can also be applied to education. For example, the use of stick men can be a quick and effective way to illustrate a point without requiring graphic skills (see the Common Craft videos at www.commoncraft.com/).

Video Techniques in Education: The Educator as Broadcaster

Modern educational practice increasingly requires lecturers and teachers to create and deliver content beyond the confines of the class or lecture theatre, making available teaching materials and learning activities online to accom-modate the flexible study patterns of modern students or as part of blended, distributed, or distance learning initiatives. This has changed the dynamic of traditional teaching activities pushing them into the realm of publishing or broadcasting.

Increasingly educators and students alike are both consumers and producers of video and audio material. Tools such as Windows Movie Maker, and iMovie for the Mac, have made rapid editing and publishing of videos to public sites such as YouTube (www.youtube.com) and Vimeo (http://vimeo.com) a straight-forward process. These tools – plus the growing availability of digital cameras, audio recorders, and smart-phones with built-in cameras – enable high quality audio and video content to be captured and distributed as podcasts which can be downloaded to a computer or mobile device using software such as iTunes.

Gradually more educators are using existing video and audio archive resources to supplement their teaching using distribution systems like iTunesU, which contains thousands of free-to-use lecture recordings, audiobooks, films, slideshows, and other educational content produced by some of the world's leading universities.

Video is often used to produce talking head lectures, lecture summaries, presentations, tutorials, and supplementary learning resources. Video provides an excellent way to capture reflective commentary (for both learner and student), case studies and as a record of performance in order to receive feedback. It can also be used to create instructional how-to guides and software walkthroughs using screen-capture software such as Camtasia or the free Jing. These tools allow the user to narrate and annotate real-time screen interactions. A common example in games, used to support reflection, is the ability for players to record and play back key moments of gameplay, such as battles, in order to analyse what went wrong and what they could do differently on a subsequent attempt; this technique of 'record and reflect' could equally well be applied to any learning situation whether analysis of performance is important. The process of video development itself can also be used to foster reflection, for example asking learners to create a video documenting a field trip or experiment that could later be used for discussion.

Game Audio Techniques in Education

Audio has had a long tradition in music and language tuition and educational radio broadcasting. The use of speech audio in education mirrors that of video in many ways, and can be used for many similar tasks. Recording and editing broadcast quality audio is achievable using free PC tools such as Audacity and Traverso, and Garage Band and Audacity on the Mac, which enables multi-track recordings to be created with ease. These tools enable users to manipulate and polish their recordings by adding sound effects and jingles.

An increasingly common use of audio in education is the podcast, where audio commentaries or lessons are made available for learners to listen to, often on their mobile phones or digital music players. This allows learners to stop, listen and reflect at a time, place and pace to suit themselves. As in games, music can be used for scene setting, to establish the tone and pace of a lecture for example, and sounds can also be used to break up a learning activity and change direction, for example using an alarm-clock sound to indicate that time on a particular activity is finished. The use of sound can also be an effective mnemonic, for example by associating a familiar tune with key points in a list. For example, when running a workshop on design in a learning environment, I introduced each of the ten learning points with a sample from a relevant (albeit tenuous in some cases) 1980s pop classic.

Game Haptic Techniques in Education

There is a long-held tradition in education – stretching back to the ancient Greeks – which extols the virtue of learning by doing. This hands-on or active approach to learning is common in primary education but becomes scarcer in tertiary education and is often relegated to fieldwork, lab work, or perhaps work-based learning. It is often seen as a better fit for vocational and practical subjects (medicine, dentistry) or certain disciplines (art and design, sciences) and increasingly disappears from classroom or lecture-based tuition as the academic level increases. Learning which relies on the sense of touch and engages students in physical activities such as building, prototyping, examining, experimenting, and repairing can be powerful. Learners who prefer to process information through the sensations they feel in their bodies (haptically) are sometimes referred by proponents of learning styles theories as 'kinaesthetic' learners. An anecdotal example of haptic techniques in lectures is of the lecturer who selects students for questions by playing 'stop the pigeon', where a stuffed toy bird is thrown around the lecture theatre until the music stops and the 'lucky' student left holding the pigeon is required to answer the question. Light interludes such as this can also be extremely effective for providing a break from learning and relieving stress.

Creating opportunities for haptic, tactile, or kinaesthetic learning can be challenging especially in a classroom setting; however there are possibilities. For example, a lecturer could bring in artifacts which are handed round the class to illustrate different concepts – I worked with a corrosion control engineer who kept examples of corroded metalwork to show students the various types of corrosion that could occur as a result of tensile stress, activity of microorganisms, weld decay, and many others. Obviously each corroded artifact was accompanied by the story of how the item had failed. The use of haptic approaches does not need to be limited to the classroom space; in the case of this example it would also be possible to send objects out by post and get students to describe or discuss them online.

In this chapter I have looked at the different ways that computer games make use of multiple media, and examined how these techniques could be used effectively in learning. Hopefully you will find some of the suggestions and ideas of use when applying these techniques to your own practice. Of course, you needn't feel constrained to focus simply on one type of media, but multiple types can be used together to create a rich and authentic learning environment, using contextual images, sounds, video. Making sense of multiple simultaneous stimuli, and sorting out what is important from what is background noise is a key skill for the modern student.

I've presented just a few ideas here, but there are many more ways in which sounds, images, and objects can be used to support learning. Look to games for inspiration: which visual or audio effects make you sit up and take notice, which make you feel emotions, which can you remember long after the game has finished? It is important to remember that high-end quality should not be seen as an insurmountable barrier to using multi-media; the focus – as the increase in popularity of low-specification games shows – should be on the underlying purpose and the effectiveness for the task in hand. Games provide a great way to stimulate creativity and generate ideas, far beyond simply using commercial-off-the-shelf games, putting the focus back on learning and the power back in the hands of the educators.

Part III
CREATING GAMES FOR LEARNING

In Part II of this book, we addressed the issue of how the average educator can use game-based learning by highlighting five areas in which we can learn from computer games and apply those lessons to teaching and learning. In Part III we return to the idea that games themselves can be used to encourage active learning and engage students, but that many off-the-shelf games are unsuitable, and the creation of quality digital games is beyond most educators. This part tackles the problem head on, giving practical advice on how teachers can create affordable games for themselves, providing the flexibility to meet their exact needs.

While there are many drawbacks to bespoke game creation in terms of technical expertise required for development, by designing their own games teachers can have far greater control than if they simply use something off-the-shelf. Many teachers have excellent ideas about how to design games that are perfect for their teaching situations but are hampered by lack of resources, skills or time to put their ideas into practice. This part of the book aims to address the limitations of high-end game design by providing examples and guidance of how lower-specification games can be used to support learning, which do not require programming or graphic design expertise, and are therefore far more universally accessible.

'I've seen some interesting games done on a shoestring budget that were very effective. You don't need to use the Unreal engine with a high-powered physics engine to get the point across. While a degree of professionalism should always be present . . . a shiny box or a realistic render don't always yield effective games.'

Kris Rockwell

There are three areas in particular that we want to highlight as presenting opportunities for game creation: alternate reality games (ARGs), virtual worlds, and traditional games.

Alternate Reality Games

ARGs are a comparatively recent genre of game, the first fully formed ARG being 2001. They are an interesting alternative to traditional computer games because they take place in both the online and real worlds, and utilize a range of accessible low-end technologies. They combine storytelling, puzzle-solving, and online community to provide a fictional game world in which narrative is interwoven with real people and events.

ARGs engage players with a series of interactive and collaborative challenges and puzzles that contribute to finding out more about the storyline as it unfolds, typically over several weeks or even months. This interwoven nature of the real, online and fantasy worlds is key to the genre, and players are often not sure what is reality or part of the game as there is no explicit distinction between the real world and the game world. Websites or locations within the game will often be indistinguishable from genuine sites, and the creators of the game often go to great lengths to ensure that they are anonymous and uphold the secrecy of the game.

An ARG will typically consist of three elements: (a) the ongoing storyline that unfolds as the game progresses (and is shaped by the actions of the players) that the players need to assemble over time, piecing together the narrative from multiple sources as the game unfolds; (b) a series of challenges or puzzles that are set to the players as the game progresses that generally require some type of collaboration to complete (either because the puzzles explicitly require more than one person or because they are so hard and cover so many domains of expertise that it is unlikely that one individual will be able to solve them alone); (c) a community that works together to solve the puzzles, supports one another and creates and elaborates on the game environment and narrative as the game progresses.

ARGs are of particular interest to the non-technical game designer because they make use of many different media types to act as a delivery mechanism for the game such as print, telephone, blogging, social networking sites, email, web pages, radio, television, and advertising, as well as actual people. This focus on player activity and collaboration, rather than high-end digital design gives ARGs particular value in an educational context.

Virtual Worlds

Virtual worlds provide another way in which educators can create game-based environments for learners, without needing high-end technical skills. A virtual world is an online space in which users can move around and explore the environment, interact with objects, and talk with other users (either via chat or voice). Some virtual worlds, such as *Second Life*, also enable users to expand the environment and create their own interactive objects, and while some technical skills need to be learned for this, they are far lower than those needed to design games from scratch.

Players are typically portrayed in a virtual world through the use of an avatar: a graphical representation of their character that can be customized by the user to varying degrees. A key benefit of these environments is that they are designed for users to travel around, discovering the environment, and communicating with other users – both significant advantages for the educational game designer.

While some virtual worlds, such as those used in multiplayer role playing games like *World of Warcraft*, are specifically developed to support a game-format and have activities and goals built into the game world; others, like *Second Life,* simply provide an environment in which users can undertake any type of activity they desire – including playing games. The use of a virtual world is not synonymous with game-based learning, but they do provide an accessible platform for game development.

Traditional Games

Advocates of digital game-based learning tend to forget that the idea of using games in education is not new, and was around long before the development of the computer. A whole host of traditional games, such as card games, board games, role playing, and puzzles have been used in education for generations. These types of game offer many of the advantages of computer games – such as active learning, collaboration, engagement – but without the drawbacks of high-development overheads.

The design and development of traditional games is also easier to undertake as prototypes are easy to create and modify, moving control away from the technology and back into the hands of the teacher. We highlight the use of traditional games here because of their simplicity, ease of creation and because there is a tendency to forget them in discussions on games and learning. Yet they offer a simple and effective way of bringing game-based learning into classroom and other face-to-face settings. There is also the option, in the digital age, to merge elements of the traditional and digital worlds, and provide interesting new forms based in traditional methodologies.

We believe that these three areas offer great opportunities for low-end development, and examples from each area are used in the chapters that follow. In the four chapters in this part, we focus on the practical issues of game design in an educational context, highlight the range of issues that need to be addressed, and aim to provide a framework for development and hints and ideas for effective educational game development.

The topics covered in this section are:

- The importance of an authentic *context* for learning, and ways in which to provide this in games (Chapter 8).
- Adding value to games by ensuring that they map to the appropriate *curriculum* and meet the intended learning outcomes (Chapter 9).
- Ways in which *assessment* can be built into game-based learning and the benefits and drawbacks of assessing learning using game-based approaches (Chapter 10).
- A model for development to support *game creation*, using the three low-specification approaches described above (Chapter 11).

We hope that reading this section will provide you with the confidence and enthusiasm to create games for yourself, using the game models and tools suggested. By providing a range of examples of the use of bespoke games in educational contexts, we also hope to stimulate your own ideas as to their potential uses.

Authentic Contextual Games for Learning

Simon Brookes and Alex Moseley

Tell me and I'll forget; show me and
I may remember; involve me and
I'll understand.

(Chinese proverb)

Context is King

Think back to your time in school (or university, or the last time you took a night-school class, depending on your power of memory) – what stands out? Chances are it will be moments of love, or hate, or embarrassment; or an outdoor trip, group project, the first teacher or topic which awakened your interest in your current line of work. What it probably won't be is the English lesson when you covered the semi-colon or the History lesson covering the Italian Wars.

For education to become meaningful (and over time pervasive and useful), we need to feel some engagement with it at the time; in the examples above, our engagement might be with our role in a social group (hence the moments of love, hate, embarrassment), or in a future or usefulness we can see for ourselves (hence the first awakening of subject interest). In each case, learning in a particular *context* is key; and we will explore this idea of *contextual learning* in this chapter.

Let's begin with an extreme case. The pinnacle of *contextual learning* would be to place learners right in the middle of the jobs or activities they need to learn about. Forget medical training – let's just put the students in white coats, and drop them next to a professional surgeon: completely immersed in the correct context. They might make mistakes, of course, but they'll be making real mistakes with real subjects and real repercussions; and as a result, they'll learn very quickly (or learn that it's not the job for them, equally quickly). Hopefully, you've spotted the slightly lethal problem with this approach; and fortunately, so have medical educators – in this and many other jobs, a period of training or *scaffolding* (gradual development of skills) takes place before students are let loose on real subjects or activities.

For centuries, though, the idea of placing students of a trade in close proximity to the trade itself has been utilized in the form of apprenticeships; and even today in the medical profession, after initial training students spend significant time shadowing doctors on wards, gradually perfecting their earlier knowledge with real-context situations. This enhanced level of learning is described by Vygotsky (1978) as occurring in a 'zone of proximal development' between the apprentice and master (when students are in the zone, they learn more effectively), an observation taken up and supported by a number of cognitive scientists and described in terms of a 'cognitive apprenticeship' by Collins et al. (1989): 'learning through guided experience' on a cognitive/metacognitive level (p. 457). This idea was developed further by Lave and Wenger (1991) with their description of a 'community of practice', where students and professionals mix in a shared context: where this context is strong, learning is more effective.

Apprenticeships are no longer an option for the vast majority of academic learning, however, so in most cases we need to find a way to create an artificial context for students that is authentic enough to improve their learning. Of course, contexts are formed from a vast array of aspects (as well as activities, materials, subjects and responses; there might be particular buildings, labs, equipment, lighting, background or foreground sounds; and any number of non-tangible elements such as emotions, feelings, etc.). A number of theorists have focused on recreating a subset of these aspects, such as Kolb (1984, drawing in turn on earlier work by Dewey, Lewin, and Piaget) who uses 'experiences': students test out their knowledge on a real-life problem and either succeed or fail, but learn from this experience, and apply it in their next real-life problem. Other approaches focus mainly on the material surroundings and a set of targeted actions, in the form of detailed 'simulations'. In some high-end cases, such as military or aviation flight simulators, these can be incredibly effective, immersing students in a highly authentic context; but this level of authenticity costs money, and many simulations in higher education tend to be produced using pseudo-realistic virtual worlds or 3D modeling – which while impressive and having a novelty value for students, often fail to create particularly authentic contexts because other aspects of the context (tactile, reactive or emotive elements) are absent or poorly implemented. (See Chapter 7 for a discussion of the relative merits of high and low production values in visual games design.)

More recently, though, researchers have attempted to capture and recreate as many aspects of a context as possible within a learning environment in what have been called 'thickly authentic' contexts. In the words of one of these researchers, 'activities are simultaneously aligned with the interests of the learners, the structure of a domain of knowledge, valued practices in the world, and the modes of assessment used' (Shaffer, 2005, p. 1). By embedding *many* aspects of the context into the course environment, the quality of each individual aspect need not be anywhere near perfect: thereby removing the need for costly simulations.

To improve student engagement with the subject context even further, Shaffer (2005) and others have designed their authentic contexts as games. Although not an obvious move for many lecturers or course designers, particularly in adult education, the use of games is not as surprising as you might at first think. Cast your mind back to some of the popular games from your childhood. Monopoly, for example, is a highly engaging game which keeps families playing for hours – but at its heart is a pretty authentic simulation of property sales: the board contains real streets, deeds are bought and sold, you hold (and lose) money, and so on. *Risk*, in a similar way, models the materials of war (maps, troops) the strategies (which form the gameplay) and the primary emotions around winning and losing. Clearly, in both cases, these games don't approach the reality of property development or war in precision terms, but by taking some of the key components of the contexts and simplifying them in the game environment, they can build up a very effective, and authentic, context overall.

Scenario-based teaching and more complex simulations (including role-play, case studies, and computer simulations) are the commonly used experiential learning tools employed in the classroom to approximate realistic, professional practice scenarios (an example would be the use of a computer game to simulate the stock market or patient simulations used in medical training). Although increasingly sophisticated (flight simulators, military training games, and medical training leading the pack), these interventions are still arguably, on the whole, unconvincing proxies for real-life experiences, often falling short on delivering the 'whole experience'. To illustrate the point let us look again at our previous example of a stock-market simulation computer game. Players of such a game might learn about how the stock market operates and could in theory, if the game provided enough detail, develop the same level of knowledge in the player as a practicing stock market trader (a trader's domain knowledge). However, there is much more to being a successful stock-market trader than having an expert knowledge base alone: their job description would mention, amongst other things, a requirement for excellent communication skills, the ability to remain calm in stressful situations, good leadership abilities, networking, and team-working skills, the ability to spot opportunities, to be adaptable, and reflective etc. We could go on, and of course you could make the same argument for any simulation of any professional authentic context. The point is that the experiential learning tools we have at hand only go so far in their ability to develop a professional mindset in our learners, a mindset that should link knowledge (knowing) with skills, values, beliefs, behaviours, and desires (doing), i.e. their whole way of thinking about themselves and their stakeholders within their chosen profession. We shall refer to these 'doing' skills as *professional competencies*. Shaffer (2005) refers to this as development of an 'epistemic frame' where 'practice, identity, interest, understanding, and epistemology are bound together' (p. 1).

Getting this mix of contextual elements right, forming a game around them, and fitting the result into an academic course, is not easy; but it can be far less costly, and potentially more effective, than taking a simulations-type approach. The rest of this chapter will explore how games can be used in this way, how existing designers have approached the problem, and give practical advice to help you start to design your own *authentic game* approaches to seemingly complex subjects.

Games and the Reality Gap

If we eschew pure simulation, where realistic environments are created by emulating and modelling reality itself, and try instead to develop a *sense* of reality within a much simpler game environment, we have to adopt a much more creative approach. Is it possible to approach reality without realism?

> 'People like things which simulate or mimic the real world, which seem a bit magical or unexpected. For example, you do something on a computer and get a phone call back – crossing boundaries.'
>
> Adrian Hon

Kriz (2008), in his introduction to design approaches to simulation games, talks about 'bridging the gap' (p. 28) between reality and the learner (with simulation used to make the bridge). This notion of bridging a *reality gap* or *contextual gap* is one we've developed in our own work: in game terms, this gap is what separates the game experience from an authentic experience (see Figure 8.1): 'the wider the gap – the harder the participant has to work to suspend their disbelief' (Brookes, 2009, p. 1). Importantly, this gap isn't just about a designed version of reality or indeed the input of the designer; it also includes anything that prevents the learner being able to engage with the intended reality – such as the learner's desires and expectations, their ideas of what is relevant to their subjects or contexts, their own perceptions of their learning potential from a particular type of activity, and a number of internal blocks that we all carry (which may include, for instance, a disdain for games as frivolous or pointless) (Moseley, 2010).

Clearly, as designers we can't design a hyper-reality *and* take on board all of our students' individual desires, expectations and hang-ups – or at least if we

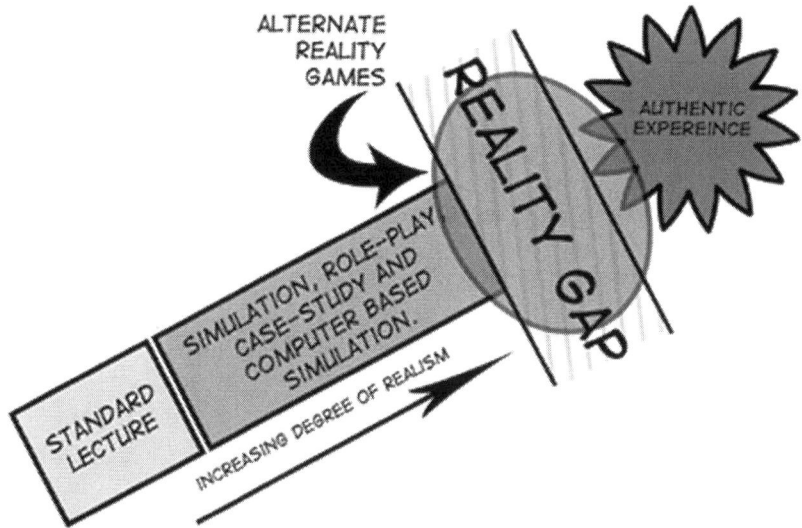

Figure 8.1 The reality gap

tried to, we'd end up with a game which would only work with one particular group at one particular time. What we can do, however, is design games that aim to fill this gap as a whole, using simple rather than complex methods to encourage the learners themselves to build their *own* realities, which are respectful to and fit within their own particular learning contexts. By blurring current realities and intended new realities in the learners' own minds, we remove the need to worry about overcoming, for example, the grey classroom, or the slow computer, or the lack of suitable tools.

As soon as we widen out our approach in this way, and are no longer concerned with developing an expensive detailed copy of a particular piece of reality, we can start to bring other useful elements into our designs. Elements that resound with a local curriculum, for instance, or the introduction of portable twenty-first-century skills that are favourites of modern employability skills agendas (such as critical thinking, problem solving, and digital literacy). We can effectively create a 'personalized learning' environment that extends beyond the classroom, as usefully described by Gershenfeld (2011, p. 1):

> Personalized learning: Games are designed to enable players to advance at their own pace, fail in a safe and supportive environment, acquire critical knowledge just-in-time (vs. just-in-case), iterate based on feedback and use this knowledge to develop mastery. Games can help teachers manage large classes with widely divergent student capabilities and learning styles . . .

This all sounds like a pipedream, as anyone who has tried to develop a course that works effectively with all students will attest. However, a particular type of learning activity, the authentic learning activity (ALA), attempts to do just that.

Authentic and Pervasive Learning Activities

> 'I like the engagement that is created between players and the game. It's an innovative manner of telling a story and letting players participate in that story. From an educational stand point, being able to leverage that idea and convey practical knowledge at the same time is not only a challenge to create, but a great experience to watch when it works well.'
>
> Kris Rockwell

An ALA is an intricate, super-rich simulation that attempts to create an authentic learning experience within the classroom: essentially trying to create an environment which is close to that which would be experienced by a participant in the real context. In a review of authentic learning approaches, Herrington and colleagues (2003) collected ten characteristics of ALAs, which include real-world relevance, activities that are ill-defined and require student co-creation, the opportunity to examine tasks from different perspectives, opportunities for collaborative and reflective activity, and complex tasks to be completed over long periods of time. They found that not all authentic activities produced positive outcomes in student learning, however; and that what made the biggest difference between an effective and non-effective activity was the 'suspension of disbelief' (p. 1). Laurel (1993) has also linked such a suspension with high engagement 'when we are able to give ourselves over to a representational action, comfortably and unambiguously' (p. 115).

It struck us that this notion of extending or blurring belief/disbelief across a 'normal' boundary between learning-in-context and being out of context bears interesting comparison with Salen and Zimmerman's idea of a 'magic circle' in gameplay (2004, pp. 94–96). In traditional games, they state 'as a player steps in and out of a game, he or she is crossing that boundary . . . that defines the game in time and space' (p. 95) – once a player sets out the board, or decides who's 'on' and starts counting to one hundred, they have stepped into the magic circle. If there is a break in the game (for snacks, mealtimes, etc.) players will step out of the circle temporarily, and re-enter it when they begin playing once more; once the game ends, they leave the circle. If we view an ALA as the magic circle, which students enter or leave as they move between learning/engaging and disengaging, then the *suspension of disbelief* sees a blurring of the perimeter of the circle: with no clear stepping into, or out of, it by the learners: it becomes a fuzzy circle. Rules, mechanics, and features of the ALA are retained, and used, by the student outside of formal learning sessions, and mix with their own reality.

Since Salen and Zimmerman described their magic circle, new forms of game have emerged which have a similar 'blurring' effect on players: alternate reality games (ARGs), immersive games, and transmedia games are all part of a group which specifically aim to suspend disbelief, and blur the boundaries between game and reality. In a close parallel with ALAs that achieve the same effect, these games generate very high levels of engagement in their players. We believe this link can be put to good effect, as we'll explain shortly.

In order to differentiate between ALAs which suspend disbelief, and those which don't, we offer the amended term *pervasive learning activities (PLAs)* to indicate instances where the activity creates an authentic context and engenders a blurring between the real and intended contexts. (We are aware that the term 'pervasive learning environments' has been used in other contexts, most notably in the blurring between real and virtual computer-based authentic techniques by Syvänen and colleagues (2005), but we feel that this approach complements rather than contradicts our ethos.)

> 'You have to find a way to connect with the player. You must give them something that they will care about – whether that is a compelling character, or story situation, or a compelling problem to solve, if you don't make a personal connection with the player, you're going to fail.'
>
> Jesse Schell

Pervasive Learning Activities and Alternate Reality Games: Useful Models?

How does one create a PLA though, rather than the standard ALA? There may be a number of approaches, and some ALAs have managed to find or approach the answer in their own ways (Herrington et al., 2003), but after exploring the similar suspension of disbelief in ARGs, we feel that ARGs offer an interesting model for PLA development. ARGs are described in the introduction to Part III, but in brief are essentially interactive stories that require players to solve a series of puzzles, often collaboratively with other players, so that eventually the end of the story is revealed. However, rather than requiring any special equipment (e.g. game boards, computer software, virtual reality headsets) ARGs use the real world as the gaming platform through which the story is communicated and played.

The following aspects of ARGs are those which we believe make them excellent candidates for promoting authentic learning, drawn from McGonigal (2003, 2011), Whitton (2007b), Moseley (2008), and Brookes (2009):

- Their realistic, immersive, interactive nature, which blurs the boundary between game and reality: 'every aspect of the player's experience [is], phenomenologically speaking, real' (McGonigal, 2003, p. 112). This extends beyond normal narrative or simulation, and creates a strong context.
- Knowing and doing are intrinsically linked. The 'doing' aspects are real 'Hacking into the in-game coroner's office fictional Web report, for example, was identical in practice to the process of hacking into a non-game coroner's office's Web site' (McGonigal, 2003, p. 112).
- Players have influence on outcomes. The game can change based on player actions and reactions; this also allows students to apply their knowledge or test approaches in a low-threat, 'real' environment.
- Players have an ownership of, and responsibility for, learning: it must be self-directed and self-organized (although encouraged within the game through the needs of puzzles or problems). Encourages critical thinking and inquiry-based research.
- Progress, competition and rewards (leader board and prizes) provide incentives and motivation to some players.
- A regular delivery of new problems/events is key to maintaining engagement and interest; problems at various levels provide an inclusive environment for all ability levels.
- Large, active communities provide all the benefits of learning in groups (collaborative, self-supportive, peer feedback, vicarious learning), and allow players to practice teamworking skills in a real setting.
- Utilizes simple, existing technologies/media intelligently. This reduces production costs, and removes barriers to entry (improving engagement).
- A novel method of delivery leads to pleasure and fun, which in turn can increase motivation (Whitton, 2007b).

There are therefore many elements within ARGs that can be combined to create an authentic learning tool which suspends disbelief – this makes them an ideal method to develop and deliver PLAs. In the next section we will take you through the steps of building your own.

How to Build a Pervasive Learning Activity: A Step-by-Step Guide

- *Set the learning objectives.* Start the process off as you would do if you were developing any course design. Think about what you want your participants to learn and write these down as learning objectives. Remember that a PLA presents an opportunity for learners to develop more than just knowledge of a professional discipline so when you are writing learning objectives be sure to include skills, abilities, and behaviours that could only be developed through 'doing', such as communicating in a professional manner or working as a member of a team.

- *Set the context*. What authentic situation/activity are you trying to recreate? Is there a particular role within a profession that is important for your learners to practice? If you are not an expert in this field yourself you will have to do some research in order to duplicate the context authentically: you need to understand how people employed in this role operate on a day-to-day basis. For example, how would these people normally communicate with colleagues/clients/members of the public (i.e. is telephone, email, online meeting, SMS, face-to-face communication the norm)? What are the common scenarios they find themselves in at work? What common problems do they have to deal with? What sort of documentation do they have to read and prepare? What are the most important/relevant elements of the situation/role you want to simulate? It is unlikely that you will be able to include everything so be selective and realistic. Understanding the context is extremely important so spend some time carefully considering it because the context feeds the rest of the process.

  Write the narrative. It is now time to start developing a scenario/story that encapsulates everything you have considered in the previous steps. Your primary consideration should be to keep the scenario as realistic as possible (you should have pinned this down in *Set the context*). You should also attempt to situate the story as near to the real-life circumstances of your participants as you can. For example, if they are full-time students, they should be expected to 'play' as full-time students in your PLA. This will help to make the activity feel much more believable to them. In common with all good stories your PLA scenario should have a beginning, middle, and an end (a 'narrative arc': see Chapter 5). However, unlike traditional stories, you may want to include a number of paths or endings which the students will have a hand in choosing or co-creating; you also need to include opportunities for your participants to learn and practice the professional competencies set out in your objectives (in-game puzzles) as well as embedding assessment artifacts (see Chapter 10). Don't forget, 'doing' is the critical component of a PLA so be sure to include lots of opportunities for contextualized practice in your narrative plan. One simple way to test your approach is by continually asking yourself, 'If my learners were doing this in a real situation, what would they be doing?'

  It is beneficial to think about this process in a linear way – plan how things will progress on a week-by-week basis; if you have built in choices or alternative endings, plan these as separate paths.

Tip: Drawing a timeline of events will help you to plan and keep track of your PLA. Use a spreadsheet or a large sheet of paper to do this.

At this stage you also need to write the characters for your story. You will probably play one of the key roles in the activity yourself but which other characters will help you to transmit your story in a realistic manner? Which characters will interact with your participants? How will this interaction be achieved? If mostly done through email, you can play these characters by setting up multiple email addresses; however, if you intend to have face-to-face or telephone contact between participants and story characters, you will need to ask other people to participate. This is often a good way to involve colleagues or central service staff (library or study support, for example) who can take on information-providing and skills-development roles.

Tip: Try to introduce as much variety into your PLA as possible. Use multiple channels of interaction. Too many emails will soon become dull and frustrating so why not send a package of materials through the post to your participants instead, or send them an urgent SMS message (further blurring the realism boundary)? Asking friends and colleagues to role-play characters (over the telephone or face-to-face) adds a convincing sense of realism and an extra dimension to the experience. Mix it up! Novelty will help maintain engagement; it provides your learners with opportunities to practice different forms of communication and, remember, this is what would happen if this were an authentic situation.

'Here I'm a fan of the ARG approach where you're not playing a different character, but an extended version of yourself. This can give enough support (or maybe enough freedom) for the more shy children to become more confident and for others to develop their listening and team-working skills. I also want to demonstrate to the staff that you can do a lot with shonky props and a slightly wobbly delivery – things really don't need to be too polished, this is play and our imaginations will gloss over the cracks.'

Nikki Pugh

• *Consider assessment and feedback.* Every learning activity should include some form of assessment and formative/summative feedback, even if it is informal in its nature. Drawing upon the context and narrative, what types of documents would a person working in this field be expected to prepare? Which activities would they be assessed or appraised on? Try to design your assessment artifacts to emulate these where possible. A lawyer's report prepared for a magistrate is very different from a marketing strategy report prepared by a marketing agency for a client. The detail is important (remember the mantra – 'context is king'). If you have access to authentic exemplars, you can use these in preparation and during teaching. Also, don't forget that PLAs are based upon a game structure, so you might want to consider designing some of your assessments using some common game strategies. For example, you could provide staged assessment throughout, gradually increasing the difficulty of tasks as the activity progresses. To design assessment and feedback opportunities to 'test' progress in the professional competencies, use higher-order techniques such as self-reflection and peer assessment.

- *Consider logistics.* Before you go any further it's time to decide how you are going to deliver the PLA. First, think about the time you have: A term/semester? Several weeks? One day? A few hours? How often will you have contact with your learners? All PLA activities, together with all assessment artifacts, need to fit within your allotted time frame and your personal schedule. How many students will be participating in your PLA? Will they work in groups or individually? Although you will be doing less 'teaching' a PLA is likely to require considerable non-classroom contact with participants (writing emails, updating blogs/websites, mailing packages, etc.). Communicating with a group is obviously less time consuming than on an individual basis, and the use of in-game peer support can help alleviate extra support load.

  Tip: A PLA is an intense, fully immersive experience which requires high levels of engagement from participants. The longer the planned activities, the less impact they are likely to have. The Phoenix UK Ltd PLA (see case study) is a twelve-week-long experience which, although proven to be successful, is, in our opinion, pushing towards the maximum length of time over which a PLA should be run.

  Develop the assets. These are all of the things that will bring your scenario to life and situate it within the real world. You can think of these as the tangible elements or the touch points with which your participants will interact. Assets have two main uses: (1) to help create the environment in which the scenario develops and where the interactions take place (the real-world equivalent of the Monopoly game board); and (2) as learning materials, or pointers to learning materials. These might include websites, blogs, maps, photographs (places and characters), videos, scripts for actors (or briefs for improvising around), letters, industry reports, newspaper articles, spreadsheets containing data, brochures, email accounts, telephone (or equivalent) numbers, fake social networking accounts, etc. (see the Phoenix UK Ltd case study for specific examples). You need to make these seem as convincingly real as is possible. Be sure to leave plenty of time to develop the assets before your activity is due to begin.

Tip: Blogging platforms such as WordPress provide a simple yet effective means of producing free websites, particularly if you have little technical web development experience.

Write the delivery plan. Finally it is important that you have a detailed plan of how you want the PLA to unfold over its duration. If you have been following these steps, you will already have a partly developed timeline of the main events in your scenario. You can simply add details to this. Note down the weeks when assessments are due for submission (clearly you need to make sure your participants are given ample opportunity to do the required learning, factoring in good reflection and preparation time). Add dates for when your various characters will interact (factor in time for responses if required). If you are delivering content as lectures add these to your plan. Quite early on in the experience you should introduce some of your 'environment' assets (the ones which help to bring the scenario to life such as company websites). Add these to your plan. Include any other learning activities that you expect your participants to complete. Finally, factor in opportunities for feedback and support. At the end of this you should have a plan that details every aspect of your PLA on a week-by-week basis.

After all that up-front planning, delivery of a PLA is relatively straightforward. Here are a few pointers that will help ensure success:

• Ideally we would like our PLA participants to believe that what they are experiencing is real. ARG designers go to great lengths to achieve this by ensuring that any reference to 'the game' is purposefully obscured from players. We do not recommend this approach when using a PLA. Learners might easily become disoriented and confused, and in extreme cases may experience stress if the situation was perceived to be real (professionals choose to inhabit their reality and are hopefully rewarded adequately for it). Ethically, this would be a step too far. So, when launching your PLA, spend the first few minutes explaining to your learners that they are about take part in a special kind of simulation and that (and this is important) in order for them to get the most out of the activity they need to play along as if the scenario was happening for real (you might even link part of your assessment with demonstration of professional behaviour as an incentive). Finally, state that, from now on, you will not refer to the activity as a simulation or game. Move into character (if required) and begin.

Stay in character and encourage your participants to do the same. Provide lots of support, particularly during the early phases of the PLA. Some learners may still be rather confused, sceptical, or even afraid to enter into the spirit of the experience. Encouragement and example set by you and other participants will help foster involvement and develop group cohesion: tangible assets can also help with this (personal in-character messages, packages in the post, etc.).

New participants may show some caution and uncertainty, which can be overcome by giving regular constructive feedback.

A Royal Solution?

We opened this chapter by demonstrating why context is king, and by the closing case study we hope that we have given compelling reason and method for introducing contextual, authentic learning into any educational environment. The development of a PLA is certainly hard work in the design stage, and we cannot recommend this approach for a quick fix or an overburdened tutor; but the rewards when the course runs in terms of student experience, learning outcomes, and personal satisfaction are certainly worth it in the long run.

Case Study: Phoenix UK Ltd

Developing an entrepreneurial mindset using a Pervasive Learning Activity

Phoenix UK Ltd is a Pervasive Learning Activity developed by Simon Brookes, University of Portsmouth, UK.

Learning Objectives

This is a first-year undergraduate unit for students on a BSc (Hons) Computer Games Enterprise course. Students taking this unit are expected to develop basic knowledge of marketing, business accounting, and some understanding of the human resources activities within a small business. It was also decided that they should practice professional communication skills (written and oral) and teamworking.

Context

There are many authentic contexts in which these skills might be developed, a small marketing agency for example, but in this case it was decided that the PLA would be based around a company that specializes in turning around failing businesses. A company of this type would have to analyse all aspects of a client's business and, as such, is a good fit with the learning objectives outlined above.

Narrative

The students are told that, as part of their studies, they are going to be working for a company called Phoenix UK Ltd who specialize in turning around the fortunes of failing businesses. The unit lecturer plays the managing director (MD) of this company. They are then given a client to work with and told that it is their job, over the next fifteen weeks, to analyse this client in detail and ultimately to present the client with a report containing recommendations on what they might do in order to turn around their fortunes. The client is a gentlemen's clothes shop (Salter & Son), which is based in a fictional town called Porthampton. Salter & Son have a new Managing Director (Craig Salter) and several employees (Christine, Barry, and Claire) who are key to providing students with information about specific areas of the business (specifically marketing, finance, and personnel). The students are required to work closely and professionally with the client, as they would do if this were a real situation. The characters provide much of the narrative (particularly the backstory) which, as students probe, research, and analyse the problems, builds into a clear picture of what has gone wrong with the business. The story is carefully managed in that it is fed gradually to the students over the full twelve teaching weeks of the unit. Students are always engaged with at least one element of the narrative and often with overlapping strands, involving multiple individuals, diverse tasks, and complex problems.

Assessment and Feedback

Four assessment artifacts test the learning in this unit:

1. *A presentation (with a twist).* The students present findings from a 'retail best practice' field trip to the MD of the company they are helping. The MD is played by a colleague.
2. *Short answer tests.* Every two weeks, students are emailed a set of five questions from a different character in the scenario (each character has an area of specialism which governs the subject matter). The students have to research the subject, provide answers then email them back to the character who marks them and then responds with feedback. The individual questions within each question set become increasingly difficult, allowing for differentiation between students. The marks are added as a score to an online leader board (see 'Assets' section below).
3. *Team work peer assessment.* Fortnightly, students are asked to assess the teamworking skills of each of the members of their team (including

themselves). They are provided with a standard assessment sheet containing ten teamworking characteristics, onto which they indicate a score (0–5). These scores are added to the online leader board which also provides students with a visual (graphical) representation of their effectiveness at team working over the duration of the unit. This helps them to produce a short reflection on this skill at the end of the unit.

4. *Final report.* This is a 'company turnaround report' of the sort produced by businesses that are working in this field. Students are marked on content as well as how professionally it is presented.

Logistics

The unit is fifteen weeks long with twelve weeks set aside for delivery. Normally a small cohort of between ten and fourteen students takes this unit. They are placed into groups of four or five depending on total numbers. Experience of running this unit for several years has proved that it is possible to deliver a PLA over this seemingly long period of time without experiencing significant problems.

Assets

A rich world, set in the fictional town of Porthampton, has been carefully created in which the PLA is situated. Websites are used extensively to help create the illusion of its existence. Porthampton has its own council website (www.porthamptoncc.org.uk) and a newspaper (www.porthamptonbugle.co.uk). The website for the town of Porthampton is shown in Figure 8.2.

Figure 8.2 The Phoneix UK Ltd PLA is set in the fictional city of Porthampton

These assets help situate the students into the fictional world but are also used to deliver potential 'solution leads,' e.g. an article in the newspaper about a new, state-of-the-art shopping centre opening in Porthampton should, if spotted by the students, present them with an opportunity which they can recommend to the client. This one article might spark off a whole new area of investigation: How much does it cost to rent? What is the potential footfall? Would the market be suitable for our client? Fictional maps of Porthampton and modified photographs of the high street (including the interior and exterior of the client's shop) are also provided. The company with which the students are employed also has a website (see Figure 8.3), along with the client of the business they are attempting to recover (www.phoenixuk.co.uk and www.salterandson.co.uk respectively). The Phoenix UK website has a section containing examples of previous reports and a blog which students are encouraged to post to.

A package of materials (marketing assets, stock list, stock images, shop layout, and an introduction letter) is posted to each student. The package is made to look like it was sent from one of the client's employees. Although not a tangible asset, conference calls are made between students and key personnel within the client business (role-played by colleagues). This is a tool that would be used in a professional setting and so this is excellent experience and a means for the students to gather important information about the client. Email is the most common method of communication used between students and scenario characters, each having individual email accounts through which they can be

Figure 8.3 The Phoenix UK Ltd company website (www.phoenixuk.co.uk)

contacted (in reality all character emails are administered by the course director). Finally, an online leader board was developed which keeps track of scores (marks from two assessments discussed above) and introduces an element of competition to the PLA (there is a prize awarded for the winner).

Delivery

Much of the learning is self-directed, guided by interactions with the characters in the narrative. An introduction session is used to set the scene (includes a conference call from a previous client). Weekly seminars are held with the whole group and the tutor which provides an opportunity for discussion of findings from the previous week and to set objectives for the coming week(s). Several lectures are used to provide a framework for the self-directed study (these are called masterclasses in this context). Email is used extensively for support and feedback, and to facilitate learning (through guidance).

9
MAPPING GAMES TO CURRICULA

ALEX MOSELEY AND ROSIE JONES

Games in the Curriculum

While any aspect of teaching and studying can be difficult at any point in time or for any individual, there are some elements that are particularly difficult for the majority of teachers *and* learners *most* of the time. Regardless of the education level (primary to tertiary) *induction, assessment and feedback, digital literacy, employability*, and *learning or research skills* all feature highly on the list of students' least engaging or most stressful sessions; and as a result on many teachers' biggest headache scale.

More often than not, students resent the fact that these elements have 'nothing to do with my studies', appear 'bolted on', or take up 'precious time'. As teachers we, of course, know that by not taking the time to engage with these elements when resources and training are available, many students will struggle with particular skills in the future.

In a similar way, the use of games within education often suffers from the same fate: particularly in higher or further education, students feel that the use of games detracts from their subject teaching, and is too frivolous for an academic degree programme (similar attitudes come from some students and – perhaps more so – parents in secondary education). There are other, significant, issues surrounding the integration of games in accredited education: how to fit them into national or local curriculum or accreditation schemes and how to persuade colleagues, department heads, and senior managers that they are a worthy addition to the menu.

In this chapter we aim to demonstrate that all of the above problems can be combated in an effectual way, and with careful design and thought to the role of games in the curriculum, they can provide engaging and highly relevant course elements, which can ultimately be flagships for your institution, rather than dirty secrets.

The Curriculum and the Wider Context

The curriculum is at the core of all formal education, although it may be more or less obvious to you as an individual depending on how and where you work. Derived originally from the Latin for *racecourse* (and interpreted wryly by many subsequent authors as a 'race to be run, a series of obstacles or hurdles . . . to be passed': Marsh, 2009, p. 3), it has variously been used to signify a wide structure for 'getting through life' – including formal schooling and outside formative experience – through to a more restricted, formalized structure that defines the courses and topics covered in a particular school or institution.

In the UK, the importance and relevance of curricula to your day to day work depends largely on your context: in primary and secondary public education, for example, the UK Government's National Curriculum (in England and Wales) defines (to quite a detailed degree) the topics, timetables, and levels toward which your teaching needs to be planned and organized. At post-secondary level, national curricula are less in evidence, although accreditation or benchmark statements tend to provide some guidance (at varying levels of detail) to particular subjects (identified professions, such as nursing or psychology, tend to provide more detailed curricula); mostly, institutions themselves tend to set local curricula.

Any new educational subject or direction needs to fit within the relevant local or national curriculum (or make a strong case to change the local curriculum if out of current scope); however, this doesn't tend to apply to new *methods* of teaching and learning. Particularly in post-secondary education, methods used to deliver the broad set topics are often left to individual teachers; and even within the National Curriculum (2011) at earlier levels, the published aims note that

> by providing rich and varied contexts for pupils to acquire, develop and apply a broad range of knowledge, understanding and skills, the curriculum should enable pupils to think creatively and critically, to solve problems and to make a difference for the better. It should give them the opportunity to become creative, innovative, enterprising and capable of leadership to equip them for their future lives as workers and citizens.
>
> (National Curriculum, 2011)

There is therefore usually little difficulty in introducing games-based methods within the curriculum structure itself. The biggest challenge in getting acceptance for games in education therefore tends to be from areas outside of the formal curriculum: the people, ideological, and administrative aspects that form the bulk of the institution as a whole. We have identified five key challenges:

- *Staff attitudes.* These cover both local staff (colleagues and local department) and important institutional figures or groups (heads, vice-chancellors, course approval groups, etc.). Getting the former on-side is crucial to the development of your idea and support for its long-term embedding and delivery; the latter are key to getting any formal approval and avoiding any scandal or complaints. Staff will want to see either some real benefit (in administration, or improving their delivery of teaching), or evidence that the approach has potential to improve student learning or the student experience.

- *Student attitudes.* The motivations to learn for any given student are many and complex, but increasingly learners respond poorly to anything which they see as 'outside the subject I signed up for' (or, more cynically, anything which isn't assessed towards their qualification). They can therefore be the most critical voices against games-based approaches if there is no clear relevance to their course. On the plus side, many students will either play games or will have played games within recent memory, and so *once they accept the relevance*, they will need little further encouragement or guidance, and may provide peer support to other less-games-savvy students.

- *Reputational attitudes.* Your institution (school, college, university, etc.) will have a reputation to uphold or improve, and (given the modern-day emphasis on marketing and public relations) will be looking to both avoid any embarrassing or horror stories about poor teaching or student complaints, and to find and promote examples of new or innovative practice, delighted student responses, high grades, or results. Clearly, any games-based approach could fit into either of these brackets, depending on its design and execution; and it is therefore in your interest to make sure it falls into the latter category. To this end, any opportunity for positive PR should be jumped upon!

- *Course design.* Any games-based approach will need to fit into, or around, the wider course context. Ideally, it should be designed as part of a wider review of an existing course (or development of a new one), but where this isn't possible, it will need to fit neatly within or alongside an existing course. If you have some ownership or influence on the wider course, this is much easier; otherwise staff attitudes will play a much bigger role and you'll need to focus your initial efforts there.

- *Course mechanics.* Surrounding the course design, but equally important in delivering a positive experience to the students, are administrative, procedural, and technical aspects. Sometimes you can design a game to fit into existing systems, but often you'll need to work with administrators and technical units to ensure that your approach can be delivered and supported effectively within the local context.

In thinking about, and responding to, these principally local concerns, it is useful to extend your view and look at current issues in the wider sector, to see whether particular themes or developments might provide a good argument or theme for your games-based activity. This, in turn, will be a persuasive argument when presenting ideas at an institutional level in particular.

Current issues will vary by sector and time, of course, but as an example we'll use our own area of activity and outline the current higher education (HE) context in the UK, which (as we'll describe throughout) contains some obvious areas with the potential for games-based approaches.

HE in England shares a number of common issues and concerns. Key concepts appearing out of the Higher Education Funding Council for England (HEFCE) and the Higher Education Academy (HEA) include *recruitment and retention, employability, developing independent autonomous learners, widening participation*, and *quality assurance*. As student engagement and motivation are key factors in almost all of these areas, educational games may have much to offer. For both *recruitment* and *retention*, games have the potential to offer a social aspect: encouraging social networking, teamworking, or aiding with orientation into a new environment. They might also offer elements of humanity or comfort through the use of narrative or stories from people and situations students can relate to. This in turn could demonstrate to students the welcoming aspects of a university and allow them to build networks to support them through their early days of university life when there is an increased likelihood of isolation or doubt.

Games offer easy deliverables for *employability* skills, in particular *digital literacy* which JISC (2011a) recognizes as a crucial employability skill in the current HE climate – asserting that '90% of new jobs will require excellent digital skills, [so] improving digital literacy is an essential component of developing employable graduates'. Digital games provide a simple platform for easy integration of learning technologies and Web 2.0, and offer new opportunities and methods to develop digital literacy by delivering challenges that encourage students to explore these new technologies and use them for academically relevant purposes.

Learner autonomy is developed through the construction, synthesis, and evaluation of deep knowledge (rather than passive reception and recall of information) and through an understanding of the learning process itself. In highly engaging ways, games can involve students in the discovery of knowledge, supporting them to transfer this knowledge and associated skills to different contexts, and take ownership and responsibility for their ongoing learning and skills.

'In terms of the work I've done applying elements of gameplay to educational settings, I think the key approaches have been to make the pupils the experts and remove myself and the other adults from being the knowledge-holders.'

Nikki Pugh

Widening access and increasing participation is acknowledged as a crucial mission for HEFCE (2011). Games can appeal to a very different audience than those who participate in traditional university learning, covering different types of motivation and learning styles; they can therefore encourage a more diverse range of students to engage in higher education (and to stay in it).

The student as 'customer' in HE is no longer a new idea: it is generally accepted that many students are juggling paid work or family commitments alongside their studies and as such are eager to learn as much as they can in as little time as possible. The idea of them demanding value for money is not new either but as students pay increased fees in the coming years they may be expecting even more for their money. Offering new and engaging methods in teaching and learning shows a university's keen commitment to, and investment in, their learners. The case studies we discuss later in this chapter show that games can fulfill this role quite effectively, with relatively low costs but reaching a large diverse audience.

Integrating Games into the Curriculum

In this section, we consider the different places where games might be integrated, and possible methods of integration.

Where can Games be Integrated?

Based on the previously identified priorities in our HE context, there are a number of potential places where games might usefully be integrated (and which resonate beyond HE). The most obvious lies in induction, an area that relates to issues such as recruitment, retention, and widening participation. Induction provides the opportunity to reach large numbers of students in one go and at a time of student need, either within or outside disciplinary boundaries, and is an area that is often delivered at varying standards and to various degrees across all subjects. Games can be launched pre-induction to encourage early socialization and can be a real selling factor for an institution (e.g. *GlamStart* at the University of Glamorgan: Chew et al., 2009); they can also provide varied levels of difficulty to ensure that all students, regardless of starting ability or knowledge, can take part on their first day.

The introduction and development of key study or research skills is also a useful area for games integration. This is an area many departments struggle to deliver on and, while often appreciating the importance of the subject, it is regularly not integrated into the curriculum. It could include skills such as research techniques, digital literacy and employability, or subject-specific skills such as practical lab or fieldwork techniques. If not properly integrated with the subject, skills sessions tend to be poorly attended or disengaging for students (who see them as 'not what I signed up to learn' or 'irrelevant to the subject'), and so using the motivational application of games in conjunction with clever subject-based design can have a real benefit to student uptake of these skills.

Both induction and skills provision offer areas without many of the barriers present in traditional education institutions, where the subject tutors have a strong sense of ownership in their particular areas. In these 'outside the core subject' areas (from a traditional education sense) subject staff are much more open to outside help or new approaches; anything that will increase student engagement or retention, and yet not increase their individual departmental workload significantly, will be gratefully received.

Games can, of course, be used in any area of education – although outside of the areas above, and related to subject-specific aspects, the barriers to engagement by staff are higher. With a well-identified area (for example, a particular subject topic or a virtual fieldwork trip) and careful development of interest within the department, very successful game approaches can be developed.

> 'If you want to teach facts, the game must not be about those facts: the game must be about something else, and the facts be merely incidental. Facts are not fun in and of themselves; people aren't going to play a game to learn facts. They're going to play a game to have fun. I can name every country in Europe. I can do this because I've played so many games that I just know what those countries are. I don't know which game in particular told me where Estonia was, but I know where it is (and that the Baltic States are arranged in alphabetical order north–south). I also know that whatever game taught me where Estonia was, it wasn't anything to do with teaching the geography of Europe.'
>
> Richard Bartle

Integration Methods

Games and game elements can be integrated into academic programmes in two principal forms. The easiest, though less effective, way is through *explicit* integration: the addition or overlaying of particular game elements such as leader boards, rewards, prizes and levels – this area is explored in detail in Chapter 10. Because this method avoids altering the underlying course, and simply overlays game elements, the design effort is minimal; but there is a danger that students and staff will dismiss the elements as disconnected from their main subject/ curriculum, or see them as trivializing elements of the curriculum.

The other form of integration is *implicit*: begin by looking at the student profile, subject area, and curriculum design; decide which areas could be integrated into a game design and build the game into the course itself. The most effective *implicit* use of games is *contextual game design* (see Chapter 8), but much simpler approaches are possible by finding particular features of a subject that relate to a game or game element. For example, a cross-European project 2 Ways produced a board game, *The Mutation Game*, to teach simple genetics principles using randomness as the game link: in simple terms, genetics is based on random mutation, so dice rolls and random card drawing in the game provided a natural game-related element (Cramer et al., 2011).

For non-subject-based skills such as induction or research skills, the greatest engagement comes when students are given a variety or choice of approaches: although some will be comfortable with 'traditional' academic methods of teaching and learning, while others may find these intimidating or disengaging, and respond positively to alternative approaches. In addition to this, any approaches used should encourage students to utilize the resources, approaches and structures which they will need to use during the rest of their course (and/or those they will need in future work or education).

Games-based approaches therefore either need to incorporate a variety of techniques and utilize existing resources as part of their design; or it may be easier to provide games-based approaches as an alternative to (and alongside) existing resources.

Dealing with the Five Challenges

Drawing on our experience in the HE sector, we suggest some possible approaches to the challenges outlined earlier:

- *Staff attitudes.* Two things are crucial in getting staff on-side with a games-based idea: (i) find a problem that needs fixing, particularly one that they find irritating, difficult or outside their areas of interest; (ii) involve as many staff as possible in the design, testing, and delivery of the game in ways they understand – for example, ask them for their favourite subject resources, find out their pet hates with current student skill levels, or involve them in awarding prizes or writing narrative or puzzles.
- *Student attitudes.* Making the game clearly relevant to their contexts of study (or their perceptions of context: they are here to study a subject, not a set of skills, remember) is crucial; it is also useful to use familiar game techniques where possible, so that a larger proportion of students will relate to them from previous experience: think *Monopoly* or *Scrabble*, rather than *Dungeons and Dragons*.

> 'For educational games we are committed to iterating between game designs and learning goals. Not putting either one out there at the expense of the other, but considering them both equally.'
>
> Eric Klopfer

- *Reputational attitudes.* If you ensure that your game fits within your institutional codes of practice, assessment criteria, and other structures – and also stays on the right side of staff and students as noted above – there should be little risk of negative PR. Avoid pushing any press releases or other PR until the game has successfully run and you have some positive student or staff feedback (or solid data such as higher registrations, retention or grades), but then push the boat out and get your press office involved in promoting press releases both internally and externally. Try to get quotes from heads of departments and students where possible, as this improves validity for academic readers.
- *Course design.* We outlined a number of areas for the integration of games above, but any form of integration needs to be considered as part of a wider consideration of the whole course design: it shouldn't come as a shock to students, and fit neatly alongside other course elements.
- *Course mechanics.* Bear in mind at all times that, while it may be innovative and exciting and have plenty of enthusiasts on hand in the first year, to be successful your game has to stand alone in future years and work with existing staff and structures. Right from the early design stage, design the game mechanics around existing resources or technologies (or develop sustainable new approaches which will save staff time or ease administration); and involve administrative staff along with subject specialists. Document any processes and/or train other staff so that the game can live beyond your involvement with it.

Supporting the Use of Games for Learning

Although it is possible to design, develop, and teach small games-based approaches yourself (particularly if you have ownership of a course or subject area), anything sizeable requires user testing/playtesting, design, or production of materials, and possibly extra assistance to run the game. Extra resource is, of course, always difficult to obtain, but two useful tips which have helped us in our projects are:

- *Use of small grant schemes.* Institutions or local and national bodies often have small grants available for developing teaching and learning initiatives; they usually ask for some kind of innovation or improvement (games-based approaches are easy to describe in these terms) and the only requirement is usually a report at the end of the project. Check your local institution, local education authority, or national teaching and learning bodies for details of current grants available.
- *Use of postgraduates, teaching assistants and other support.* Postgraduate students, classroom assistants, or teachers-in-training make excellent assistants for games-based approaches, and not just because they have

spare time, cost relatively little and are grateful for extra paid work: because they have recently been through the same educational context as your students, and have emerged as 'new experts', their understanding of the students' needs (and their rapport with the students) is invaluable. Such assistants can be used to moderate or guide student work or discussion; play roles within the game; and even help to mark and provide quick feedback on assessment.

Case Studies

The authors have been involved in the design and integration of two games-based approaches to course delivery in HE, and to close this chapter we will discuss our approaches to curriculum integration within them – illustrating some of the techniques and issues described above. The first case study describes a central (non-subject-based) course which teaches induction, library, and digital literacy skills to first-year undergraduates at the Manchester Metropolitan University; the second is a subject-based course which teaches historical research skills to History undergraduates at the University of Leicester.

Case Study 1: ARGOSI

The JISC (a UK-based organization supporting the use of technology in further and higher education) funded ARGOSI project used an alternate reality game (ARG) to support the student induction process, with a particular focus on information literacy. A collaboration between Manchester Metropolitan University (MMU) and the University of Bolton, it aimed to offer an alternative to traditional induction for new students encouraging them to get to know the city of Manchester, meet other people and to deliver more serious InfoSkills (MMU's Information Literacy) learning outcomes. The design process and issues arising during this project are also discussed in Chapter 11, so we will focus specifically on issues of integration here.

ARGOSI aimed to support the MMU induction process, in particular the issues the library faces when delivering information in these early weeks. Typically time available for library induction and InfoSkills sessions is short during the first weeks of university entry. Students are also bombarded with information during this period and rarely see the relevance that a university library has to them, nor its importance to their studies. A lot of this is down to lack of context: students are not applying the information they are taught immediately, they most likely have much more important tasks to carry out like familiarizing themselves with their accommodation or locating a supermarket; where to take a book out is not particularly high on their list of priorities. ARGOSI aimed to contextualize the library information they were receiving and offer them a way to engage with materials. It was offered as an addition to library induction information, not as a replacement.

The ARGOSI game, *ViolaQuest*, follows the mystery of a first-year student at MMU who has a puzzle to solve. She receives assistance from a librarian based in Manchester who sets up a website to help her in her quest and also to set some puzzles of his own which fit the library learning outcomes. The game originally ran over a ten-week period releasing library challenges gradually over this time frame while progressing a central storyline. The library challenges came from Induction and InfoSkills level 1 learning outcomes, which proved at times quite difficult to incorporate into the game for the designers. The mapping grid in Table 9.1 shows how the challenges mapped to the library learning outcomes.

Table 9.1 *Mapping learning outcomes to challenges*

Learning outcomes	1	2	3	4	5	6	7	8	9
Define topic and plan search									
Specify an information need								X	
Choose relevant keywords from an assignment title								X	
Be aware of print and electronic resources for finding information								X	
Use general reference resources to increase their familiarity with a topic			X						
Plan a simple search strategy to find information for an assignment								X	
Get hold of information									
Be aware of relevant holdings and collections in the library for assignments									X
Use online reading lists		X							
Use library catalogue to find specific items and do keyword searches	X								
Find a printed journal and electronic journal									X
Be aware of the library website as the key route to finding information	X					X			
Use one subject database to find information for an assignment: keyword search, phrase search, truncation, limit searches by year									X

(*Continued overleaf*)

Table 9.1 Continued

Learning outcomes	1	2	3	4	5	6	7	8	9
Be aware of the advantages and disadvantages of using information gateways and search engines to find information on the Internet						X			
Evaluate information									
Be aware of why evaluating information is important								X	
Recognize good and poor quality information					X			X	
Be aware of quality specifically in relation to information found on the Internet								X	
Organize and use information									
Be aware of why records of searches and resources are important							X		X
Be aware of why referencing is important in academic work					X				X
Be aware of the basic laws of copyright in relation to printing from a book or a journal					X				
Awareness of tools to help with referencing									X

Challenges

Here are brief summaries of the nine curriculum challenges developed:

1. Classification code. Use cryptic clues to identify the call number, page, line and paragraph of a specific document.
2. Reading list messages. Find a single item that appears on three different reading lists.
3. A strange letter. Make sense of an obscure letter requiring thesaurus or other library resources.
4. Support mix-up. Uncover an anagrammed message hidden on six student support officers' door stickers.
5. Find the errors. Identification of different types of errors in document.
6. Coded message. Work through a treasure hunt on the library website to decode a secret message.

7. Following the trail. Discovering what someone is looking for based on their search history.
8. True or false. Evaluate the authenticity of different websites.
9. Missing reference. Complete a set of inaccurate references to find another complete reference.

Attempting to make some library outcomes (like finding a book on the library catalogue) into a fun engaging game was extremely difficult but the game at least managed to cover all the outcomes and made a good attempt at making these entertaining.

Two examples of how learning outcomes were made into challenges are shown in Table 9.2.

Table 9.2 *Two challenges, and their link to learning outcomes*

Challenge name	Classification code	Missing reference
Learning Outcome	Use library catalogue to find specific items and do keyword searches.	Be aware of relevant holdings and collections in the library for assignments
Challenge description	I've lost my glasses – can you help? I think they're in the library safe but I don't know the combination. I know that the combination is a nine digit number – and I found this pinned to the notice-board.	Each of the following references has one piece of information missing. If you find the missing information from each reference you can put them together to find another item.
	Clues to the safe combination: Find the classification numbers for the following books:	You will find all of them using the library catalogue (you may need to use the advanced search), electronic journals, and the Emerald database.
	1. Title: *The Study Skills Handbook* 2. Author: Harper Lee 3. Keyword: Barosaurus	How do I know what's missing? [www.library.mmu.ac.uk/eresource/bibcit.html]
	Add the three classification numbers together to get the code for the safe.	1. Austen, J. (1906). London: Dent. (1998). *The Spirit of the Child*. London: Fount. 2. Joint, N. (2008). It is all not all free on the web: advocacy for library funding in the digital age. 57(4), 270–275.

(*Continued overleaf*)

Table 9.2 Continued

Challenge name	Classification code	Missing reference
		3. Sillitoe, Alan. *Key to the door.* London: Macmillan.
		4. McFarland, Ross. (1943). Medical program for aviation. *Harvard Business Review.* 93–127.
		5. Spector, Michael. (2002). Introduction. *Journal of Educational Technology and Society.* 5 (2).
		Your answer should be the ISSN number of the item you find with all the missing pieces of information (remove the hyphen).
Connection to Learning Outcome	To find each classification players had to understand how to search for a specific item and how to do a keyword search.	Players had to search a range of library resources in order to ascertain the final ISSN.

There were still challenges that were hard to disguise as fun activities and it was hoped that players would still be motivated by the desire to collect full sets and complete the game. Whether this worked was hard to judge due to small take up for the game. These small numbers were the biggest hindrance to the success of the game: without high player numbers aspects such as collaborative challenges, message boards and competitive elements were lost and this made it extremely difficult to know for certain if the game could have been a successful and viable alternative to the induction process. A consideration of the reasons behind the small numbers is discussed in Whitton (2011).

With the right support and stronger institutional backing, embedding a game like ViolaQuest into the curriculum could really enhance the students' experience and offer them a much more fun and engaging way to learn about library information.

Case Study 2: The Great History Conundrum

At the University of Leicester, there was a need within a first-year undergraduate History module to improve student take-up of, and engagement with, the critical analysis and filtering of internet-based historical resources: essentially a core research skills module. The module had previously been taught in large (200-student) lectures and small tutorial groups, and students regularly complained about the relevance of the course to their academic subject.

Looking for models of high engagement and collaboration that would work in an online/blended context, we used some of the key features offered by ARGs (graded puzzle solving, competition involving leader boards and prizes, minor narrative/story elements, and community/collaboration aspects) to create a four-week-long activity based in problem solving, collaboration, and competitive play, combined with subject-specific and research skills elements already used in the original course. This design process was aided by a successful bid to the university's local teaching enhancement fund, which provided me with time and a research assistant to develop the project over the course of a year.

Within this 'research year', three activities were essential to the success of the project. First, at the very start of the process, we contacted all teaching staff within the department, and asked them to provide a list of the subject resources (books, websites, journals, etc.) which they would most like their students to access, and their top three gripes about students' abilities in the second year of study (recurring themes like an inability to cite and reference correctly, or unwillingness to use print resources, emerged). This not only provided us with a source of material for the project, but also ensured that all staff in the department felt that they, and their particular interests, were being involved: this simple step paved the way for subsequent smooth integration of the project into the department with buy-in from all staff.

Second, we spent some considerable time thinking about accessibility and inclusion: ensuring that all students, regardless of their interests, abilities or learning styles, would find some parts of the course engaging and suited to their needs. This approach went across the whole design phase, and encouraged us to add in flexibility and variety wherever possible.

Third, two pilot runs were arranged during the year. The first with ten second-year students who had been through the existing course the previous year, and the second with twenty first-year students who had just completed the existing course. This allowed us to test the gameplay, flexibility, technical aspects, and assessment/reward schemes (we offered prizes for the winners), and obtain invaluable feedback via individual interviews and focus groups.

These steps meant that when we were ready to present the course to the head of department, and start to embed it into the degree course for its first real run, we had confidence in the design, delivery, accessibility, and academic usefulness; we also had buy-in from departmental staff.

In its final form, *The Great History Conundrum* (*GHC*) takes place over four weeks – principally online, but bookended by an introduction and prize-giving in a lecture theatre. Students are provided with a number of puzzles of varying difficulty, which can be solved at any time of day or night, and these are immediately marked on a leader board, and replaced with new puzzles to solve via email (the instant reward and delivery of new problems key to maintaining engagement). The puzzles are graded in levels of difficulty, and also cover different cognitive skills (searching, selection, filtering, criticism, and application) to ensure inclusion of different interests and learning styles across the large cohort. Collaboration is encouraged through the use of a 'swapping' element (students trading puzzles with their peers), discussion forums (moderated by postgraduates), and the construction of a collective wiki (a resource the students will be able to use throughout the rest of their degree). Carefully constructed assessment criteria and rubrics were developed to encourage and assess engagement with the activity and concepts (with marks directly linked to each solution and discussion post; higher marks awarded for higher levels of understanding or critical reflection: see Table 9.3). It covers three broad types of post: requests for help, an evaluation of a puzzle solution, and general hints and tips.

The initial effort we put in during the design stage to fit the GHC into the curriculum and (as importantly) into the particular needs of the students and

Table 9.3 *Rubric to map The Great History Conundrum discussion posts onto academic assessment grades. It covers three broad types of post: requests for help, an evaluation of a puzzle solution, or general hints and tips*

Mark	Requests for help	Evaluation of puzzle	Hints and tips
2	A straightforward request, e.g. 'I think I know what this is, but I can't find out the answer.'	A simple opinion, e.g. 'This is really useful.'	A clear and useful tip, e.g. 'X' will lead you to the answer."
4	As for 2 points, but show you know how you might try to find the answer.	As for 2 points, but give a reason for the opinion.	As for 2 points, but also show you know why the resource is useful.
6	As for 4 points, but with a description of your work on the problem to date.	As for 4 points, but also say what sort of information the resource provides.	As for 4 points, but also give a clue as to the type of information the resource provides.
8	As for 6 points, but *either* show you understand the issues underlying the problem *or* detail the steps you might take/ have taken to solve it.	As for 6 points, but also relate the resource either to your current work or to the wider context of historical research.	As for 6 points, but also hint at the usefulness of this resource to general historical research.

10	As for 8 points, but show you *both* understand the issues underlying the problem *and* detail the steps you might take/ have taken to solve it.	As for 8 points, but also reflect on the processes you went through to access and use this resource, and evaluate the pros and cons of the resource for current and future study.	As for 8 points, but also describe the pros and cons of this resource.

departmental staff meant that the course effectively justified itself within its first year. As we had anticipated (and modelled) in the pilots, the students were far more engaged in the course than in previous years, and returned not only a higher pass rate, but a higher mean in the pass grades (good for the head of department and administrators); there is also anecdotal evidence from tutors of follow-on courses that students are a highly engaged, highly performing cohort with increased critical understanding of key concepts, when compared to previous years (good for the teaching staff). Because of the careful assessment design and use of postgraduate students as markers, teaching staff also found they had a much lighter yet more interesting marking load than previously.

In combination with the department, we issued both internal and external press releases to describe the *GHC*, with a focus on positive student and staff quotes, which generated some interest nationally. This not only gave the department further ownership and pride in the course, but also raised the awareness of curriculum-embedded games-based learning and its effectiveness locally and nationally.

Through a combination of careful design, consideration of the five challenges outlined previously (in particular the focus on student and staff benefits and buy-in) and promotion of beneficial aspects, this games-based course is now successfully integrated within the mainstream curriculum in a traditional academic department.

In Conclusion

In this chapter we have explored some of the problem areas when attempting to integrate games-based learning into the curriculum. We hope that we have offered some useful information, based on our experience, on how to approach – and surmount – key barriers; and that the case studies have provided further ideas for you to take and adapt within your own local context. We can confidently say that, despite the challenges, the end result – with all staff on board and students receiving an integrated course – is certainly worth it.

10
ASSESSMENT AND GAMES

ALEX MOSELEY

Assessment in Learning

Assessment takes up a significant portion of time in many areas of primary, secondary, and tertiary education (and to a varying extent, in other areas such as work-based or lifelong learning). For students, exams/essays/coursework/ tests all dominate thoughts, fears, and triumphs as the years progress (indeed, a growing number of students focus not on the weekly subject teaching, but on the assessment itself); for staff, the designing, setting, validating, and marking of these fills evenings and weekends.

It is no wonder that there is much concern around the design and delivery of both assessment, and (its close neighbor) feedback, nationally, and with good reason: in higher education in the UK, the annual National Student Survey (NSS, 2011) has, over the past five years, revealed assessment and feedback as the area students are most dissatisfied with across the sector (in 2009 and 2010 they produced the lowest average score for all areas of student satisfaction: 65 per cent and 67 per cent satisfaction respectively). In UK secondary education, OFSTED reported as far back as 1996 that marking 'fails to offer guidance on how work can be improved' and 'reinforced under-achievement and under-expectation by being too generous or unfocussed' (cited by Black and colleagues in their 2003 review of existing practice, which revealed similar concerns across the sector).

Assessment has many roles in the learning and teaching process, from short-term formative tests which may be student-focused: 'Did I understand the lecture today?' or staff-focused: 'Did my students understand the lecture today?'; to broader summative ones: has this student gained the knowledge and under-standing necessary to pass the course? In form assessment has the potential to be similarly varied, but tends towards the predominant 'end of unit test' or 'final exam' at tertiary level: assessment of knowledge and understanding at a given point; although an increasing number of sectors (such as English secondary education) have moved to forms of continuous or portfolio-based assessment.

Playing such a role as assessment does in many educational contexts, therefore, how does it fit with the course itself? Talking about UK HE, Ramsden (1992) writes, 'From our students' point of view, assessment always defines the actual curriculum' (p. 187). As a course designer, I might flip that around and say that 'the curriculum always defines the assessment', at least when designed well. Assessment should be considered right at the start of the learning design process, as soon as the learning outcomes have been set and designed to help the students achieve them (Biggs' (1999) model of constructive alignment sees learning outcomes, teaching and assessment all interlinked). As Price and colleagues (2011) noted in their critique of current assessment practice, however, 'in practice one aspect of the model – that is teaching methods – is habitually privileged over the other two' (p. 480).

Without wanting to dwell too deeply on the current problems in assessment, the two things which we'll need to bear in mind through this chapter are that *assessment and feedback are at the core of learning*, and that *if this isn't borne in mind, poor assessment methods, and subsequently poor or irrelevant learning, are the result*.

Where do games come into this, and can they help? In the next section, I'll discuss why assessment is one of the easiest things to cover or find parallels for in game design; but before that I'll finish this overview on a high note.

In the light of the heightened interest in assessment, and the growing tendency towards strategic learning (i.e. focusing on assessment) among older students, there has been a reawakening of interest in assessment and feedback design, with practices such as feed-forward and ipsative assessment (which both use feedback to encourage tailored individual development of students) gaining momentum, and a wide range of other creative and cleverly designed approaches which can be broadly grouped into cognitive assessment (assessing higher-order learning), performance assessment (measuring process or activity rather than an end result), and portfolio assessment (long-term collection and review of work to look at both the process and product) (after Reeves, 2000). These new forms are also being augmented by technological advances: either to improve administration, clarity, and speed, or to utilize new media or approaches. In the UK, the Re-engineering Assessment Practices in Scottish Higher Education (REAP) project is collecting and documenting many of these for HE (JISC, 2011b).

All this means that education as a whole is now more open to creative, well-designed forms of assessment; and as I hope to demonstrate in the rest of this chapter, this provides a fertile platform to build some highly engaging games upon.

Assessment and Feedback in Games

You might not immediately think of assessment in relation to the games you play or have played, but it only takes a very short stretch of the imagination.

I only have to mention points, levels and scoreboards/leader boards for example, and you should be able to see the link. Feedback, too, plays a big part in successful games, but is more of a mystery – as both *positive* and *negative feedback* are used heavily in game design. Chris Hazard, a designer for Hazardous Software Ltd, gives a good example of negative feedback:

> Think of the racing games you may have played. If you've noticed that the computer players tend to perform better when you're winning, this is a typical example of negative feedback. This particular scenario is often referred to as the 'elastic band'; imagine a rubber band keeping the computer players with a certain distance of the lead. When negative feedback is done right, the player doesn't really notice and the game remains engaging and competitive.
>
> (Hazard, 2010)

Positive feedback, conversely, is when a particular effect is amplified (whether good or bad): for example, collecting five coins in a maze gives you a special ability; or bumping into a wall the first three times causes minor injuries, but the fourth time breaks your arm. The two combine in many scenarios – think about that bridge you couldn't jump across, or the 'boss' at the end of the level who you couldn't defeat. Repeated plays (and deaths) gave you clues about how to approach it next time round, and each time got a little bit easier (keeping you motivated to have 'just one more go: this time'). Feedback as a whole therefore helps to guide players through a game, learn its rules, and keep them engaged (see 'Some of the benefits of games for learning' in Chapter 2 for more information on feedback).

Assessment itself tends to be explicit in games. I mentioned points, levels, and leader boards: these are obvious, continuous, and help the player (and the game) monitor progress or growing ability. In some cases this may be personal advancement: levels, in particular, are used as personal 'rewards' for performing various tasks or achieving certain points totals; rising in levels helps you track your personal performance irrespective of any other players or opponents. Whereas in others they may have a social element – comparisons of point scores on leader boards, for example. Both levels and leader boards are inherently motivating for many (though not all) people: leader boards, particularly in a friendship or peer group – can provide high levels of motivation, regardless of where a player happens to be on the board: being 254th and aiming for 253rd can be as motivating as being in second place and aiming for first. Both have a direct or indirect effect on success in the game (players need to either reach a particular score or level, or achieve a certain point in the game which will see the player generate a score or level as a side effect).

What's particularly interesting in game assessment though, and what differentiates it from formal assessment in education, is that almost all of it is *contextual* and *open*: points are awarded for completing particular actions vital to the gameplay (such as defeating enemies, collecting jewels, or reaching the end of levels) and are awarded instantaneously and obviously (players will see their score appear as soon as they complete the action, and be able to see its point value); they will receive immediate feedback if they approach a task incorrectly. Levels in role-playing-style games are even more interesting: players gain *experience* through various in-character tasks to progress through levels, and as they do so they become more versed with the skills and attributes needed to be successful as that character. Levels therefore represent a true reflection of player development in the game role they have chosen. These notions of *contextual* (always relating to skills or activities in the game) and *open* (you see how much you score, when you score it) are important: we'll come back to these later.

Explicit Assessment: Pointsification

You may have heard the term 'gamification', and maybe caught a whiff of the controversy that surrounds it. Coined sometime around 2008, but gaining interest in 2010 with mobile applications such as Foursquare (which provides points and badges for visiting and 'checking in' at certain locations) and a number of Facebook games, gamification describes the 'integration of Game Mechanics and game-thinking in non-game environments to boost Engagement, Loyalty and Fun!' (gamification.org). Rewind a little though – didn't we decide that an important aspect of points and scoring in games was their close relation to the gameplay, or context of the game? Just taking the idea of points and scoring out of a game, and adding them to something which doesn't have similar gameplay elements (like mundane tasks or chores) will only transfer the limited inherent motivation of points and leader boards, and not the powerful elements which make them into a highly engaging game. Robertson (2010), a game designer with Hide and Seek, notes:

> Points and badges have no closer a relationship to games than they do to websites and fitness apps and loyalty cards. They're great tools for communicating progress and acknowledging effort, but neither points nor badges in any way constitute a game.

But she goes on to say:

> It's crucial that we stop conflating points and games. Firstly, because it devalues points. Points are great. So are badges . . . Game designers resort to them . . . so often because they're fantastic tools, and as with all tools there is real art and science behind deploying them well. They deserve to be studied, refined and adapted on their own terms, with their own vocabulary.
>
> (Robertson, 2010)

She coined the term 'pointsification' to better describe this use.

'I think games can be a very useful tool for engaging the learner so long as the game is properly applied to the subject manner. I don't support the idea of 'gamification' because I don't think it goes deep enough to provide a truly memorable experience but rather feel that a game experience designed specifically to an education concept can be very effective.'

Kris Rockwell

In these terms, points in themselves can have some useful applications within education. A couple of interesting academic-related applications use pointsification to provide leader boards and badges for non-gaming activity:

- *750words.com* is a site which encourages writing: giving points every time you write something in a day, more points if you write 750 words, and bonuses/badges if you do this over many consecutive days – a simple reward system which is, effectively, assessing the quantity you write. I have academic colleagues writing books and Ph.D.s who use the site regularly and find the points motivating (occasionally boasting about gaining a particular badge).
- *The Neverending Uni Quiz.* At the University of Brighton, Katie Piatt introduced a novel way to engage students with the barrage of information they need as first year entrants (such as local town information, how much the printing costs, what a lecture is like, etc.). She packaged these snippets of information up as online multiple-choice questions, and added leader boards to keep track of each student's scores. What made things more interesting (and raised the students' interest in the site) was adding group-levels to the leader boards: divided into their houses, students played the game regularly to raise their group scores and beat rival houses. *The Never-Ending Uni Quiz* (see Figure 10.1) is unashamedly points-based (rather than games-based) but has done its job extremely well and engaged the students into the bargain (1500 users after a year). Katie notes:

> Initial analysis of players' behaviour, and feedback, shows bursts of intense activity – often playing for over an hour in a session until a target (e.g. top of the leader board for their team) is achieved. The model of attaching a leader board to a 'standard' activity, such as an online multiple choice quiz, does seem to transform the activity into something substantially more motivating to players than without.
>
> (In Moseley et al., 2009, p. 6)

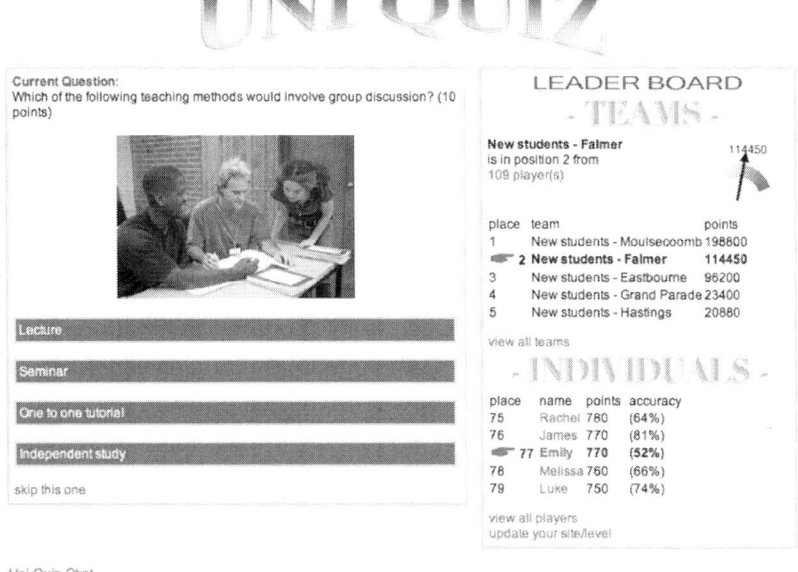

Figure 10.1 *The Never Ending Uni Quiz*, with leader board

In his popular book *Game Frame* (2011), Dignan proposes a theoretical framework which moves beyond pointsification, and aims to incorporate more gaming elements in other contexts (business training or informal child learning, for example) through the design of 'behavioural games' which follow a ten-step design process not dissimilar to game development. Although the case he makes is not yet grounded on any real success, the examples he takes from games and applies to real-world situations are compelling and suggest that there may be a place for more considered gamification in wider contexts, including education.

The application of the game-derived ideas of points, leader boards, and similarly engaging features therefore clearly has a role to play in education, and should not be discounted. But their use alone, without even the *contextual* aspect that points have in games (although both examples above utilize the *open* aspect to good effect) does not make a game – and as such the levels of engagement and relevance to the subject are less than might be possible with a higher level of game-based input.

Game Concepts as Assessment

In an education context, *game-based learning and assessment* could refer to several different things; crucially, there are two distinct uses: (a) the assessment of game-based learning activities, and (b) the use of games as an assessment tool. Table 10.1 categorizes this range of use. The matrix in the table shows, for simplicity, two teaching methods: game-based and traditional (i.e. lectures, tutorials, seminars, etc.) and two assessment methods: in-game and external to the game. In-game refers to the built-in features of the game, such as scoring or levelling-up, which could be used to assess progress; external to the game refers to a variety of assessment methods that can potentially be integrated into or around a game-based learning scenario (such as a reflective discussion or written report after playing the game). In practice, courses may mix and match different teaching and assessment methods.

The discussion of assessment present within games (including pointsification) in the previous section all fits within the bottom row on the matrix: in an educational context, these features would provide in-game assessment. While it can offer a host of pedagogic advantages (briefly touched in the section above and expanded later) and certain benefits in administration and consistency of marking, game-based assessment is typically very poor at fostering reflection or meta-cognition around the learning process (there are no natural pauses or gaps, or accompanying instruction, in which such practice can be encouraged in traditional assessment). There may also be factors outside of the subject learning which affect game-based assessment (the students' engagement with the game, their skill or experience with some of the game mechanics, usability issues, etc.). Any assessment of games that relies solely on player performance in the game may also be problematic unless there is a very tight mapping between assessed game goals and learning outcomes; there also

Table 10.1 *Forms of game-based learning and assessment*

		Teaching method	
		Game-based	*Traditional*
Assessment method	*External*	Game-based learning and traditional assessment	Traditional learning and assessment
	In-game	Game-based learning and assessment	Traditional learning and game-based assessment

Source: after Whitton, 2010b

needs to be space in the game for learning through mistake-making before assessment begins.

Traditional forms of assessment, however, are equipped to capture a wide range of outputs, including reflection and critical thinking as well as knowledge-checking. When used most effectively, they allow a wider view of assessment as part of the learning process – building in feedback and development over a number of assessment points, and enabling application to other contexts. Core to this is the human factor: skilled tutors setting, marking and feeding back to individual students, enabling individually structured development and support.

There is current bad practice in both game-based and traditional assessment: most of us will have experienced poorly designed or lazy traditional assessment and feedback; and many of us may have experienced educational games which provide a meaningless score at the end of a learning task. There is potential, therefore, to utilize the best parts of both game-based and traditional assessment to create something better all round for both students and tutors.

Key to any successful assessment strategy is careful design, as described in the opening section to this chapter. From that basis, there are two ways in which game-based and traditional approaches can be combined to offer effective assessment. The first is to use a combination of in-game game-based assessment (quantitative, lower order tests) with external traditional assessment (adding higher order, qualitative elements and widening to other contexts). In-game assessment is discussed at length in the next section; external assessments will be familiar to practising tutors but might include:

- Reports on actions taken and decisions made in the game, with critical analysis of the consequences of decisions, or personal reflection on them.
- Creation of artifacts based on and extending the action in the game (e.g. posters, digital video, audio, graphics).
- Discussion posts can be assessed for their contribution, critical engagement with and reflection on the game.
- Narratives associated with the action in the game (e.g. characterizations, back stories, future scenarios).
- Portfolios detailing the use of the game, decisions made, artifacts created, consequences and learning.

The second approach is to use what I term *implicit* or *invisible* assessment: assessment which is designed alongside the game design and so closely with the learning outcomes and wider course, that the lines are blurred between in-game and external. In this way the whole range of assessment methods can be utilized, with no apparent break or in-game/external split to the student. This approach is detailed later.

In-game Assessment

In this section I'm going to focus on how game elements can be mapped *directly* to assessment as used in education; rather than be applied as a layer or outside element (pointsification). This isn't as difficult as it might initially sound: most assessment systems within formal education allocate marks (out of 10, 100, or other nominal scales; even when there is a simple pass/fail, there are usually hidden grades behind there) to rate a student's performance in particular learning outcomes on a scale. There is little difference between this and awarding points for completing a particular action in a game; particularly as many games give more points for better efforts or higher achievements. The idea of progression too, where academic assessment gradually raises the bar to improve students' performance over the longer term (e.g. harder, or more critical, or more reflective, skills are required as the course progresses) has an almost direct parallel in certain games: the use of levels or stages of increasing difficulty, where players are tested, and rewarded, at a higher level, as they progress through the game.

> 'Never forget they are there. Take them places they have never been. Empower them to acts greater than they can perform in real life. Reward them for their efforts.'
>
> Lee Sheldon

As discussed above, however, this is where the parallels tend to diverge. Points in games are awarded in real time, as players complete a task, and in direct relation to that task; feedback on the task is instantaneous; and new levels or stages are awarded as soon as the player achieves the required level – the notions of *contextual* and *open* which we discussed earlier. In contrast, formal assessment in education tends to be at certain fixed points within the course (usually at the end of a long period of learning), tends to assess many aspects of work within one assessment mark (such as content, style, grammar, understanding, critical awareness, reflection, etc.), and the majority of students progress to the next year or level of study together, at the same time.

There is no reason, though, why we can't utilize some of the *contextual* and *open* aspects of game scoring and feedback, and mould them to fit an educational context. In particular:

- *Contextual assessment:* designing assessment to match the subject or skills the students are learning. For example, on a business studies course, assess students' ability to produce reports, or present to shareholders. For more information on context in learning, see Chapter 8.

- *Open assessment:* marking students on particular activities *as they do them*, and on broken down scales (e.g. separate marks for content and style, *or* a clear matching of the mark to a particular level of expertise, through a rubric or similar). This will provide immediate feedback on particular activity, and gives the option of opening up marks to a group and using leader boards or similar devices.
- *Negative feedback:* giving students gradually harder or easier tasks depending on their performance in the previous one (always pushing or scaffolding them a little more) – this would move beyond something like ipsative assessment (or feed-forward) by amending the assessments themselves in relation to the student.
- *Positive feedback:* already built in to many assessment schemes in a simplistic way (e.g. high scores in four courses result in a higher overall mark); but this could be more creative and engaging: for example, learning four different skills or topics, or finding and analysing particular resources, gains a special mark, award or useful tool.

Some of these elements have already been used in educational environments (contextual assessment in particular), but a fascinating redesign of assessment for a whole course by Lee Sheldon at Indiana University utilizes several of them. Sheldon had the advantage that his course was 'Multiplayer Game Design': an easy subject to introduce contextual games approaches to, which would reduce the need to persuade staff and students of its academic suitability (a problem described in Chapter 9); but nevertheless his approach (now in its third year of use) provides a working case study for the use of game concepts as assessment.

Instead of grades, Sheldon assigns *experience points* to his students for their academic work (experience points being the equivalent of gaining experience in the academic and practical sides of the subject); when students amass a certain number of experience points, they rise in *levels*. Well before the end of the course, students can see which level they are on (and what they need to do to rise in level), and so have far greater visibility of their progress (see Table 10.2). Furthering the concept, Sheldon uses guilds rather than group work, and a variety of other games-based terms for course activities. What is interesting about Sheldon's assessment design is the way that individual grades or experience are far less important than the gradually increasing levels – which help to show students that essays and other assessment points are just elements (or *side quests*) within the greater aim (or *campaign*) of development as experts in the subject.

Implicit (Invisible) Assessment

The use of game concepts as a way to rethink assessment design and make it more relevant and useful for students is a compelling one, moving on a stage

Table 10.2 *Assessment grades based on experience points*

Level	Experience points	Grade
12	1860	A
11	1800	A−
10	1740	B+
9	1664	B
8	1600	B−
7	1540	C+
6	1460	C
5	1400	C−
4	1340	D+
3	1260	D
2	1200	D−
1	0	F

Source: adapted from Sheldon, 2011

from simple pointsification, and approaching what might be termed *implicit assessment*: assessment which is woven into the subject and students' activity so closely that it becomes almost invisible.

Even greater 'invisibility' can be obtained when games-based approaches are applied to the course as a whole, assessment included. More than a combination of game-based learning and traditional assessment, this approach uses game concepts alongside traditional learning and teaching concepts during the course design phase, so that the resulting teaching, learning and assessment are invisibly entwined.

Having undertaken this process myself for a course I designed four years ago at the University of Leicester (*The Great History Conundrum*, or *GHC*; see the case study in Chapter 9 for more details about the overall design), I will elaborate on the assessment design and give practical tips which may be useful for your own context.

A Case in Implicit Assessment Design

In brief, the *GHC* teaches critical research skills to 200 History undergraduates using a games-based approach. Puzzles which introduce students to real-life research problems are solved for points, and further points are obtained by discussing the puzzles and research issues within a group discussion board. Gradually, the students collect knowledge and techniques and build them into a shared wiki, which they can use as a reference in their continuing studies. The game process is outlined in Figure 10.2.

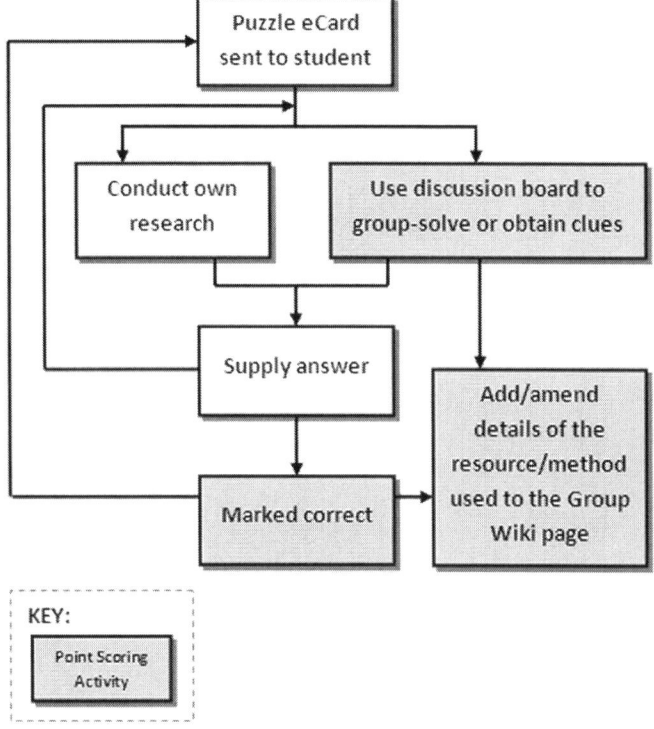

Figure 10.2 Overview of the GHC activity cycle, showing point scoring (assessed) elements

Assessment design played a key part in the development of this course, and (most crucially) was designed right at the beginning, along with the gameplay. I used some key principles when considering the assessment methods:

- students should be assessed on real and identifiable activity, and should know what is required of them for a particular score;
- students should receive immediate or close-to-immediate feedback on their activity;
- students should be able to select a level and type of activity comfortable to them at the start of the course, and be able to choose an appropriate development path through it; this should be supported, not hindered, by assessment;
- students should know at all times what their current achievement level is, and what they need to attain for success.

You'll notice that many of these draw from the four game concepts outlined in 'Assessment and Feedback in Games' above (contextual and open assessment, and positive and negative feedback).

From these principles, I arrived at the following assessment design. I found that the most successful strategy was to keep things simple – think about scoring systems used in games, think about the skills and activity I actually wanted to assess, and then think of the most direct way to link these together.

Assessment is linked directly to the three main areas of the activity, and marks are awarded continuously as it progresses:

- Each puzzle carries a points total indicative of its level of difficulty (1–10): when successfully solved, these points are immediately added to a student's *puzzle score*, which is their assessed mark for this aspect of the course.

  This direct link between assessment score and *higher points for higher difficulty*, which comes directly from games, means that students immediately see both the difficulty *and* value of the puzzle to their overall assessment/development. It also means the students can self-select their difficulty level – they may choose to start with 1 or 2 point puzzles, but will realize that to achieve a pass mark of 40 per cent they'll need to attempt some 4, 5, 6+ point puzzles before too long. When they attempt the higher levels, and how many puzzles they attempt, is up to the individual student (which provides flexibility for different learning styles).

- Once they have solved a puzzle (or if they are stuck on one), students are encouraged to post hints, resources, or requests for help within a group discussion forum. Each forum post is marked with brief feedback by a postgraduate moderator within twenty-four hours of posting, based on a visible rubric (see Table 9.3 in Chapter 9) which awards higher marks for increasing depth of understanding and critical thinking. These marks are added to the student's *discussion score*, which is their assessed mark for this aspect of the course. The visible rubric, and swift marking and supportive feedback by the moderators, means that students are always aware of what they need to do to be successful in the subject; and how to develop to the higher levels. Like the puzzle marks, they are also being marked directly, and openly, on a specific contextual activity.

- Each student's current puzzle score and discussion score are visible at all times on the student's GHC home page (instantly updated), and also on an overall leader board, where they can see where they lie alongside friends and peers in the cohort. The top three students in puzzle and discussion scores at the end of the course receive prizes. This open leader board is designed to provide competitive and motivating elements to the course (from game design principles). In practice, we found this to be very true: students voted this the most motivating aspect of the course behind the open assessment scores, and each year we see a big rise in activity on the final two to three days as students try to raise their place on the leader board above friends and peers. The leader board has a secondary advantage: it shows a combined average for the puzzle and discussion scores, which gives the student a current aggregate score for the whole course. In this way, students get obvious indication that they can specialize in either puzzles or discussion (as befits their learning style) and yet arrive at the same final mark as a friend who specialized the other way round.

- The group-produced wikis form the final portion of assessment. These are marked by teaching staff within the department, to a visible rubric, and a group mark and feedback is provided to all students who contributed to the wiki. This assessment is more traditional, in that it marks a final product and is awarded around a week after the students submit. In many ways the inclusion of this alongside the other open/immediate assessment helped to give the course a 'trustworthy' academic grounding in the department; although it also fits well alongside our initial principles as the activity and method of assessment models a 'research group output': the production and assessment of a final resource. It is however, like much group work, the one area that students complain about in end-of-course questionnaires, and is the section we constantly tweak each year.

Rethinking Assessment

In this chapter, my aim has been to show how time-honored game elements can add a fresh and useful dimension to assessment design; not – as is the current trend in a number of sectors – by adding a layer over the top of an existing course, but by using lessons and features from game design as part of the overall course-design process. Although this approach will undoubtedly take more time and effort in the design stage, it should provide far more effective and appropriate assessment for your students, and hopefully some savings in administration for yourself with each iteration. Even if you don't have the time or option to redevelop a course at present, I hope that some of the game and design techniques discussed might add an extra dimension to your current teaching and assessment practice.

11

DESIGNING LOW-COST GAMES FOR LEARNING

NICOLA WHITTON AND ALEX MOSELEY

The Problem of Designing Computer Games for Learning

Computer games offer exciting and active ways for students to learn, both informally and within the boundaries of formal education. By their very nature, they adopt problem-based, collaborative, and experiential pedagogic approaches, supporting learners seamlessly in their transition from novice to expert in an engaging and stimulating way. However, when it comes to formal learning, big problems exist with finding and using appropriate games, or games appropriately.

Commercial off-the-shelf games have been used in school contexts (see, for example, Squire (2005) and Rylands (2011)) but it can be difficult to find a commercial entertainment game that maps to the required curriculum, can be played within the time and technological constraints of the school classroom, and doesn't require lots of irrelevant gameplay. For this reason, the use of commercial games tends to be limited to stimulating ideas or discussion rather than engaging directly with learning content. There are examples for bespoke games being used effectively (Ebner and Holzinger, 2007; Yaneske, 2010) but these tend to be limited to disciplines such as engineering or computing, because of the specialist expertise needed to design and develop computer games. The opportunity to create bespoke fit-for-purpose computer games is beyond the technical capabilities and time limitations of most teaching staff and outside of the capability of most learning technology teams. Effective digital games need games design expertise – many expensive in-house or designed-for-education games simply aren't games.

However, traditional-style games, such as board games or card games, have had a long history in learning and teaching because they are easy to create, easy to play, and effective. Indeed, they stretch at least as far back as the early board and war games in use in China from 3000BC (Wolfe, 1993) although the first formal 'educative' game with a rulebook is generally agreed to be *New Kriegspiel* invented in 1798. By 1872, games were being used by the British military, and made the trip over to America shortly after (Cohen and Rhenman, 1961) and it was to be a century later, with the advent of home computers, that these war simulation games came into widespread use for pleasure rather than training.

Business or management training has also made use of traditional games, or paper-based games with simple rules, for over fifty years; the first was derived from military stock-taking (*Monopologs* in 1955), but the first widely used one was the *Top Management Decision Simulation* developed by the American Management Association in 1956, which was followed by a wide and rapid spread in the early 1960s (in 1961 there were estimated to be a hundred different management games, with over 30,000 employees playing them) – and more recently, 97.5 per cent of management schools use games/simulations in their training (Faria and Nulsen 1996).

Keeping it Simple: Traditional Games for Learning

'The most recent game I worked on was a card game that helped people formulate strategies for a mobile learning development plan called *A Game of Phones*. What was so surprising (and exciting) was the social interaction that occurred between people as they worked out their respective plans. I think that we have grown to rely on computers to the point that we tend to forget about the importance of actual face to face human interactions within gameplay. According to the players, it was this interaction that made the game so interesting and fun. This was an important lesson to me and reminded me that the traditional board game is an often overlooked solution that can be very effective.'

Kris Rockwell

In education, traditional games are often used at primary level (either standard games such as *snakes and ladders* or *matching pairs*, or those developed specifically for young child education, such as number or word games). At secondary level and above, however, traditional games are only kept alive in the main by student-led clubs and societies. This is a shame, as traditional games (see Figure 11.1) offer a number of distinct benefits for education:

1. They require no technical knowledge to create or play.
2. They can be produced cheaply and easily using readily available materials.
3. Inspiration and working gameplay approaches can be readily sourced from existing board, card or other games.
4. They can encourage group working and discussion.
5. They can be reproduced and amended easily.

Figure 11.1 Traditional game pieces

In addition, recent theory and practice has suggested that simple traditional games can be used to very quickly create authentic learning contexts for the participants (Moseley, 2010) without the expense and development timescales of full-scale simulation games.

In the last few years, a growing number of traditional games have been developed for learning, covering a variety of subject areas but all based on simple ideas and cheap production:

- *First Aid Training.* Charlier and Clarebout (2009) designed and used a board game to formally assess the understanding of key first aid and basic life support concepts in third world countries. Their game was found to increase mean scores when compared to traditional paper-based tests; and the authors speculate that this may be a result of both a reduction of fear/stress (games are 'fun, motivating, challenging' when compared to the 'fear of examination') but also of peer discussion and feedback during the game.

- *Mutation!* A pan-European partnership of university Genetics departments collaborated on the development of a board game to teach school-age pupils about the principles of genetics. Using the idea of 'randomness' within genetics as the basis for their game (dice rolls and card draws dictate how amusing alien species mutate and reproduce over time), it provides a basis for discussion about deeper genetics elements during and after the game (Cramer et al., 2011).

- *Of Course!* and *Accreditation!* are two board games developed at the University of Leicester and Manchester Metropolitan University, respectively, which teach university staff about elements of course design. Staff feedback, after playing *Of Course!* as a course team, reflected on the way the game opened their eyes to real issues and helped them to open out their own ideas and prejudices: 'You have to make pay-offs between elements of the course – and that reveals preferences and prejudices within a course team about what kinds of teaching mode you prefer' (staff quote from Moseley, 2010, p. 7).

- *Game of Phones.* In adult training within education, Kris Rockwell (*Hybrid Learning*) and Alicia Sanchez (*Czarina Games*) used a deck of cards (see Figure 11.2), containing real practical issues and potential solutions around mobile learning. The game is played in small groups, and at its launch at mLearnCon in 2011 it generated animated discussions and some interesting solutions from participants. Two of the most interesting aspects of this simple yet powerful game are the design process (Rockwell and Sanchez reduced the game down from

Figure 11.2 *Game of Phones* cards

Source: reproduced with permission of Kris Rockwell

an original phone-based approach, through progressively simplified forms until they arrived at a set of playing cards and the inclusion of blank cards so that players can create their own elements which can feed into future games).

Creating Your Own Traditional Game

As can be seen from the small but varied selection above, traditional approaches can be used in a variety of settings and for a whole range of subjects. If you are inspired to try some development in your own area, the following tips may be of help:

- Think about good game design. The best way to do this, bar none, is to dust off your old board games, or think back to the favourite games of your youth. What kept you going back, what motivated you to have 'just one more go', and which parts did you always find irritating? If you want to take things further, Caillois's *Man, Play and Games* (2001) is a fascinating study of games and how humans interact with them; whilst Salen and Zimmerman's *Rules of Play* (2004) and Schell's *Art of Game Design* (2008) are both inspiring guides on how to design games – written by academics who are also active game designers.
- Think about the principal ideas you are trying to teach, and distill these down to their simplest form; then try to link them to game elements. For example: to denote random or surprising events, use dice rolls; if you need to cover budgets or costs, turn these into easy units (Monopoly money-style) and use them as your scoring system, etc.

> 'You need to understand who is going to play your game. Everything flows from that. A game you make because a piece of gameplay is interesting, or because you like a particular setting, or because you want to see how systems will interact, can result in a game that is fun to play. However, unless you know who is going to play it, you can't say anything meaningful to them. Games aren't designed for you to play, they're designed for people to play.'
>
> Richard Bartle

- Create prototypes using card, felt-tip pens, and counters/dice from existing board games. Once you know how your game works, you can produce more robust, designed versions for repeatable use; as your budget allows.
- Playtest, test, and test again: use friends and colleagues to test your game with. Make notes, adjust the gameplay, rules or elements accordingly, and test again.

Traditional games therefore have much potential in learning contexts. However, they tend to require a classroom environment and limited numbers of players; and therefore do not necessarily meet the needs of distributed, mass and self-paced learners which now make up the fabric of modern education. Some traditional games have made the leap from board to screen quite successfully (Scrabble on Facebook, for example; or versions of Monopoly or Risk on mobile devices) and therefore mix traditional simple gameplay with widespread communities of players. However, this sort of game development and network technology requires high levels of skill, and so as yet such cross-over games are out of reach of the educator.

Mixing Media

One approach that incorporates the best features of computer and traditional games, in a way that is easy to develop and does not require high levels of technical skill, and can operate with small or large numbers of local or distributed players, is the use of mixed-media games. A prime example of this type of game is the alternate reality game (ARG), which is covered in the next section of this chapter. ARGs use narrative, community and problem-solving in a game that unfolds over weeks and months, combining the real and virtual worlds. The players work together to solve the puzzles and develop the story themselves through the creation of artifacts, both digital and real-world, and the mythologies that surround the game (see Chapter 12 for a fuller description, and background, of ARGs).

Chapter 8 has already looked in depth at the reasons why ARGs provide the potential to be excellent learning tools. In the sections that follow, we will present a design process that can be applied to the development of ARGs, as one model for creating low-cost games that meet the needs of learners in a creative way.

Designing Alternate Reality Games

ARGs provide a way to harness the potential of computer games for learning without the typical development overheads required for commercial or high-end computer games. This model also provides teaching staff with a great deal more control to design and tweak the game they want to use for themselves. We present a documented case study here of an ARG used at Manchester Metropolitan University to support student induction, which should provide you with a flavour of the nature and potential of the format, as well as gaining an understanding of one possible development process.

The Alternate Reality Games for Orientation, Socialisation and Induction (ARGOSI) project ran over one year from 2008 to 2009 and was funded by JISC, a UK-based organization that supports technological innovation in further and higher education. The aim of the project was to develop a game to support new students at the university getting to know the city and meeting other people. It was also seen as an alternative way of presenting basic library and information literacy skills that were typically taught as a short face-to-face session during induction week. The game ran for ten weeks at the start of term and we hoped that the format would provide context for a range of activities that supported the informal objectives of orientation to the city and socialization with others, as well as the formal objectives of the information literacy curriculum.

In the sections that follow, we will describe the process that the development team went through in order to create *ViolaQuest*, the game created as part of the project (see summary in Figure 11.3). Player engagement in the game was less than hoped (for reasons discussed in Whitton (2011)) – as might be expected given that this was an experimental project and one of the first of its kind – but the process of development was sound and effective, and this is the focus of the rest of this section.

The steps described here should not be viewed as a restrictive methodology, nor should they be seen as unique to ARGs, but they are simply the process that the development team worked through and found to be effective. While they are presented as discrete steps here, there was in actuality a great deal of iteration, and movement backwards and forwards from one step to another. You may wish to work from the broad principles here and fit them to your own context or any institutional course development cycles.

As ARGOSI was a funded project we were lucky to be able to afford to bring in a range of people with different skills, which we realize may not be possible for individuals or small teams who want to create their own ARGs. Realistically,

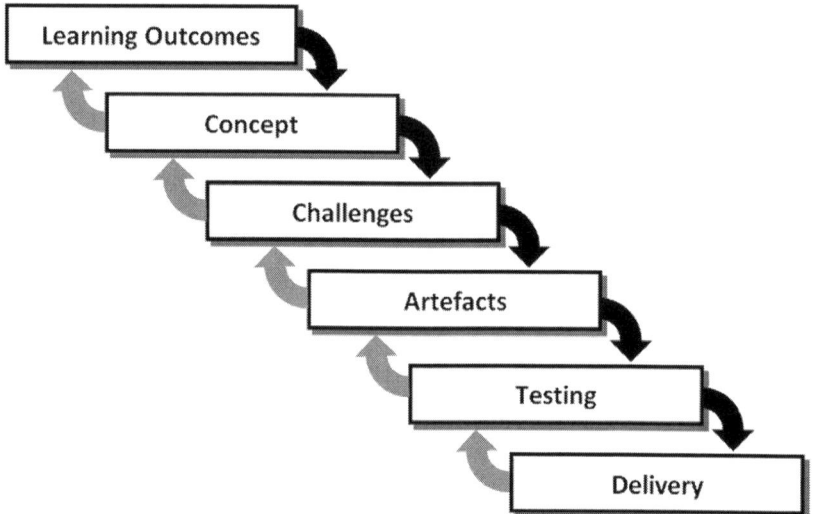

Figure 11.3 A design process for alternate reality games

however, there are some core skills you will need, including someone who can handle graphics, people who can come up with ideas for puzzles or challenges, and someone who can write a storyline. You will also need a small amount of technical expertise and familiarity with the web and other media you might wish to use. However, more important than all of these skills, creativity and enthusiasm will go a long way to developing a successful game. The development of the *ViolaQuest* game produced for the ARGOSI project was done in cycles of team away days (three in total), in which the core creative work was undertaken and direction and actions agreed as a group, followed by allocation of tasks and individual development work. All work was shared on a collaborative site between meetings (the team were geographically dispersed so face-to-face meetings between away days were limited) and this proved to be a very effective way of sharing ideas in progress, getting feedback, testing challenges, and keeping in touch with the rest of the team.

Learning Outcomes and Limitations

It is important to be clear about the purpose of the game being created right from the outset. While the game should be fun to play in its own right, its primary objective is that the players will learn something by playing it. Therefore, explicitly specifying the learning outcomes at the start is a crucial part of the process. In the case of the ARGOSI project, there were two informal outcomes – to get students to meet others and find their way around the city – and formal learning outcomes that mapped to the information literacy curriculum (see Chapter 9 for more detail). By having these outcomes clearly defined at the start of the project, it was easier to ensure that the game and challenge design facilitated learning in these areas.

Once the learning outcomes were fixed, the next step was to be clear about the limitations and scope of the game, including timescale and resources available (including people). In the case of ARGOSI we had a small team and small budget, but anything that involved lots of technical development was out of the question. We had six months to develop and test the game and ten weeks in which it could be played (the first ten weeks of term). Again, being explicit about the limitations up front will help ensure that the game can actually be developed and delivered in the time scales available.

Initial Game Concept and Narrative

The second stage, once the learning outcomes and limitations were determined, was to start the creative process of developing an initial game concept and storyline. For the ARGOSI project we wanted a story that would run for around ten weeks, be based around characters who were students at the university, and focus on a mystery that needed to be solved. The model that the project used for the narrative design was one of a backbone with sub-plots (see Figure 11.4).

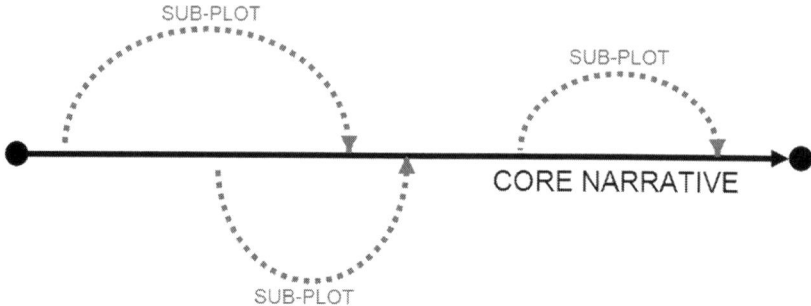

Figure 11.4 Backbone and sub-plots narrative model

This meant that there was an overarching plot and storyline that made up the main game (and met the two informal learning outcomes) with the potential for multiple sub-plots (in this case a single sub-plot that met the formal learning outcomes). This narrative model was designed to be extensible so that different sub-plot challenge blocks could be brought in to map to different curriculum areas without affecting the overall plot structure. There would be regular plot-points on the main narrative, mapping to weeks of gameplay, when parts of the story would be revealed. We decided to use a 'map' as a device to hold the story together, so that at each plot point another map piece would be revealed to the players, which would move the narrative forward (as well as stimulating the desire to collect things and make sets).

Creating the main narrative was carried out at our first face-to-face meeting, working in small groups to develop several different narratives, then coming together to agree on one, and taking additional ideas from the others. Once an overall narrative structure was agreed, based on student Viola Proctor solving a mystery from the past, with plot points, this was written up outside the meeting. The narrative structure used various fantasy elements to bring together the real and fictional worlds, outlining the key plot points and the information given to the player in order to progress the story at each point.

Backstory

At the end of the nineteenth century a group of six Manchester industrialists collaborated on a project to produce a super-efficient weaving machine, but by accident created a device that would allow them to communicate through time with dinosaurs. The Society for Communication with Intelligent Dinosaurs (SCWID) was formed and a long and happy relationship developed with man and dinosaur sharing information and technology. Sadly the dinosaurs entered a period of environmental crisis: they have discovered the secret to reversing the disaster but it is too late to save themselves; however they offer their secret to SCWID: limit industrialization. The society prefer progress (and money) so they cut off all communication with the dinosaurs and hide the communication device. However, just in case it was needed again they created a map with clues to the whereabouts of the device, which was cut into six pieces; one for each society member. These map pieces have been passed down through subsequent generations.

The Present Day

Our story starts when student Viola Proctor inherits a letter containing a map piece from her grandfather, a descendant of an original SCWID member. The letter is cryptic and mentions a secret society and a powerful device. Viola sets up a website to recruit others to help her solve the mystery.

0. Pre-game

Before the game starts lots of information is seeded across the web, suggesting the presence of SCWID, the possibility of communicating with dinosaurs, etc.

1. The First Piece of the Jigsaw

Viola makes her letter public and sets up the blog to get people to help her. At this stage players know that there is a map that needs all the pieces collecting, that there was some sort of secret society, and that there is some sort of object that is important.

2. Tracing the Descendants

The second piece comes with an old diary from the SCWID days, many of the entries have been removed, but there are references to hiding the machine and a clue to another descendant. Players find out that each piece of the map is in the keeping of one of the descendants of each of the original SCWID members, that the map shows the location of the secret object and the object is hidden somewhere in Manchester.

3. The Secret Society

The third piece of the map contains the word SCWID. Players find out that the secret society was called SCWID, it was made up of prominent industrialists at the end of the nineteenth century, and the object was powerful and had to be hidden to avert a crisis of some sort.

4. Communicating with the Past

The fourth piece of the map is accompanied by plans and a journal entry. Players find out that the object was created by accident as part of an industrial project, it enabled the members of SCWID to communicate with the past, and successful communication over a number of years furthered the industrial revolution in Manchester.

5. The Dinosaurs Revealed

The fifth piece of the map is accompanied by an original audio recording from the dinosaurs. Players discover that SCWID stands for the Society for Communication with Intelligent Dinosaurs, the dinosaurs had the secret to saving the planet but left it too late, and fueled by greed, SCWID did not want this secret made public so hid the machine.

6. The Final Showdown

Using the map, the location of the communicator can be found. If enough people meet at a certain point at a certain time, they will be able to, once again, communicate with the dinosaurs and learn their secrets. The secrets are presented via a dinosaur video.

In reality, the hidden object described in the narrative was a street art installation near to the university campus, but in an area that students might not typically visit.

Once the main narrative was developed, the plot for the sub-plot was devised, which centred around a librarian, Percy Root, who wanted to help with Viola's quest but had a variety of his own problems that needed to be resolved first. The sub-plot was designed so that it could tie in with the main plot but was not integral to it. The core narrative was delivered through two blogs, one belonging to Viola and one by Percy.

Designing Challenges

After the main narrative structure was developed, this provided a framework from which to build the challenges. The model used in the project was that for the core narrative there would be one challenge for each of the main plot points, making six in all, each delivered every one to two weeks. The sub-plot challenges (related to the formal learning outcomes) were provided separately (to test the idea of modular sub-plot challenges) and made available throughout the game rather than being drip-fed to players over time. The intention of this model was that keen players could keep themselves busy on the additional challenges, while less active players could concentrate on the core.

The core challenges were all designed so that they fitted in with the plot and allowed the players to uncover additional map pieces, as well as encouraging them to meet other people and get to know the city. We also tried to provide a range in terms of online and offline and individual and collaborative challenges. The challenges are:

1. A coded message hidden in a letter.
2. A treasure hunt around Manchester.
3. Uncovering a hidden password by solving a series of puzzles on a website.

4. Finding the location of a place, based on four photographs of place in the city.
5. Taking a photograph for an entry in a new Manchester A–Z.
6. Using the map pieces to find an encoded location of the hidden object and having your photograph taken beside it.

The library challenges were developed as a separate set, including sixteen different challenges: some that mapped directly on to the information literacy learning outcomes and others that simply provided additional puzzles for fun. More detail can be found about the design of this challenge set and how it was mapped to the library curriculum in Chapter 9.

There were three main types of challenge used in the game:

- Knowledge – challenges that require certain information to be discovered or researched.
- Puzzle-solving – challenges that involve solving puzzles or riddles, such as codes or logic puzzles.
- Creative – challenges that involve developing artifacts, which can include photographs, videos, stories, poems or websites.

Different players will prefer different types of puzzles, so it is good to try and design the game so that there is a good mixture of different types. Other aspects that we considered (and which form a useful checklist for your own developments) are:

- The level of difficulty – making a large number of relatively easy challenges available at the beginning will help players to make quick initial gains, see themselves progressing, and hopefully help them to become immersed in the game. However, it is also important that a range of challenges are available at different levels so that players at all levels can be kept engaged.
- Balancing types of challenge – it is important to provide a balance of types of challenges that require different skills and previous knowledge (e.g. literary and scientific, mathematical and musical), take place online or in the real world, and are individual or collaborative. Starting with individual online challenges and building to real-world collaborative challenges enables players to engage gradually.
- How many challenges you make available – consider how many challenges are made available at any one time so that new players won't be overwhelmed but that established players still have something to keep them occupied.
- Moderation – some challenges can be moderated automatically and it is ideal if the majority work in this manner; however, some (e.g. those that require the creation of artifacts) require manual moderation. This

allows a greater variety in challenge type but also increases the amount of time required to run the game.

- Accessibility – it can be difficult to make all challenges accessible, particularly those that rely on a specific medium, without making the solution obvious. Two solutions are: a) provide an alternative version of the challenge; or b) accept that a specific challenge cannot be made universally accessible without spoiling it and assume that collaboration is integral to the challenge.
- Other information – which links or other resources would be useful to solve the challenge.

The challenges were delivered using a bespoke challenge engine, developed as part of the project (and available open source at http://argosi.playthinklearn. net/resources.htm). This engine allowed players to create profiles, log when they had completed challenges and share that information on a leader board for other players to see. There was also a community forum where they could share hints, tips, and ideas with other players, and the administrators' interface allows challenges to be moderated or marked automatically. The prototype (along with all challenges) is freely available at www.violaquest.org.

Creating Artifacts

The main storyline was delivered through Viola's blog, with challenges provided via the challenge engine. In order to add colour to the narrative and support both the provision of information about the story and the challenges themselves, a series of artifacts were developed by a graphic design specialist on the team. The artifacts were all created as editable graphics so that they could be reused in other contexts or easily re-edited by other members of the team (these are also all freely available). The artifacts included the map itself (see Figure 11.5), letters, diary pages, newspaper articles and blueprints for the communication machine itself.

As well as graphical images, the project also used audio and video files as well as a bespoke website for one of the puzzles. These were all made by members of the team, and the ethos was very much to produce things that were in keeping with the feeling of the game, and amusing, rather than try to produce anything of professional standards.

Testing and Refining Design

It is difficult to overstate the importance of ongoing and iterative testing at all stages of the game development. Ideally, end users should participate in the whole development process (unfortunately this wasn't possible in the ARGOSI project). Without thorough and rigorous testing, it is impossible to get the game right for the users and easy for developers to make lots of assumptions about puzzle difficulty, plot coherence, and so on.

Figure 11.5 The map piece that starts the game

'When you come up with a design, play test it extensively and don't be afraid to experiment with new ideas. Klaus Teuber refined *Settlers of Catan* over a period of two years to come up with the final design!'

Kris Rockwell

There are three specific areas that you should think about testing:

- Usability – whether the game is usable by and accessible to players. Do they understand what they have to do? Does the narrative make sense? Is the online interface fit-for-purpose?
- Gameplay – whether the game is playable. Is it enjoyable and engaging? Are the challenges pitched at the correct difficulty? Is the pace too slow or too fast?
- Learning – whether players engage with the learning outcomes. Do players learn what you intend them to learn? Could they apply it in other situations? What else have they learned?

For the ARGOSI project we used three phases of prototyping and user testing to look at these questions. Two of these involved players being observed using the game in an experimental environment and taking part in focus groups afterwards. We also ran a short pilot of the complete game with a set of volunteers who took part in telephone interviews afterwards. After each pilot, the game was modified to take account of the findings.

Delivery

Once the game has been designed and tested it can go live. One advantage of ARGs is that although the structure and core challenges need to be created in advance, because it is played out over several weeks, changes can be made in response to users. New challenges can be created, additional information provided or alternative directions opened up. It is important, however, that there are people who are given responsibilities for monitoring and supporting the game as it progresses.

The marketing strategy for the game should be considered very early on, as it may involve getting support from academics, other university staff, and the students' union. In the case of ARGOSI we opted for a cryptic strategy (a mistake in retrospect) using physical map pieces, teaser stickers, posters, and flyers distributed by students in *ViolaQuest* t-shirts, along with an interview with 'Viola' on student radio and in the student newspaper. In hindsight it would have been preferable to have been more explicit about the nature and purpose of the game in the marketing.

The types of activities that are required once the game has started are:

- releasing information;
- updating blog posts;
- moderating challenges;
- controlling character emails and social network sites;
- monitoring player progress and speed of completion of the challenges;
- moderating and taking part in community discussions.

This part of the game support is time consuming and we would recommend that at least two people are involved in this stage. For *ViolaQuest* two individuals had responsibility each for playing the role of Viola and Percy, while several others took on player roles to seed discussion and get the game started.

Technology

A key advantage of the ARG format, which combines virtual and real-world technologies, is that the choice of technologies used as part of the game is limited only by the imagination (and budget, although there are many free or cheap options) of the creator. The ideas that follow provide an overview of the different types of technology that can be used to convey information to players, or as the basis for puzzles, but again these should be seen as an idea to build on rather than the limits of the genre.

Real life technologies can be used very effectively in combination with online technologies, as they really help to get across the idea of an 'alternate' reality, somewhere between fiction and the real world. This can include use of the telephone, such as the secret message left on a mobile phone in a venue toilet (Rose, 2007), messages in print media such as newspaper articles or advertisements, radio interviews, materials such as posters, stickers, and leaflets, or clothes such as t-shirts, hats, or wristbands. It can even include interacting with real people, acting as characters in the game, to pass on secret codes or messages, or getting groups of people together in events such as flash mobs.

Social networking sites can be used to create fictional personae, as was done in *ViolaQuest* where the main character Viola had her own Facebook identity, so that players again experience this overlap between what is real and what is not (be careful though as the creation of non-real identities is outside the terms and conditions of some sites). They can also be used to organize groups and collaborative activities within the game.

Online media sharing sites allow different types of video, audio, images, presentations, and so on, to be shared with other people. In *ViolaQuest*, YouTube was used to share a video that passed on key information to players, and one of the challenges involved a collaborative photography task where players had to upload their images to a Flickr group. Using multiple media types to pass on information to players is much more interesting than text alone, and the creation and sharing of media artifacts is also a great way to embed creative challenges in the game.

Other collaborative sites, such as blogs, wikis, shared documents, and microblogging sites, can be used in a variety of ways. This includes building up the virtual persona of characters in the game, by using Twitter for example, providing information on the game progress as was done in *ViolaQuest* through the use of Viola's blog, or providing a platform for challenges or problems that need to be solved in the game.

Bespoke websites take a bit more time and expertise to develop, but can add colour and a sense of realism to the design of an ARG. In *ViolaQuest*, searching for the initial SCWID (previously provided as a clue) will lead players to the History Mystery website (see www.historymysteries.net), which contains a puzzle that will further the game. There is nothing in the site to tell players that this is part of the game, and in fact any web user could find it and believe it to be real (if they were particularly gullible). This also means that sites of this type may have to be created a long time before the game actually starts so that they become established and picked up by search engines.

Virtual worlds such as *Second Life*, or even virtual gaming worlds, can be used to bring people together in virtual environments for activities such as treasure hunts, collaborative tasks or group events. Much of the types of activities that can be carried out in the real world can be replicated in the virtual without the physical barriers of space, but the nature and value of the activity has to be such that it is worth the player going to the trouble of signing up to access the world, and learning how to operate within it (more detail on assessing the effectiveness of virtual worlds is given in Chapter 13).

Hopefully this has given you some idea of the wide range of technologies that can be used to support the mixed-reality format. Of course, getting the technology right is only one part of the game design, and the ARGOSI project taught us some important things about the design of ARGs, which are discussed in the next section.

Tips for Designing Alternate Reality Games

While ARGs offer a different approach to engaging learners, combining the benefits of game-based learning with the ease of development of traditional materials, they are not without their drawbacks or potential pitfalls. Many lessons were learned from the ARGOSI project about how – and how not – to apply this type of game format in education. The following three points are, we feel, the three key lessons learned from the project:

- *Have a clear purpose.* It is all very well to be cryptic, but if students don't know how to access the game, understand what they are supposed to do, or actually play the game then no amount of good design up-front will make it a success. The secretive nature of this type of game, blurring reality and fiction, may simply not be appropriate for education, where learners are more strategic and want to know *why* they should engage in an activity; we can't assume that everyone simply likes to play games for their own sake. Explicit and accessible marketing, or tie-in to specific curricula, is important to ensure student buy-in.
- *Get learners involved in design.* Getting students involved as early as possible and throughout the development process is the ideal. As well as highlighting the importance of testing with your intended users, getting student representatives involved in designing and running the game is helpful for ensuring that it appeals to the right demographic and adding legitimacy within the target group. This is true of all game types, but particularly so when the audience may be unfamiliar with the genre.
- *Make it easy to start playing.* Provide lots of simple ways for players to do things that do not require too much effort, especially early on. Easy challenges and tasks with quick rewards allow players to see that they have achieved something quickly and seeing initial progress makes them increasingly likely to engage further with the more challenging aspects of the game. Straightforward tasks that involve simple

interaction with the community are also key to building players' confidence and getting them to collaborate with others.

Keep It Simple

In this chapter we have aimed to show two workable options for the creation of games that are affordable, both in terms of development time and overheads and in terms of running and maintenance costs: from the simplest of board or card games, to detailed but low-tech ARGs. By creating games that do not rely heavily on technical systems or high end production values, the ability to develop fit-for-purpose games becomes a reality for all educators. The ideas and processes described here should not be seen as definitive, or followed to the letter; we merely aim to provide an overview of two practical ways to approach game design and development, and hope to convince readers that the design of games for learning is not such an onerous task after all.

Part IV
GAMES IN PRACTICE

In Parts II and III of this book, we have looked at the ways game-based learning can become accessible to educators with all levels of technical skill, experience, and confidence. We hope that after engaging with these two sections you will be at least partially convinced that games have something to offer for your own practice.

In this fourth part, we hand over the microphone to researchers and practitioners in the field to show how the ideas and techniques presented in the previous parts of the book can be applied. Three areas in particular have been highlighted: the design of low-fidelity games in practice; the applicability of virtual worlds; and the use of narrative to support game-based learning. Each case pulls together the theory and practice of the individual situation, and is presented from the perspective of the authors, providing a taste of the issues encountered when developing games for applying game-based techniques in the real world.

The approaches presented in this section are:

- An examination of the practice and theory of *developing alternate reality games for learning* (Chapter 12).
- A discussion of how to evaluate the benefits and affordances of *gameplay in virtual worlds*, when considering their applicability for learning in a specific context (Chapter 13).
- The use of *narrative in a gaming context*, and the practicalities and advantages of taking a narrative approach to learning (Chapter 14).

We hope that reading this section will provide you with in-depth insights about the applicability of different gaming techniques in specific situations, and the benefits – as well as the drawbacks – of each particular approach.

12

DEVELOPING ALTERNATE REALITY GAMES FOR LEARNING

KATIE PIATT

Introduction to Alternate Reality Games and their History

The reality: A group of students on campus with spoons strapped to their heads.

The alternate reality: Education Detective Recruits working together to foil a conspiracy of pirates from the future set to destroy the university.

This is the heart of an alternate reality game (ARG): players working together in the real world to complete the challenges of the game.

Figure 12.1 Reality and alternate reality

The differentiation of ARGs from more traditional board games or computer games is that they use the world around you to deliver the game experience, which adds a game layer over perfectly normal activities. For example, you might be reading a blog post on an otherwise normal site, but you are prompted to solve an anagram of all the initial letters. Or that seemingly normal phone call at work takes on special significance when you find you are speaking to someone from the future. This boundary blurring between real life and the game is key – using real life resources, but for you they have an 'alternate' meaning than to people not playing the game. In contrast to many commercial games, ARGs can exist simply with a few web pages and making 'alternate' use of pre-existing, more expensive resources: providing a format with a much wider range of budget and resource needs; key in education, which we will come to later in this chapter.

ARGs began in early 2000, growing in popularity through their use in advertising campaigns for films and games such as *The Beast* for the film *A.I.* and *I Love Bees* for the computer game *Halo 2* (Szulborski, 2005). These games deliberately blurred the lines between the players' experiences both within and outside of the game, exploring many different forms of media in parallel. 'Alternate Reality Games are games that are cross-media and that blur the line between the game space and the real world experience' (de Freitas, 2006). Still a relatively new game format to many people, ARGs are still very much in trend, with many new companies being set up to provide rich, multi-media experiences to television programmes, films, and games. The various elements included in the game, and evaluations of their effectiveness, are not yet well studied and this is a growing field in media and education. 'I know it's a game, and you know it's a game, but the game doesn't know it's a game' (Microsoft ARG designer Elan Lee, cited in MacDougall, 2011).

Part of the uniqueness of an ARG is that as a player you don't always know what is or isn't part of the game. When playing, you never admit you are playing – the mantra 'This is not a game' allows you to immerse yourself and act within the game as if it were real, providing extreme levels of engagement and motivation in some players: you are allowed to act as if it is not a game. Over the years this mantra has been relaxed: after all players know it's a game and yet still find the experience fun; plus it's very hard to attract players if designers spend too much effort on being cryptic and not actually telling the players what they are involved in or need to do. This becomes even harder in an educational context where you want your students to participate in the game for their own learning, so in learning modes you can relax this mantra and let students know it's a game.

> 'In ARGs, people get engaged deeply with the characters/story, which is always surprising and results in surprising levels of engagement or activity.'
>
> Adrian Hon

Examples of Alternate Reality Games

The following four examples of ARGs, two from the commercial world and two from education, have been chosen to highlight the practical and logistical issues of creating an ARG as well as a range of contexts where ARGS can be effective. I'll start by looking at two ARGs from the commercial sector.

PerplexCity

Games development company Mind Candy released *PerplexCity* in the UK in 2005. The story of the game revolved around finding a priceless cube that had been stolen and buried somewhere on earth. Using blogs, puzzles, and other media, players were encouraged to complete the game and win a real-life £100,000 prize.

Players bought collectible cards, each with a different numbered puzzle, and solved the puzzles through the website to earn points on an in-game leader board and reveal a map formed from the images on the back of the cards. The cards ranged from simple brainteasers, through hidden features only revealed

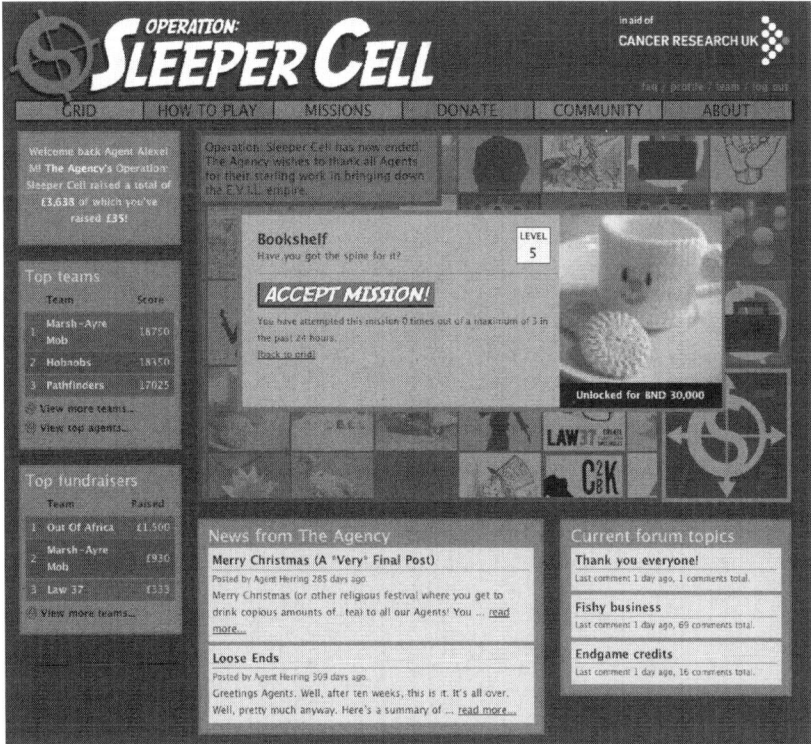

Figure 12.2 *Operation: Sleeper Cell*

under ultraviolet light, to an international search for one man on earth with only a photo to go on. In parallel to the cards, the larger story unravelled through blogs, websites, and some real-life events.

Moseley's (2008) investigations into the high levels of motivation and engagement demonstrated by players of *PerplexCity* found several key elements of the format of interest to education: problem solving at various levels, progress through the game and rewards, the story/plot, a regular delivery of new challenges, the large active community, and the influence the players had on the game outcomes.

Operation: Sleeper Cell

By using a spoof spy theme for an ARG, *Operation: Sleeper Cell* became the first game to directly incorporate fundraising for charity, in this case for Cancer Research UK. Teams of players either donated to the game to unlock new puzzle cells or could be sponsored by their friends and families. Unlocking the puzzles also released the next part of the spy story – defeating the forces of 'E.V.I.L' – through websites, blogs, and Twitter. The game ran for a fixed period of ten weeks, culminating in a live event.

> '*Operation: Sleeper Cell* shows that games can be a real force for good in the world.'
>
> Adrian Hon

The game raised just over £3600, and suffered from some of the common problems experienced by designers trying to build a community of ARG players: if there aren't enough people playing then there will be little activity and the story will unfold too slowly.

The game has now finished but most of the missions and the story are still available at www.operationsleepercell.com/.

Despite stereotypes of gamers, it is now well established that games are not a waste of time, or just for fun. If you want to find a way to provide high levels of engagement and motivation for your students, games are increasingly an option you can turn to. Studies looking at the use of 'play' and 'games' in higher education have shown increased engagement and task completion (Colarusso, 1993). However, as Whitton (2007a) showed, when games are used to merge entertainment and education, despite the highly increased engagement, the potential of the game was often limited by cost-effectiveness and accessibility. The two educational examples that follow have been selected for their ability to overcome these barriers within institutions.

Enterprise in Content

It would be ideal to be able to involve and immerse our students in real-world experiences, to make the learning feel as real as possible. In education, ARGs can be used to easily set an authentic context where this would otherwise be impractical and therefore close the gap between the simulation and reality (see Figure 8.1, Chapter 8).

At the University of Portsmouth, Simon Brookes' work to close the reality gap for his enterprise students led to the creating of an ARG to allow the students to work with a business, using the normal communication channels – but in this case, the business was not actually real.

In small groups, the students were tasked to help a struggling company, 'Salter & Son', a fictitious clothing shop, to turn around their failing business. In response to triggers and workshops from employees at the company and consultants (provided by role-playing academics) the student teams needed to complete their own research and undertake communications in order to make recommendations back to the company. The triggers came as packages through the post as well as online using email, chat, and video.

Matching the self-directed learning tasks to the unit learning outcomes progressed the students through the basics of marketing, finance, business management, and personnel. The unit was assessed by peer assessment, a group presentation, short answers tests, reflective essays, and a group report. There were also prizes awarded to the highest scoring team. Student feedback showed the students actually cared about the client, including defending them against criticisms – despite being fully aware they were fictional. This model of teaching the unit produced considerably higher assessment marks across the board than in previous years. The investment work of the fictional company and the city (Porthampton) in which it sits can now be expanded on and the resources used within this and other units, even across institutions. Over time this world will grow into a rich set of interlinked sites and resources to easily extend into new contexts.

Who is Herring Hale?

The University of Brighton was looking at non-traditional ways to support students' induction, and games were seen as a likely candidate to improve engagement. I identified ARGs as a way to offset the cost and accessibility issues of development, by using familiar, established web technologies and enabling game design to make use of existing physical and virtual resources on and around the university campus. The total budget for the game was £1000, entirely spent on prizes.

The format of the ARG was a series of nine tasks, one per week over the first term, with an underlying time-travel storyline and a supporting online community on the campus social network. The content was designed to allow in-depth and physical exploration of selected support services and resources. In total forty-two students completed at least one task in the game with twelve students completing all nine tasks. There follows the initial posting on the game's community area from the 'Education Detective' Herring Hale, illustrating the tone and storyline for the game:

> I am the Education Time Detective (3006) and I am writing to you for your help. Join me on my Community now.
>
> In 3006 the University of Brighton has become the Earth Intellectual Curiosity Centre, helping to bring wisdom to all. The Education saboteurs are trying to undermine the Centre by travelling back in time and infiltrating the work of the University in 2006 to stop its amazing progress through history. You are needed to help the Time Detective catch these saboteurs by revealing their identities and reporting back to Education Headquarters. Time is of the essence – we must be subtle yet quick and save the University of Brighton before Christmas 2006 when the infiltration will have been successful.
>
> History shows that there are 9 saboteurs we need to reveal over the next 9 weeks. I will reward my recruits as best as I can by scoring your contribution to the mission and providing prizes of an advanced technology appropriate for this time period to the highest scorers.

Emails triggering each task and student responses to the tasks were handled via a dedicated 'Education Detective' email address and managed by the project team. Each task covered one of the major support services at the university, and was designed to feature an aspect of the service that was felt to benefit from additional highlighting. The clues all involved finding codes and cryptic content that were hidden within 'normal' information about the featured service, e.g. find and apply for a specific job at the careers centre, locate a desk loan book in the library, and find a specific name.

'Right now what's most interesting for me about games is the way that they can provide a different sort of a lens through which to view your surroundings. I'm interested in how being tasked to find certain things, or running to evade capture, or simply gathering with others to behave in a conspicuously odd manner in public space, can shift different elements of the city in and out of focus.'

Nikki Pugh

Here is some sample feedback from the twelve students who completed all tasks:

- 'In induction week they tell you where to go to get help, Careers for instance. But you forget it all five minutes after you've left. This was brilliant – now I really know where to go.'
- 'I was wrapped up in too much programming, it helped give me a break and get a new perspective.'
- '. . . a really good way to learn.'
- 'Thank you all for a wonderful and inspiring term! From chasing orange techie people to strapping spoons on my forehead, its been fun:).'

A similar example to this took place at Manchester Metropolitan University, where the ARGOSI project (Whitton, 2009) produced an ARG to induct new students into the city and university life. Players had to fully explore the city to complete the clues and collect the cards. Both of these projects attracted a small but enthusiastic following. Students were observed to fully engage with the quest, and to go as far as meeting and offering hints to fellow players fully in the theme of the story.

Advice for using Alternate Reality Games in Learning

It is clear that the often cryptic nature of ARGs does not appeal to everyone and has its critics: 'This might be the curricular equivalent of walking into a room and stating: the theme is physics, work out the questions, and then leaving the students to "discover" the subject' (O'Donovan et al., 2009). And a balance needs to be struck to make sure the fun and the education are well matched and enticing from both the student and academic sides. The educational examples described above provide evidence that the ARG formats can provide an interesting alternative to existing mechanisms for introducing students to certain types of skills, information, or services. This format does not appeal to all students, but is very effective for those that like it. The format also provides students with something special to feel part of. The use of existing technologies and tools within the institution for interacting with and supporting the players is both practical and effective.

One of the factors identified as affecting retention is the quality of the induction process; and this model may be able to appeal to an increasingly diverse student population. Several students in the *Herring Hale* ARG commented on the feeling of 'fun' and 'being part of something special'. It would be hoped that this could be built on and possibly linked to student retention, meeting a key issue in higher education.

Tips for Using Alternate Reality Games in Education

1. *Have realistic expectations*. Don't be disappointed by low take-up: mysteries and puzzles just don't appeal to everyone. Consider how

many players you would consider enough to justify the staff time and resource required to create and run the game. In the case of *Herring Hale*, the twelve players who completed the challenge was too low considering the time invested.

2. *Raising the profile of the game.* It is worth investing time and money in marketing the game to make sure potential players are aware of it. If there aren't enough people playing then there will be little activity and the story will unfold slowly. It's ok to say that this *is* a game, even if you are concerned it destroys some of the illusion of the 'alternate' reality.

3. *Avoid criticism.* Make any scoring completely fair and transparent and if there is an online discussion element to your game, make sure you respond quickly to any questions or concerns raised. In *Herring Hale* there was originally a 'speed' bonus for completing challenges, but this benefited students who didn't have a lecture at 1p.m. on Wednesday when the tasks were released and so this was withdrawn.

4. *Design for action.* Plan the tasks in your game to provide a way for the students to share and collaborate on tasks, or target other skills you wish to encourage. The final task in *Herring Hale* which involved working with other 'recruits' to take photos on campus (as seen in the opening photo for this chapter) was identified as being particularly successful, encouraging creativity and collaboration.

5. *Go with the flow.* Hopefully you will get plenty of players, so plan your resources to be responsive if the player numbers get higher without needing to modify your planned storyline too much. It is also good to remain flexible around the direction of your story and the details of tasks: you might want to introduce topical posters around the campus in response to particular events, or to increase take-up at certain points, for example.

6. *Use what you've got.* Many logistical problems with using campus services were highlighted over the course of the *Herring Hale* game, such as physical delivery of items, but the format of an ARG using existing tools and services still makes it much quicker and cheaper to create than a more traditional game. Staff, for example in our careers office, or on catering tills, were more than happy to be involved and give scripted responses or hand out clues when the format was explained.

13
EVALUATING IMMERSIVE VIRTUAL ENVIRONMENTS FOR LEARNING

SARAH SMITH-ROBBINS

Immersive virtual learning environments, virtual or synthetic worlds such as *Second Life* and *Opensim*, and immersive virtual game environments such as *World of Warcraft* have, over the last decade or so, emerged as authentic digital tools for those engaged in the practice of teaching, learning and research. Now that the hyperbole that inevitably surrounds early adoption of any new technology has subsided use in education is tentatively venturing on to the 'plateau of productivity'.

> 'I believe that the future of gaming will be a mesh of real world and virtual components. This can certainly be seen in new technologies such as Augmented Reality (AR), but I believe this will extend to real life sensor data as sensors become more affordable and designers integrate them into games (think about Nike+ as one common example). The integration of virtual and real life pieces (and, in some cases, sensors) can be seen in arcade games like *Sangokushi Taisen* (www.sangoku-wars.com/sangoku-wars01/game_main.html) or with the integration of boardgames and computer games such as Ex Illis (http://ex-illis.com/wikien/Main_Page).'
>
> Kris Rockwell

Early use of these environments in educational settings, arguably, focused primarily on the novelty of integrating new tools into learning experiences or the efficacy of the environments in improving engagement and interaction with students but should now be considered as part of a much wider challenge to established practice. The use of digital technologies brings into question our existing notions of curriculum design and delivery, challenges the digital literacy of tutors and students alike, opens up new pedagogic possibilities, and in times of austerity may provide our education institutions with a scalable opportunity to widen participation within constrained budgets.

The efficacy of educational activities within these environments is largely dependent on a combination of the affordances (Hollins and Robbins, 2009) provided by the environment's mechanics, the literacy of both faculty and students engaged in the activity, and, significantly, the emergent complexity produced by the interactions between them. In this chapter, I explore the relationship between the mechanics in game-based immersive virtual environments, the designers' or tutors' intended objectives or learning outcomes, and the student.

Utilizing activity theory (AT) and genre ecology models (GEMs), this chapter suggests a model of immersive environment mechanical and social literacy beneficial to designers, instructors, and students. This literacy is used to analyse and evaluate learning potential within such an environment, explore potential activity designs within the space, and hasten the necessary acquisition of skills within the space. Via an examination of the genres of commonly known virtual environments (both designer-provided and user-created) made possible by the mechanics of the environment, faculty and instructional designers will learn to make use of this model in their own work.

Evaluating a New Immersive Space

Before we can integrate a new tool, such as a virtual world (VW), into our classrooms we have to evaluate its potential to support our learning objectives. To evaluate a tool we must first become literate in the tool. But who has the time to play a game for months just to become literate enough to evaluate it? We need a better, more efficient, way to evaluate tools and hit the ground running.

This chapter is dedicated to explaining a method to do so. Based on AT and the GEM, the technology adaption and adoption model (TAAM) is designed as a process to help instructors evaluate and leverage new tools as quickly and as effectively as possible.

Activity Theory: An Introduction

Although average users have preconceived motivations for entering a VW (e.g. the world's marketing materials, the suggestions of friends and colleagues), the world itself must provide a satisfying activity for the user if that user is to have a fulfilling experience. In terms of AT, the world not only is the tool with which the subject interacts, but also provides the object that initially engages the user. Most worlds do this through a tutorial, or set of basic activities designed to introduce the user to the interface and tools and engage them in common objects/ objectives. These objects/objectives and the means to achieve them not only give the user a satisfying experience, but also provide a path to engage in further activities as intended by the world's creators and enabled by the world's tools.

Activity is fluid in VWs in part because VWs are a product of rhetorical activity. Without the communicative acts of users, VWs would be ghost towns of code waiting to be inhabited. The activities of the user are what bring a VW to life, bring meaning to the constructs created by designers, and uncover the truths about the reality within the world. Without user activities, a VW is just a potential reality.

AT is a framework to describe the cyclical and reciprocal interactions among subjects (actors/individuals), the objects of the interaction (the purpose or objective of the activity), and the tools used to facilitate the activity (software, concept, etc.) as shown in Figure 13.1 (Koschmann, 1996). AT suggests that subjects do not merely interact with the world according to a simple cause–effect relationship; rather, the relationships within an activity constitute a complex, layered, continuous process of learning and situational or cultural influences. In its simplest form, AT focuses on the relationship among a single subject, object, and tool and the context in which an activity occurs (Kaptelinin and Nardi, 2006).

AT stresses that tools alter our activities, which in turn, alter our tools (Nardi, 2010). For example, I need to write an email, and I have an internet-connected computer, an email client, and my native language (the tools), which allow me to convey the message I need to send (the object). As I use the tools successfully or unsuccessfully, I gather feedback and alter my actions to improve my use of the tools and to get closer to completing my object. If I try to send the message without first typing in the recipient's email address, the software will alert me that I am missing a critical part of the message. After entering the address, I can successfully send the email.

AT also suggests that individuals take into account the context of the activity, such as the cultural or environmental factors that influence the relationships in the activity. Writing an email using my iPhone's small keyboard or an unfamiliar email client would introduce new factors into the performance of the activity. Given the situation and my need to send the message, my ability to use

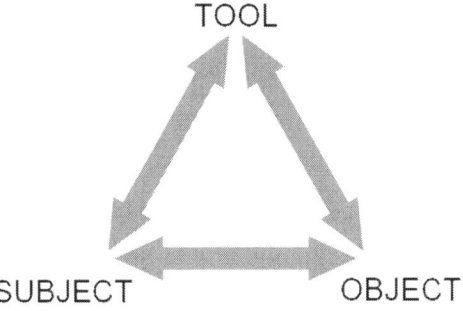

Figure 13.1 Diagram of the relationships in activity theory

the device and the client improves through effort and trial and error. The activity itself results in learning. 'Activity Theory posits that conscious learning emerges from activity (performance) not as a precursor to it' (Jonassen and Rohrer-Murphy, 2008, p. 62).

A critical element of AT is the view that the tool itself is part of a larger cultural system. The tool limits the object by mediating what is possible. Tools may be physical objects (such as a hammer or lever) or mental devices (such as language or philosophy). They are the product of human activity and develop as they are used within a community or culture. Tools are shaped as they accumulate the social context in which they are used (Joyes and Chen, 2007).

Focusing on only the subject, tool, and object is suitable for examining the activity of an individual. However, individuals live in communities, and their activities are always intertwined with the activities, expectations, and influences of others.

According to the framework of AT, the tasks we undertake to accomplish our objectives also exist in a cyclical system of growth and change. We construct our activities to achieve our goals, but those constructions are combinations of actions and operations. Operations are simple acts that we perform unconsciously or autonomically, such as holding a pencil or taking a step. If we combine those operations into more complex acts such as writing an essay or dancing, we create actions. Perform an action often enough, and it becomes operationalized (Jonassen and Rohrer-Murphy, 2008) as shown in Figure 13.2

AT posits that we only learn about a process by performing it (Jonassen and Rohrer-Murphy, 2008). This cyclical process of moving from action to operation in pursuit of accomplishing a goal results in learning. Our orientation is the mental plan created to accomplish an action. Orientation recedes as actions become habituated and operationalized. Should an operation fail to produce the expected results, individuals encounter a contradiction, and the operation again unfolds into action. Development occurs within these contradictions (Kuutti 1996).

AT stresses that the whole of the relationship among subject, tool, and object should be the focus of analysis. However, in this case, the subject seems to recede into the background. All new users in a VW are treated the same by the software. Thus, the VW is not concerned with an individual user's motivation for logging in. Rather, the system of the VW treats all users equally and assumes that the designers' intended objectives are the objectives of the user. Because of this, the tool and object come to the forefront in the analysis – so much so that the line between them becomes somewhat blurred in the discussion of VW tutorials, which are an introduction to the tools and intended objects within the world.

Tools and objects are tied closely to the rules of the space. These rules are not merely behavioural suggestions, but also limitations and abilities programmed

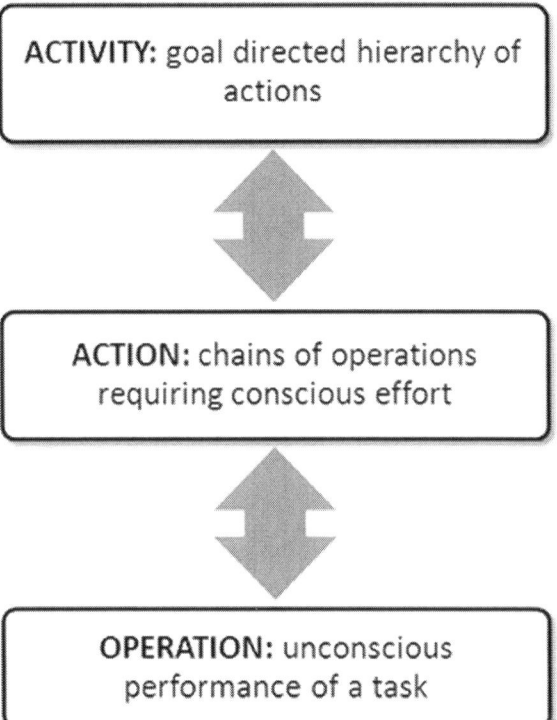

Figure 13.2 Activity, action, and operation are related

Source: Jonassen & Rohrer-Murphy, 2008

into the world, which users do not have the choice to accept or reject. Nardi (2010) claimed that individuals see the limitations set by rules as 'resources preserving good design' (p. 74). I argue that, in the early space of the tutorial, rules are the guiding posts that ensure a user has the experience intended by the designers. Rather than preserving the design for the new user, rules preserve the experience.

It should be noted though, that the distinctions among rules, tools, and objects in a VW is weak. The tools are the source of the rules (i.e. *Second Life* has a rule that allows users to fly, whereas in *World of Warcraft* flight is only allowed using a mount and only for users at high levels). The result of limiting flight to high-level characters in *World of Warcraft* preserves the hierarchy of players and provides motivation to low-level users to continue playing. Objects arise at the crossroads between rules and tools, such as the goal to reach the level at which *World of Warcraft* users may purchase a flying mount. The rules in a VW enable or inhibit activities and are created by the tools and intended objects.

Genre Ecology Models: The Next Step in Activity Theory

AT helps us quickly see the system of tools provided by the designers of a VW. However, because educators are most often leveraging VWs to do things other than what the designers intended, we need an easy way to see not only what's possible, but what else is possible.

AT analysis provides insights into the way that individuals, their tools, and their objectives are connected. Through this lens, we can learn about the activities that designers provide to new users. However, because tutorials are constructed with prescriptive activities provided by designers, tutorials say little about the activities that make up the remainder of the user experience. In an effort to see the larger context of these activities, we turn to the GEM to examine what happens after the objective is reached. By focusing on the communicative results of activities, the GEM explores how patterns of recurrent activities form stable, repeating forms of communication. Creating genre ecologies adds a layer to VW analysis by going beyond intended activities and intended genres to what is possible to create specifically to support our learning objectives.

Spinuzzi et al. (2006) offers a four-step process to creating a GEM:

1. Identify genres.
2. Identify relationships among genres as sequential, modifying, or categorizing.
3. Develop the GEM.
4. Detect discoordinations.

In addition, Zachry and colleagues (2008, p. 244) define three levels of work activity to classify the motivations and intentions, as well as the scope and impact, of the work.

1. Strategic: established by managers or leaders to define organizational objectives.
2. Tactical: established to accomplish specific projects in support of greater goals.
3. Operational: executed by teams or individuals to build to tactical accomplishments.

These three levels are drawn from the ways large organizations stay on track and move forward. However, the levels also easily apply to other organizations and their goals. For example, when they are applied to VWs, strategic activities are the work done by designers, who decide what users should accomplish, while being mindful about how the accomplishments support the overall purpose of the world. Tactical activities are the objectives assigned to users when entering the world. Users learn to navigate, survive, and communicate (operational activities), which aggregate to accomplish the tactical goals provided.

A hallmark of the development of the culture of a VW is the growth of user-defined activities, either to augment or circumvent the designer-provided goals or to satisfy other interests using the VW. If these activities are to take place, they must be supported by the genres within the world.

TAAM: Tool Adoption and Alignment Model

Now, let's put all of these pieces into our toolbox and put them to work. As educators evaluating a VW as an educational tool our next step, once a promising world is found, is to start designing learning experiences and ensuring that those experiences will be effective.

We should be clear about the questions we'll need to answer:

- What are our learning objectives?
- Will the affordances (designer-provided genres) of the VW support/allow the creation of the learning experiences to accomplish our objectives?
- Will engaging in these learning experiences conflict with the culture of the VW's existing users?
- Will the learners understand why the VW is being used for class? Will they be willing to engage in the experience? If the VW is game-based will learners be willing to play and to accept playful behaviour as worthwhile in a course?

Combining the insights from AT and GEMs can help us answer these questions. First, we should understand the relationship between the user-created genres that we will use in the VW and the designer-provided genres. To be successful (i.e. useful, entertaining, and not disruptive or pointless), user-designed activities cannot conflict with or be overshadowed by designer-provided activities. There are four types of relationships between them. Table 13.1 shows each of the four categories and provides users' perceptions and examples. For simplicity, I focus on *World of Warcraft* and not a range of VWs.

Educational applications within VWs succeed when they fall into the categories of complementary and additional. Educational experiences that fall into the conflict and overshadow categories will fail to achieve their learning goals. Incommensurate activities are not limited to conflicts between user-created activities and designer-provided activities. The consideration of educational experiences requires consideration of the relationship between the activities provided by the instructor and the students' perception of the activities within the context of the course. The VW's designer-provided goals are a layer placed on top of the course. Table 13.2 shows Zachry and colleagues (2008) terminology for the motivations and expected outcomes of activities (strategic, tactical, and operational). Coordination in each column and row

Table 13.1 *User-created activities defined by relationship to designer-provided goals*

Label	Role of user-created activity	General user perception of activity	Example
Conflict	Conflicts with designer-provided activity	Negative	Gold farming
Overshadow	Is overshadowed by designer-provided activity	Easily ignored	Chatting on public channels about topics unrelated to designer-provided activities
Complementary	Complements or assists designer-provided activity	Useful, positive	Quest tracking and map add-ons
Additional	Neither conflicts with nor complements designer-provided activity	Engaging if justified or entertaining	Social gatherings such as parties or funerals

are necessary for a successful educational experience. Instructors are familiar with the issues resulting from discoordinations between the 'Course/Instructor' column and the 'Student' column. For example, if students do not feel that the material in the course is relevant to their career or that a particular assignment does not contribute to the learning objectives of the course, they may feel dissatisfied with the class. If an assignment contributes only slightly toward the overall learning objectives of a course but requires a long time to complete, students may feel that the assignment is not worth doing. It is also possible, in game-based worlds, for the mechanics (skills necessary to play) to feel unnecessarily difficult or not aligned with the learning objectives which may cause learners to reject the entire experience.

VWs add a third layer with its own dominant activities, introducing further potential discoordinations. Learning to use the mechanics of a complex VW such as *Second Life* to accomplish a course task worth only a few grade points represents an operational discoordination between the student and the VW. An inability to observe students engaging in an activity in order to assess them illustrates a tactical conflict between the VW and the course. This framework can be used to assist in the identification of factors that contribute to the success or failure of VW instructional design.

The bulk of discoordinations occur due to conflicts between the VW and student activities. Within worlds where designer-provided activities are

Table 13.2 *Strategic, tactical, and operational goals and activities across virtual worlds, courses, and students*

	Virtual world	*Course/instructor*	*Student*
Strategic	'Success' and enjoyment High engagement and prolonged use	Learning objectives Disciplinary discourse Career preparation	Course completion Satisfactory grade Better or higher paying job Return on investment of time or effort Enjoyment
Tactical	Socialization Exploration Creation Quests	Assessments Assignments	Efficient completion of course tactical goals Understanding course mechanics (rubrics, grading, etc.) Connecting course objectives and assignments to long-term personal goals
Operational	Learning to use genres and mechanics to achieve tactics	Information Experiences Rubrics Skills	Attendance Note taking Learning facts Allotting adequate time for completion Understanding assessment requirements

dominant (often, game worlds where user-to-environment and user-to-user relationships are conditional or competitive), there is a danger of creating course activities that easily conflict with the provided activities of the world – including the game experience. While the genres of the world may support an activity, such as using guild chat as a class discussion space, the activities of the world may prove too distracting or too contrasting to the class activity.

However, the inverse also seems to be true. Activities created in VWs that complement the designer-provided objectives may benefit from the engrossing nature of activities such as quests and exploration. Designing learning activities that coordinate with designer-provided activities creates a compelling learning experience. In worlds where there is no set of dominant designer-provided activities, such as social VWs like *Second Life*, there is little danger that the world's activities will crowd out the educational applications.

Nevertheless, discoordinations are possible. Conflict can arise between student objectives and course objectives, rather than between the course and the VW. If the instructor does not make a solid connection between the course's tactical and operation goals and the students' tactical and operational goals, then students will disengage or misunderstand the purpose of the activities. On the other hand, worlds such as *Second Life* that lack dominant goals also offer easily manipulated genres that may be leveraged to design creative learning activities – but only if students see the purpose and are not overwhelmed by the world's operational learning curve.

Using Activity and Genre to Choose Virtual Worlds for Educational Applications

Given the difficulty of designing an effective course, even without the complications of using a VW, the choice of whether to use a VW as a course tool is a difficult one. Critical examination of the course and student objectives (strategic, tactical, and operational) can assure that the basic course design is sound. Checking for alignment, both vertical and horizontal, ensures that the learning objectives and associated exercises fit together.

Adding a VW to a course can complicate learning. However, instructors can prevent discoordinations between the course and the VW's activities by using Table 13.1. The operational activities are largely the result of identifying the mechanics of the world and using the designer-provided genres.

After identifying a VW, instructors should look at the activity coordinations column to discover if the genres support the operational activities of the course or may be manipulated to create new genres, as well as if the VW's tactical activities will accommodate the course activities without overshadowing or conflicting with them. If there are too many discoordinations, the instructor is faced with three choices. First, if the operational activities (genres) do not coordinate well, but the tactical activities do, then the instructor should consider using outside tools to provide the necessary genres. Second, the instructor should examine a VW with different facets to look for a better fit. If the course activities require specialized spaces and the VW does not allow the construction of spaces, then the instructor should choose one that is and examine if it would allow the creation of the spaces necessary for the course. Lastly, it would be wise for the instructor to consider that a VW is not a proper tool to augment the course.

The TAAM process isn't only useful for ensuring that our learning experiences will be effective within a VW. It can also serve in the opposite function to diagnose why an exercise isn't working or why a tool that's been provided to us may not be the right choice. Explaining to administrators, for example, that a learning management system is discoordinant with necessary learning experiences may assist them in providing a more effective tool.

Conclusion

Understanding the connections between the affordances and mechanics of an immersive world and our learning objectives are merely the first step. This connection only proves that it's possible to achieve those goals within the world. Using TAAM we can see that the motivations behind the tool, the learning objectives, and learner opinions form a complex web that must coordinate to allow the highest quality learning experience to occur, whilst maintaining the game experience of the original immersive world.

14

ALTERNATE REALITY GAMES AND LITERATURE

DANIELLE BARRIOS-O'NEILL AND ALAN HOOK

Imagine this: Tomorrow morning, you check your email as you always do, and you see you've received a puzzling message from an unfamiliar sender. The email, when you open it, tells you the beginning of a story in which a shy student named Ana (searching for a book on the Pleiades star cluster at the university library in Belfast) happened to stumble upon a different book instead. Ana flipped through the pages of this book, entitled *The Star Factory*. It appeared to have been recently altered with strange diagrams and messages in code. Curious, Ana opened it to the back. She found, handwritten on the final page of the book, addressed to her, a note (see Figure 14.1).

You have come to the end of the email, which ends with a link. You click on this, and a page loads with the words '[in]visible Belfast' in bold black text. In the centre of the web page is an embedded secret-surveillance video of a girl (Ana, you presume?) that plays automatically. From behind a bookcase, the video watches Ana in a dark corner of the library; then flashes a view of her from a distance, as she hurries fearfully through the streets of Belfast; then, she is being chased; in the last moments, she finds herself cornered in an alley, and begins to turn to the camera . . . The screen goes dark.

Text below the video welcomes you, if you dare to enter, into a mystery. Register your details and you become a 'Conspirator'. Your purpose will be to help the vulnerable Ana discover what lies at the heart of the city of Belfast, and to protect her from her ominous watcher, the 'beast stirring in the labyrinth'. The last words on the page read simply, 'Good luck to you' (*InvisibleBelfast*, 2011).

Through the Rabbit Hole

This was one of the rabbit holes orchestrated as an introduction to *[in]visible belfast*, an alternate reality game (ARG) which ran in Belfast from 12 May to 19 June 2011. Through a combination of various media, including websites, email, postal mail, radio, graffiti, dead drops (USB memory pens embedded and

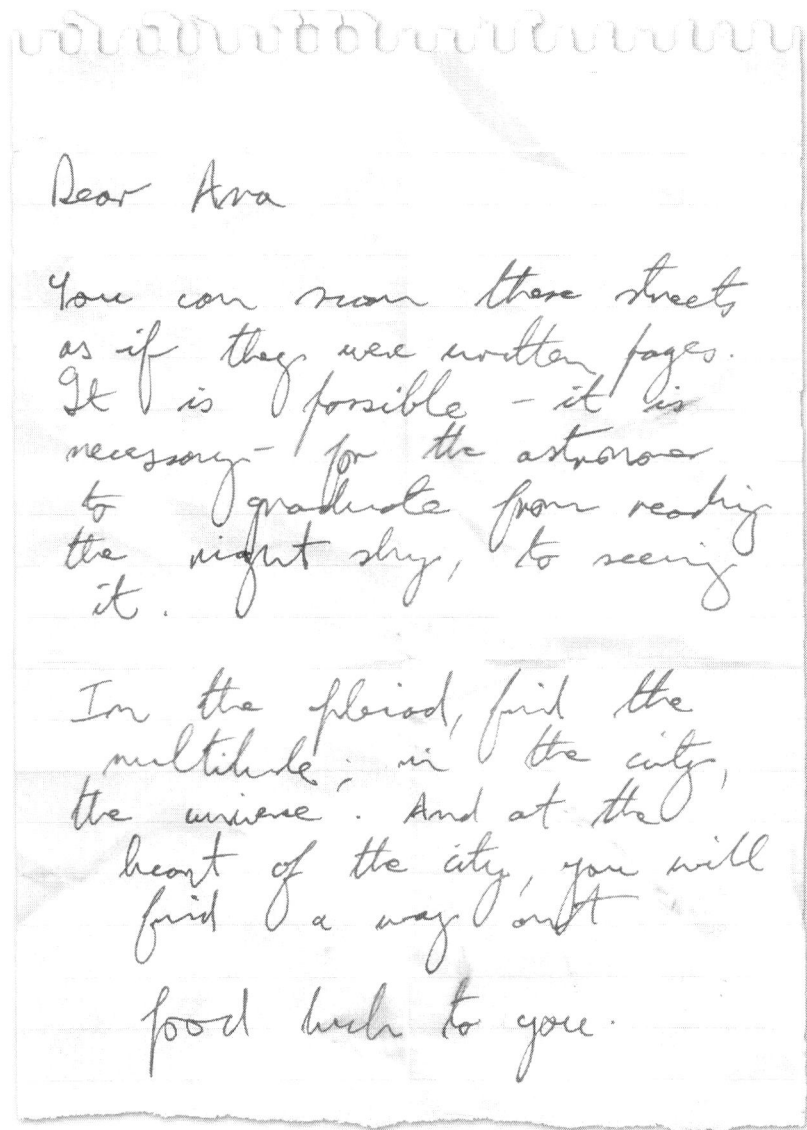

Figure 14.1 The original drafted letter to Ana. This was later replaced with an inscription directly onto the back pages of the game's central artifact, a copy of *The Star Factory*

secured into existing cracks in walls within the city), and live events, game Conspirators joined Ana's quest through the virtual and real spaces of Belfast, helping to build her adventure as they joined in, solving a trail of clues based on the web and in real space.

As an educational and literary project, the *[in]visible belfast* was a reimagining of Belfast writer Ciaran Carson's 1998 novel *The Star Factory*, a book that characterizes Belfast as a 'collapsing city', poised between layers of reality, whose architectural landscape is also a virtual labyrinth, containing 'the city's unconscious, its dark double' (Horton, 1999, p. 342). In designing the game, we sought to create the elaborate, 'many-toothed' beast haunting Carson's Belfast in the form of our Antagonist and ostensible puppet-master, known only by the title '[in]visible belfast', and to employ this multilayered presence as an Antagonist in spurring players through a labyrinth of their own creation (Horton, 1999, p. 343).

From an educational perspective, we hoped to motivate collaborative problem-solving and dispersed story-building, to increase awareness of regional literature and its relationships with world literature, and to challenge players' use of virtual and real space. From a critical-theoretical perspective, we wanted to find out what happens when you place narrative in the hands of players, and to explore new ways of expressing the realities of urban space. The task was an ambitious one, but a fascinating project for us in all its creative and critical facets, from beginning to end, and our responses from players, both during and after the game, have been overwhelmingly positive.

But that isn't to downplay the effort involved. There are countless unpredictable factors in game design when using the real world as a platform, and also infinite provisionality when allowing players to influence the development of a narrative. Because of this, within the ARG, everything is provisional; the form is part story, part game, and part puzzle. We challenged players to find, 'in the city, the universe' – a tall order, for them and for us.

But, let's begin at the beginning. On 8 March 2010, Alan Hook (future 'Antagonist') and Danielle Barrios (future 'Protagonist') decide to create an ARG (see Figure 14.2) . . .

Day –399: Mapping Belfast

The project, in its earliest stages, was a series of variations on the concept of a virtual, literary map of Belfast. We were interested in creating a tool for understanding Belfast through both its geography and its literature, and in the primordial soup of early planning, this had the potential to take several forms. Among the more modest of these was a map of the Falls Road with geo-cached bits of poetry, a sort of poetic route through the city accessible via Google; among the more ambitious, a version of Carson's labyrinthine, rhizomatic Belfast fleshed out (so to speak) in the virtual platform *Second Life*. In the end, what the Belfast-based ARG could have which the other versions of a 'Carsonian' Belfast could not was groundedness in the actual city, and impetus for players to explore real places along with virtual spaces. Experiencing the actual city in new ways, we felt, would be crucial to deepening understanding of its literature.

Figure 14.2 We used a range of means to draw attention to the game, for example stencil graffiti with water soluble paints, which washed off in the rain

It was also important that Ana, the name eventually given to our Protagonist, had much to learn about the city as well. We brought Ana from Canada, made her an international student based in the Astronomy department at Queen's University, a character as foreign to the urban landscape of Belfast as possible. This gave players a fresh set of eyes through which to re-learn Belfast. Ana was also effectively detached from the politics and history of the city by being an outsider, giving her a neutral relationship to any inherent regional politics in the game. As the Protagonist of the game narrative, Ana would be an identity designed to interact with players, a character on the internet by various social networking sites (Twitter, Facebook, Blogger), and also a character available for in-person interaction at live events. She was to be a resource to help players through the maze as an ally, and also a source of information that would deepen the narrative: her experiences, past and present, would be revealed on an emerging, textual and posttextual map of the city.

'Engaging players in a game story – if the game is good – shouldn't be too hard. The game's done half your work for you. The most important thing is to think about character, to make your characters real, rounded, with both light and shade to them.'

Naomi Alderman

On the book itself: *The Star Factory*, a portrait of Belfast in thirty-two parts, is spatially organized and driven, and in reading it we make excursions 'into the imagined and remembered fabric' (Stainer, 2005, p. 376) of Carson's city. It's a book that owes something to the novel *Invisible Cities* (Calvino, 2009) in which Marco Polo describes fifty-five versions of Venice to emperor Kublai Khan, frustrating and complicating the concept of empire. In his many descriptions of his own versions of Belfast, Carson engages in what Neal Alexander calls a 'utopian spatial politics,' whereby he 'precludes any privileged position of detached objectivity in favour of active engagement in the writing and re-writing of the city-text' (Alexander, 2008, p. 42), engaging the place while challenging the status quo. Carson's 'somewhat wayward and disorienting textual strategy' creates a sense of 'searching, of constant reordering and redefinition' (Stainer, 2005, p. 376).

We agreed that any transference of Carson's Belfast would have to reflect the nature of Carson's work, and stay true to its style and form. We based much of the game's design from Carson's version of Belfast, including Ana's backstory (she is the invented daughter of a friend of Carson's actual father, a friend who is mentioned in the book), to the themes of our live events (halfway through the game, Ana and the Conspirators attended a play entitled *The Water Clock* (Barrios-O'Neill, 2011), its content based on the section of *The Star Factory* titled 'The Star Factory I' (Carson, 1998, pp. 61–70). We also continually sent players to the book for bits of information and story that would provide answers to the clues (and sometimes sections that would disorientate them further).

True to Carson's style, players would need to learn through involvement, engage through action and take to the streets they investigated. In an ARG, both designers and players learn by doing; in the case of *[in]visible belfast*, we would endeavor to write and re-write (translate) the city-text according to our own methods of tra(ns)versing. We set out to help make the city real for players in a new way, by cutting across administrated boundaries and allowing them to piece it together themselves; thus, they would have new ownership of the city.

Day –236: The Protagonist Comes to Life

On 18 August 2010, Ana initiated her YouTube video blog, a series of videos that is intended (she explains in the first video) as a way to stay in touch with her cousin in America. It is in this vlog that Ana makes her first observations about the city. 'It's really rainy, and really cold . . .,' she says, with a hint of awkwardness, 'but the people seem nice' (AnaDanika49, 2010). In a video uploaded a month into the vlog, still several months before gameplay begins, Ana admits it's still difficult to feel acquainted with the many-faceted Belfast, and she comments that she has a sense of much going on 'under the surface'. Ana also admits to being lonely, which has motivated her to join Facebook.

Leading into the game, we created Ana with as many social media portals as we felt we could effectively manage. In addition to her YouTube channel and active Facebook account, Ana was vocal on Twitter and kept a regular blog. Our use of several modes of communication between Ana and players was intended to give her character depth and believability, and to place her comfortably within the (virtual) landscape of Belfast before the story began. Well before game launch we coordinated with local festivals to drive a long publicity campaign for the game, which also provided ways of making Ana, as well as her Antagonist '[in]visible belfast', emerging presences in the city.

Day –40: [in]visible belfast is Watching

On 2 April 2011, @visiblebelfast made the following post on Twitter: 'At the heart of the city, you will find a way out. www.invisiblebelfast.com.'

The six weeks leading up to launch consisted largely in attempting to attract attention to the game, particularly to the main characters: Protagonist Ana and our Antagonist, known only by the '@visiblebelfast' Twitter ID and the '[in]visible Belfast' signature on emails. The registration page for *[in]visible belfast* was available on the website well before game launch, so [in]visible belfast as a character or entity was in touch with players even before launch. Players could also get in touch with Ana before launch, if they were so inclined, through her social media platforms. It was our prerogative to establish a core player base, and begin encouraging cohesiveness a solid month before the game actually began. We worked hard to create collegiality among early joiners first by keeping a light but continuous dialogue that foreshadowed the launch, and eventually assigning them a collective identity and name ('the Conspirators').

By the nature of their fluid structure, ARGs can be confusing: they tend to be cross-platform and networked, with ample opportunity for players to become lost in the maze. By encouraging cohesion, we hoped to counteract any sense of alienation resulting from this, and to help them learn to rely on the network for support. Inventing the cooperative group identity of the Conspirators was one part of this strategy, clearly suggesting their existence as an entity upon the start of the game, but leaving open their specific purpose.

Communications on multiple platforms were used from the pre-launch period to create ambience around the narrative, meanwhile establishing relationships among the Protagonist, Antagonist, and Conspirators, a means of setting the stage, so to speak, for the coming story. Ana's role was to deliver segments of narrative, to serve as a focal point within the story (both online and in person), and to be afraid; she served to heighten suspense by seeming chased, anxious, and potentially unstable, as [in]visible belfast seemed increasingly threatening. From the start, we intended the relationships and roles of the Antagonist and Protagonist to appear clear-cut, but to become increasingly ambiguous (e.g. for the Protagonist to lose credibility and the Antagonist to take her place as ally to the Conspirators). In the end, however, player response dictated this element of the narrative more than we did.

> 'Games can also provide frameworks for supporting people at the edges of their comfort zones: encouraging them to step beyond and do things they might not otherwise consider doing. This, opportunities for collaboration around creative problem-solving, and the potential for players to take rulesets and run with them are also, I think, very interesting.'
>
> Nikki Pugh

Our player base turned out to be quite active and engaged, so it was important for us to be flexible with story structure, scale, puzzle difficulty, and implementation. This approach led to short production cycles on each segment of the puzzle sequence, in which we wrote new bits of narrative and developing narrative trajectories on the fly – in other words, plenty of late nights and long hours. For us, it was a fairly steady process of responding to players' needs, expectations, and desires. The role of puppet-master is a challenging and exciting space to inhabit, as an educator or theorist, and it's one of the elements that makes the ARG an extraordinary format for learning. Human cognition and machine processing are very different, and we can always sense this gap when using an automated format, for example a computer game. But in the ARG, both sides of the playing field are populated by living creatures, and every move in the game is, to borrow from Katherine Hayles, 'mediated through emotions and the complexities of bodily processing.' (Hayles, 2008, p. 183) An ARG, in other words, is a particularly human form of writing/reading/play.

Day –30: Mapping [in]visible belfast

Our ARG had a sizeable run of five and a half weeks. Throughout the development of the game, it would be paramount to have consistent narrative flexibility (in other words, to keep our plan as specific as possible, but not become attached to it), to have strong recurrent themes, to believably reach key points in the narrative, and to coordinate rewards or milestones with the solving of puzzle sequences. For all of these reasons, having a game map in place was requisite for us.

The planning document can take any form that's comfortable and accessible for puppet-masters; for us, the simplest solution was a sheaf of A4 paper, one leaf for each day of gameplay. Each day was marked with key events, actions required by the puppet-masters, descriptions of how elements would be delivered to players (e.g. 'via Facebook comment and blog post'), calculations of solve times for puzzles, and contingency plans for any failures we could foresee. We would try and ensure that key events were mentioned and supported on a number of channels; for instance, Ana would update her Facebook status to mention her blog or vlog update. This meant that the social media streams supported one another, and players wouldn't miss important parts of the narrative if they weren't active on one or another media platform. This also meant that each event in the game needed a strict solve plan in place ahead of time (with a range of contingencies, depending on the difficulty and importance of the event) to ensure that the narrative trajectory ran smoothly.

As we neared our launch date, Ana was increasingly watched and filmed by [in]visible belfast, always without her knowledge and always in Belfast locales that would become relevant to the game later. These surveillances were made public at www.invisiblebelfast.com. The purpose of the short films we posted was to gain publicity, but the early use of surveillance was also designed to contribute to the ambience that would characterize the game: a sense of paranoia, of stalking and being stalked. Simultaneously, this was a means of generating and maintaining interest from players who registered early.

> 'Invest your best efforts in engaging players at the start of the game and not the end. There's no point creating an amazing finale for your game if players are struggling to get past the first level. It might sound obvious, but it's a surprisingly common mistake made by many commercial games – including some I've worked on!'
>
> Jacob Habgood

Day –15: Buying time – the Precious Bottleneck

Within the narrative and play structures of *[in]visible belfast*, a number of key strands drawn from the literature of the city were woven through the game. Each aspect required different skill sets to tackle the tasks, be that technical expertise, prior knowledge of the works, a diverse approach to research or the ability to think laterally (or sidewise) about the challenges. Often due to the structure of the game, our puzzles worked in what we might call puzzle chains; we produced a series of online puzzles which would lead to an end point that required players to await an event. These puzzle chains were surrounded by narrative progression on the surrounding networked platforms (blog posts, Facebook updates, vlogs and Tweets). Each puzzle in the sequence would yield a new password, and when entered into the website this password would unlock a new page and a new puzzle in the chain. This helped us keep the game pace from spinning out of control: because some players devoted a large amount of time to solving puzzles and raced through the sequences, the waiting period before each event gave other players time to catch up, and gave us time to manage the narrative and upcoming tasks.

The puzzle sequence that launched the ARG established our pattern, where each puzzle was accompanied with some ambient context that sometimes included instructions or clues. This first sequence began with an email sent by [in]visible belfast to registered players, providing the first clue and starting point for the story.

Upon entering the password '666', players were taken to the new page, featuring a section of *The Star Factory*, from which all reference to the name of the book and location the section referred to had been removed. Overlaid on this page was a 1932 city map, featuring the original Star Factory building. If players identified the building or text and entered 'thestarfactory', it would lead to the next puzzle and so on.

The final puzzle in this sequence consisted of a page torn from *The Star Factory*, scanned and with a message imprinted in Braille, which translated read:

FOLLOW VISIBLE BELFAST YOUR NEXT CODE WILL BE RELEASED AT 12 NOON WEDNESDAY THE 18 OF MAY GOOD LUCK TO YOU

This would delay all players moving forward until others had caught up on the puzzles and narrative. We used this simple puzzle chain not only to work as a bottleneck, but also to introduce players to some of the ideas, sequences, tools, and patterns that they would need later in the narrative; these included, for a few examples, the use of Twitter, the recurrent use of codes and ciphers, and notions of the city changing with time. These bottlenecks were a useful tool during the game, although admittedly, they can be frustrating for players who work fast.

Day 0: Game Launch

Repeatedly during the process of promoting *[in]visible belfast*, we were faced with competing and often conflicting goals. One problem that arose frequently was determining how to attract interest in the new and somewhat confusing concept of an ARG, while also creating suspense by not giving too much away. In many places as in Belfast, there is no substantial existing ARG player base, so a large part of our task was to attract people who had never heard of an ARG to play one. With marketing, as with many other aspects of game design, we were obliged to mix traditional and non-traditional methods.

On 9 May, we were offered a next-day slot to promote the game on BBC's *Arts Extra* programme with Radio Ulster. This would need to be a short piece in which Ana would be discovered and approached in a Belfast bookshop, and informed that she is the focus of a growing conspiracy called '[in]visible belfast'. In the same broadcast, we had to find a way to make it somewhat clear what *[in]visible belfast* actually was, and attempt to attract players. It was a golden opportunity with some daunting strings attached.

In effect, we had roughly eight minutes to explain the concept of an ARG to the reporter as well as to Northern Ireland, to give our Protagonist and Antagonist a public voice without spoiling the game launch in two days' time, and, most importantly, to try to convince the radio-listening public to get on board with future media.

> 'Are you Ana?' you hear the reporter ask. 'I have a message for you.'
> 'Who are you?' Ana asks falteringly.
> 'It doesn't matter. I was told to give you this message: Look carefully at everything you receive.'
> 'I don't understand,' Ana says. 'Who are you? . . . Are you one of them?'
>
> (*Arts Extra*, 2011)

The clue from the radio broadcast, in combination with a clue sent to Ana in the post two days later which Conspirators helped her examine carefully, led them to Belfast's famous Linen Hall Library, where she came upon the altered copy of *The Star Factory*. Crucially, this was a central artifact of the game which gave us some control over the narrative: Ana was the only one with access to the book, and she could release its information at will.

In the first week, Ana encouraged the Conspirators to start a game wiki as a bank of useful information. This became an extremely useful resource for players in solving puzzles, and for us when deciding how to craft a narrative line or puzzle sequence that would address players' questions and interests. It also encouraged players to become independent of our direct guidance, by asking them to forge their own set of goals and values within the game. This, in turn, influenced the direction of the narrative.

Day 12: Lost in the Labyrinth

The inner workings of the ARG require that, at least some of the time, players feel disoriented and lost. This is a necessary condition of coming to see the context (in our case, Belfast) differently. But it can be challenging for new players to embrace the labyrinth, with its rhizomatic sequences of clues, a narrative that jumps back and forth between virtual and real-world layers at will, characters that exist in multiple realities. One way of approaching this was to make our Protagonist a bit of a lost soul herself. On 22 May Ana blogs:

> This game sometimes feels like a sort of maze. I'm often confused. It's clear that some people are in their element and discover things quickly, but many like me are usually lost. I have to say, I'm not used to asking for or accepting help. I hate it, in fact, and always have. But in this case, if I'm to be any kind of proper protagonist, I do need help.
>
> (Danika, 2010)

Eventually, players will hopefully catch on that the game doesn't follow a traditional, linear pattern, that this is part of the point. In effect, they're learning to trust guided, but largely unstructured, learning paths. The end result will ideally be that players hone skills associated with creating and implementing their own structures (the wiki, for instance). But the period before this happens can be a drop-off point for many players, so addressing the issue of 'lostness' was for us an ongoing effort.

The main narrative ran as a thread through the game structure to facilitate and anchor play, but as the narrative progressed and players became more involved, our authorial role became less 'ours' and more dispersed among ourselves and players. The Conspirators were apt to create new lines of flight via alternative interpretations of the story which we hadn't foreseen. Players were also encouraged to create videos that directly gave their explicit views on what in the game was interesting, and what might be most important to solving the central mystery of the game.

Both the creators and players established a number of spaces to communicate and collaborate. Some of these were necessary from the beginning (e.g. the emails from [in]visible belfast; Ana's blog and its comments section) and tended to be more hierarchical. Some that gained momentum further into gameplay, like Twitter and the wiki, were more leveling in their structure, and put the Antagonist, Protagonist, and Conspirators on a similar level. At times, the variety of modes was confusing for both players and producers, but we held that it was important to have different forms of communication, across multiple platforms, to provide players with a richer narrative experience.

Day 30: Letting Go of the Pen

On June 11, a Conspirator added a post on the wiki (see Figure 14.3). That wasn't what was supposed to be happening in the game at the time; we intended no specific connection between the photographs that the player refers to and Ana's father. However, this was one of many valuable opportunities to play to the Conspirators' observations, instincts, and interests. Two days later, Ana Tweets that she seems to see her father everywhere; four days later, she is obsessed with a sense of his presence in Belfast, the past invading the present. It's not definite whether the insightful Conspirator put the idea in Ana's head, or in ours.

We were often consciously working against players' competing habit of focusing on ideas of qualifiable correct answers ('Am I doing this right?'), traditional linear narrative structures ('Was I supposed to find this now?'), and fixed outcomes ('This isn't what I expected to happen now').

It's to be expected that many players' approach to the narrative structure, puzzle mechanics, and player interaction will be heavily anchored by traditional forms of media, and they won't expect to have much agency in the story-writing process. But very often, in our case, things happened at the wrong

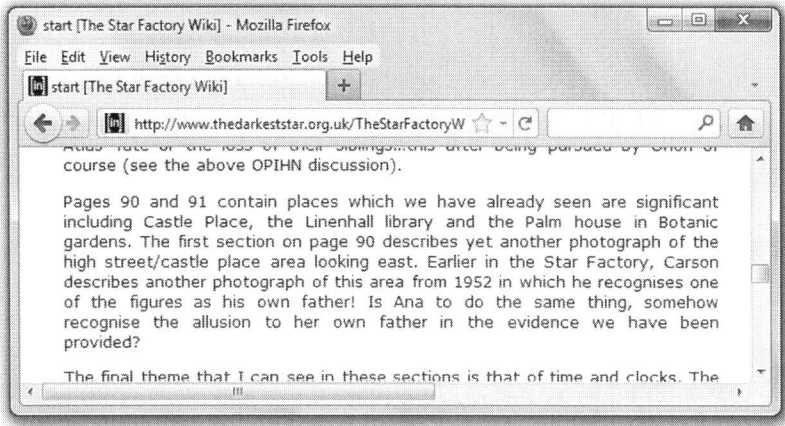

Figure 14.3 The player Richard Thompson's reflections on events within the narrative which we used to develop our story

times, people found things that we never knew to hide, and stories appeared in their investigations that were better than what we had planned. The choices of what to play up to were of course, ultimately ours, but if the story faltered logically or the storyline got lost, or even simply became less interesting, players were vocal – and we had to respond.

In one sense, managing the *[in]visible belfast* narrative was less a matter of writing it, and more a matter of composing a meaningful amalgamation of our own ideas and those of the players as they came to light – expressing, variously, our own goals, and the players' concerns. This isn't to say we indulged every question or prediction with an affirming event, but rather that we continually managed desire and expectation, which is sometimes about subverting them.

All of the above refers to the way that the Antagonist, Protagonist, and side characters communicated the narrative. But the Conspirators also had opportunities to directly communicate the story to the group: in the wiki, through Twitter and Facebook, in the videos they created, and following each live event. In such ways, their interpretations formed the 'alternate' reality. The game became an ongoing system for creating meaning, whereby players would catch us up, we would catch them up, or we would catch each other up; and each time this happened, some element of the story had to change. The narrative outcomes of the change would then drive the next part of the game.

Day 45: The Loose Ends of Non-linear Narrative

All of that said; it was still in our interest to deliver a satisfying ending to players, a problematic goal in a non-traditional, non-linear medium. In a story that was intended to have many interweaving threads, rather than a single line, it was impossible to fashion a neat ending, or induce the cathartic moment that the members of almost any narrative audience will be hoping for.

For us, the defining features of *[in]visible belfast* were everything that happened between the storylines: ambient exchange in dialogue, breaks from original narrative intent, jumps between layers of reality. We were always most interested, not in the success or failure of the story-as-game, but rather in the game-as-storytelling machine: the game that builds a story rather than the story that limits a game.

At least for us, the game was never about catharsis, or a moment of change; the game was itself a process of change. To try to produce a traditional, closed ending felt not only artificial but precisely counter to what our ARG's structure was about. As a potential solution to this, at a final live event we brought together the main characters and central elements of the game, gathered the players into a creative mass in person, and hoped they would write their own ending, if indeed they needed one. This final event resulted in the spontaneous construction of some very entertaining tales – some that offered closure, and some that did not.

Back to Reality

It may be rhetorical to now attempt to consider the success or failure of *[in]visible belfast* as an ARG. Surely it was successful in some ways; at least as often, it was a more enjoyable experience where the narrative or puzzles failed, players responded, and we integrated their responses into the game design. It's our contention that there is no way to 'fail,' so to speak at an ARG, unless it's by creating something which isn't an ARG: in other words, something that isn't flexible, open, and responsive. This aspect of its nature is empowering for those who choose to make an ARG, and those who choose to play.

[in]visible belfast had a small, solid player base, with over 100 enrolled players, and a small core group that were steadily engaged for the duration of gameplay. Having a small core group meant that we could personalize the experience for the most involved players, react directly to their questions, and respond quickly to their input. Within the core player group there were Conspirators from across Europe and the United States. For this reason, it was important for us to balance the interactions between online and live events, so not to exclude players unable to attend live events.

As for our specific goals – to encourage explorations of the urban space, to encourage explorations of the literature we engaged – undoubtedly the game did that. It was entertaining for us all, we think, to take gaming out of the SimCity-esque non-space of the digital world, into the real space of Belfast, complex palimpsest that it turned out to be. As an educational tool, gaming provides something that a classroom struggles to produce, and that even adults need, which is an area for play. In some senses at least, we did make a play-ground of Belfast within the context of the game, and, we hope, outside the game as well. Last year, street artist Banksy told a writer of the *Sunday Times*, 'I still paint graffiti because I genuinely think the side of a canal is a more inter-esting place to have art than a museum' (Mills, 2010). For that reason and others, we enjoyed opening the book, the art-ifact, onto the interactive, real space of the city.

Part V

Conclusions

15
CONCLUSIONS

NICOLA WHITTON AND ALEX MOSELEY

This book has examined whether and how games can inform and support learning, first by drawing on five of the key principles of games that can be applied to education, and second, by looking at practical ways in which low-cost games can be integrated into learning and teaching contexts. In this final chapter, we will draw together some of the overarching themes from across the book as a whole, and reflect on the current challenges in the field of learning and games.

In this book, we hope to have moved beyond the common view of game-based learning as necessarily using high-end commercial games, with the associated high production values and development costs, to discussing a range of options that put the control for design back in the hands of educators. Using mixed reality games, such as alternate reality games (ARGs), virtual worlds and traditional games allows the focus of game development to move from the design of the media to focus on what we believe to be the more crucial aspects of game design and learning design.

Throughout this book, six key themes have emerged, which are at the heart of how we see games can best be used to support learning in all contexts.

Pedagogy

The pedagogic approach and value must underpin the use of games for learning. The assumption that games will automatically motivate learners is flawed. In Chapter 2 we saw how good games in themselves exemplify good learning design; and this is fundamental to our approach to games and learning. While the theme of appropriate pedagogy is embedded throughout most of the book, it stands out in particular in Chapter 4, where the importance of community and collaboration (and what we can learning from games in this respect) is discussed, and in Chapter 8, which highlights the importance of authentic contexts for ensuring that learning is based in reality and transferable. Chapter 13, which focused on the affordances of virtual worlds for creating learning games, also puts their pedagogic potential to the fore. The key message, for us, is that the game and the medium must be pedagogically appropriate for the learners and the learning outcomes; without that, the value of using games is lost.

Integration

The issue of how to appropriately integrate games into a curriculum is addressed throughout the book; this is a fundamental aspect of game-based learning and one that is problematic. Using commercial-off-the-shelf games offers limited opportunities to tailor the timing or gameplay to particular teaching settings, but bespoke game design puts much of this control back in the hands of the teacher. The appropriate use of games, their acceptance as purposeful by learners, and the practicalities of their use, all need to be considered before they can reach their full potential as learning tools. Chapters that particularly focus on ways in which to achieve successful integration are Chapter 9, which looks at how a game can be designed to map on to a specific curriculum, and Chapter 10, which highlights the importance of assessment and games.

Motivation

A third theme that occurs throughout the book is how to motivate learners to engage with the learning process; and this is a particular area in which games can offer insights that can be applied to learning. While games cannot be considered to be universally motivating (particularly in terms of motivation to play in the first place), they embed different ways of supporting sustained engagement and motivation to continue. Chapter 3 examines the ways in which challenge is designed into games to support the transition from novice to expert and keep users playing 'just one more level', and Chapter 6 focuses on competition in games and its appropriate transition to learning situations; both highlight the importance of motivation in learning and what can be learned from games.

Affordability

The theme of affordability of games also runs throughout. This book aimed to take the emphasis from expensive commercially produced games, to those which can be developed locally by teachers, students, or small teams. This focus on simple, affordable approaches is a crucial step in aligning the pedagogic role of the game with the needs of the learner and teacher in a specific situation. While this theme is alluded to in almost every chapter, it is Chapters 11 and 12 (showing how traditional and ARGs can be developed and employed) and Chapter 13 (which focuses on the role and value of virtual worlds for gaming and learning) that show how straightforward it can be for anyone to implement game-based approaches.

Creativity

A key principle that we have also tried to embed throughout is that game-based learning is not simply about using games to convey content, but is also about designing and building games (both for learners and teachers) and using game principles in as many creative ways as possible. Learners are unique and teaching contexts vary from institution to institution, so the notion of a 'one-size-fits-all' game simply doesn't apply; teachers have to be able to adapt and customize, tailor, and tweak. Two chapters in which the creativity angle particularly comes out are in Chapter 5, where the value and design of narrative is discussed, and Chapter 14, which shows its effective application – limited only by the creativity of the game designers – in a learning game.

> 'It's very easy to get tunnel-vision (e.g. we have to make this game about piracy): let the idea go, and let it come to you – the best ideas often come in from the side. I have one good idea in 3-6 months. But then you have to make it. Something really good doesn't come quickly. So my main advice is: be patient. Let the ideas come to you.'
>
> Adrian Hon

Technology

Finally, the theme of technology – or lack of it – is one that we hope cuts right across the book. While game-based learning has been dominated in recent years by big-budget, high-production-value games, and simulation-games, it is crucial to remember that the field of games and learning started long before the popularity of computers. Simple, low-technology, low-production-value solutions, offer an opportunity for teachers and educators to start designing games for themselves. The value of simple technology is highlighted in Chapter 7, which looks at the value of multiple media and makes the case for low-specification games, and Chapter 11, which discusses the design process for mixed-media and traditional games.

We hope that after reading this book you will be at least some way convinced that games can be an effective tool to support and enhance learning and teaching in a variety of educational sectors and contexts. However, their use is not without its drawbacks, and there are a number of major challenges that we see in the field that need to be overcome before the use of games for learning can reach its full potential.

First, the use of games in learning suffers an image problem, with the media prepared to blame computer games for a whole range of ills, from obesity to illiteracy. This means that the role of games (and particularly digital games) in learning is hampered by the negative attitudes of staff, parents, and learners themselves.

Although in recent years game-based learning has grown in acceptability and strength as a field, it will always be hampered by the media image of video games, despite the fact that the vast majority of commercial games are not violent, sexual, or in any way offensive. This challenge – one of educating people and winning hearts and minds – may take a long time to overcome. We suggest some ways that this can be approached at a local institution level in Chapter 9, and this bottom-up approach may be the best way to counter such attitudes in the long run.

A second challenge in the field is the current predominance and emphasis on educational games that adopt a behaviourist model, and focus on lower-level learning skills such as recognition and recall. Games that adopt this model are tried-and-tested, and are relatively easy to develop (commonly being based on standard templates) and evaluate (using a pre-test/post-test design). While we would not argue that these types of game are ineffective, they are merely scratching the surface of what game-based learning has the potential to achieve. It is games that foster deep learning through collaboration, discussion, problem-solving, and creativity that have the power to truly engage students in learning; unfortunately designing and developing this type of game is not an easy task.

Third, there is still a lack of robust research evidence showing the value and efficacy of games for learning. This is particularly true of large-scale and longitudinal studies, and those that compare games with more traditional learning and teaching methods. While there is much evidence that (at least some) learners find games enjoyable, there is little evidence that they are an effective way to learn. This links to our second point above; while the focus of learning games is on behaviourist pedagogic models, it will be difficult to show the true learning benefits that we believe games can bring, when created as active, collaborative, and authentic learning environments.

What this book has achieved, however, is in showing that there are ways in which teachers and educational designers can overcome a fourth problem: that of the difficulty, technical challenges, and expertise required to create bespoke games. By using approaches such as ARGs, virtual worlds, and traditional games, the power to develop can be moved back into the hands of those who best know how to effectively teach the subject, and the diverse needs of their learners. These low-cost approaches enable educators to develop their own games, control how these games integrate with the curriculum, assessment practices and learning contexts, and focus on the aspects – such as creative game and learning design – that really matter in terms of game-based learning. We very much hope that after reading this book you are (at least some way) convinced of the value of games in learning, and enthused to have a go at integrating them into your own practice.

'Games are like magic. They make whole worlds out of almost nothing.'
Jesse Schell

REFERENCES

Alexander, N. (2008). Deviations from the known route: writing and walking in Ciaran Carson's Belfast. *Irish Studies Review*, 16/1, 41–54.

AnaDanika49. (2010). 18 August 2010. [Online] www.youtube.com/watch?v=YcqIGIL-Kik (accessed 11 September 2011).

Arts Extra. (2011). BBC Radio Ulster, Tuesday 10 May.

Bandura, A. and Walters, R.H. (1963) *Social learning and personality development*. New York: Holt, Rinehart & Winston.

Barnett, J. and Coulson, M. (2010). Virtually real: a psychological perspective on massively multiplayer online games. *Review of General Psychology*, 14/2, 167–179.

Barrios-O'Neil, D. (2011). *The Water Clock*. First produced 18 May. Brian Friel Theatre, University Road, Belfast. Performers: Emma Copland, Roger Dane, Mary-Frances Doherty, Charmaine McBride, Kim Moylan, Cathy Quinn. Director: Jack Geary.

Bekebrede, G., Warmelink, H.J.G., and Mayer, I.S. (2011) Reviewing the need for gaming in education to accommodate the net generation. *Computers & Education*, 57/2, 1521–1529.

Biggs, J. (1999). *Teaching for quality learning at university*. Milton Keynes: Open University Press.

Black, P., Harrison, C., Lee, C., Marshall, B., and William, D. (2003) *Assessment for learning: putting it into practice*. Milton Keynes: Open University Press.

Bottino, R.M. and Ott, M. (2006) Mind games, reasoning skills, and the primary school curriculum. *Learning, Media and Technology*, 31/4, 359–375.

Bourdieu, P. (2002). The forms of capital. In N.W. Biggart (ed.) *Readings in Economic Sociology*, 280–291. Oxford, UK: Blackwell.

Bowlby, J. (1958). The nature of the child's tie to his mother. *International Journal of Psycho-Analysis*, 39, 350–373.

Boyer B. (2008) Ubisoft: Wii to rule them all, Microsoft/Sony battle split in U.S/Europe. [Online] www.gamasutra.com/php-bin/news_index.php?story=18389.

Brookes, S. (2009) Using an alternate reality game to teach enterprise. Learning and Teaching in HE blog entry posted 3 November. [Online] http://simonbrookes.wordpress.com/2009/11/03/using-an-alternate-reality-game-to-teach-enterprise/ (accessed 8 August 2011).

Brown, E., and Cairns, P. (2004). A grounded investigation of game immersion. In *CHI '04 extended abstracts on human factors in computing systems*, 1297–1300. New York: ACM.

Brown, J.S. and Adler, R.P. (2008). Minds on fire: open education, the long tail, and learning 2.0. *EDUCAUSE Review*, 43/1. [Online] http://connect.educause.edu/Library/EDUCAUSE+Review/MindsonFireOpenEducationt/45823 (accessed 26 July 2011).

Brown, J.S. and Thomas, D. (2006). You play world of warcraft? You're hired! *Wired*, 14 April. [Online] www.wired.com/wired/archive/14.04/learn.html (accessed 26 July 2011).

Bruner, J.S. (1966). *Toward a theory of instruction*. Oxford: Oxford University Press.

Caillois, R. (2001) *Man, play and games*. New York: Free Press.

Calvino, I. (2009). *Invisible cities: new edition*. London: Vintage Classics.

Campbell, J. (1993). *The hero with a thousand faces*. London: Fontana Press. Carr, C. (2006) Games and narrative. In D. Carr, D. Buckingham, A, Burn, and G. Schott (eds) *Computer games: text, narrative and play*. Cambridge: Polity.

Carson, C. (1998). *The star factory: new edition*. London: Granta Books.

Charlier, N. and Clarebout, G. (2009). Game-based assessment: can games themselves act as assessment mechanisms? A case study. In *Proceedings of the 3rd European Conference on Games Based Learning*. Graz: Academic Conferences.

Charlier, N. and De Fraine, B. (2010). Games based learning as a vehicle to teach new content: a case study. In B. Meyer (ed.) *Proceedings of the 4th European Conference on Games Based Learning*. Reading: Academic Publishing Ltd.

Chew, E., Jones, N., and Blackey, H. (2009). A UK case study – technology enhances educational experiences in the University of Glamorgan. In *Proceedings of 2009 International Conference on Future Computer and Communication*, 212–216. Wuhan, China.

Cohen, K. and Rhenman, E. (1961). The role of management games in education and research. *Management Science*, 7/2, 131–166.

Colarusso, C.A. (1993). Play in adulthood. *Psychoanalytic Study of the Child*, 48, 225–245.

Collins, A., Brown, J.S., and Newman, S.E. (1989). Cognitive apprenticeship: teaching the craft of reading, writing and mathematics! In L.B. Resnick (ed.) *Knowing, learning, and instruction: essays in honor of Robert Glaser*, 452–493. Hillsdale, NJ: Erlbaum.

Connolly, T.M., Stansfield, M., and Hainey, T. (2011) An alternate reality game for language learning: ARGuing for multilingual motivation. *Computers & Education*, 57 (1), 1389–1415.

Cooper, P.A. (1993). Paradigm shifts in designed instruction: from behaviorism to cognitivism to constructivism. *Educational Technology*, 33/5, 12–19.

Cormier, D. (2008). Rhizomatic education: community as curriculum. *Innovation*, 4/5. [Online] www.innovateonline.info/index.php?view=article&id=550 (accessed 27 July 2011).

Cramer, K., Suter-Giorgini, N., Moss, K., Gill, E., and Donegan, S. (2011). Serious (but fun) games for effective learning in genetics. In *Proceedings of the Effective Learning in the Biosciences Conference 2011*, 23.

Csikszentmihalyi, M. (1992). *Flow: the classic work on how to achieve happiness*. London: Random House.

Danika, A. (2011). Starfish signs: the moving staircase of the beast. Starfish Signs. [Online] http://anadanika49.blogspot.com/2011/05/moving-staircase-of-beast.html (accessed 11 September 2011).

Dansky, R. (2007). Introduction to game narrative. In C.M. Bateman (ed.) *Game writing: narrative skills for videogames*. Boston, MA: Charles River Media.

de Freitas, S. (2006). *Learning in immersive worlds*. JISC report. [Online] www.jisc.ac.uk/eli_outcomes.html (accessed 11 September 2007).

Dignan, A. (2011) Game frame: using games as a strategy for success. New York: Free Press.

Douglas, Y. and Hargadon, A. (2000). The pleasure principle: immersion, engagement, flow. In *Proceedings of the eleventh ACM on hypertext and hypermedia*, HYPERTEXT '00, 153–160. New York: ACM.

Downes, S. (2007). What connectivism is. Half an Hour blog entry posted 3 February. [Online] http://halfanhour.blogspot.com/2007/02/what-connectivism-is.html (accessed 25 July 2011).

Ducheneaut, N., Yee, N., Nickell, E., and Moore, R. J. (2006) 'Alone Together?' Exploring the social dynamics of massively multiplayer online game. In *Proceedings of the SIGCHI Conference on Human Factors in Computing Systems (SIGCHI 2006)*. New York: ACM.

Dunlop, F. (1976). Competition in education. *Cambridge Journal of Education*, 6/3, 127–134.

Ebner, M. and Holzinger, A. (2007). Successful implementation of user-centred game based learning in higher education: an example from civil engineering. *Computers & Education*, 49(3), 873–890.

Egenfeldt-Nielsen, S., Smith, J. H., and Tosca, S. P. (2008). *Understanding video games: the essential introduction*. New York: Taylor & Francis.

Elliott, J., Adams, L., and Bruckman, A. (2002). No magic bullet: 3D video games in education. In *Proceedings of ICLS 2002*. Seattle, WA, October. [Online] www.cc.gatech.edu/elc/aquamoose/pubs/amicls2002.pdf (accessed 9 September 2002).

Faria, A. and Nulsen, R. (1996). Business simulation games: current usage levels – a ten year update. *Developments in Business Simulation & Experiential Exercises*, 23, 22–28.

Folmann, T. (2004). Vocalized game audio. *Official BLOG of Troels Folmann* blog entry posted November 8. [Online] http://troelsfolmann.blogspot.com/2004/11/vocalized-game-audio.html (accessed 9 September 2011).

Gardner, H. (1993). *Frames of mind: the theory of multiple intelligences*. New York: Basic Books.

Gee, J. P. (2003). *What video games have to teach us about learning and literacy*. New York: Palgrave Macmillan.

Gee, J. P. (2007a) Affinity spaces: from age of mythology to today's schools. In *Good video games + good learning: collected essays on video games, learning, and literacy*, 87–103. New York: Peter Lang.

Gee, J.P. (2007b). *What video games have to teach us about learning and literacy*, 2nd ed. New York: Palgrave Macmillan.

Gershenfeld, A. (2011) Game-based learning: hype vs reality. *Huffington Post* blog entry posted 3 April. [Online] www.huffingtonpost.com/alan-gershenfeld/game-based-learning-education_b_843001.html (accessed 5 August 2011).

Gillespie, L. and Lawson, C. (2011). *WoWinSchool: a hero's journey: a middle grades language arts adventure*. [Online] http://wowinschool.pbworks.com/f/WoWinSchool-A-Heros-Journey.pdf (accessed 26 July 2011).

Hagel, J. and Brown, J.S. (2009). How *World of Warcraft* promotes innovation. *Business Week Online*, 14 January. [Online]. www.businessweek.com/innovate/content/jan2009/id20090114_362962.htm (accessed 26 July 2011).

Harp S.F. and Mayer R.E. (1998) How seductive details do their damage: a theory of cognitive interest in science learning. *Journal of Educational Psychology*, 90/3, 414–434.

Hayles, K. (2008). The future of literature: complex surfaces of electronic texts and print books. In J.J. Bono, T. Dean, and E. P. Ziarek, (eds) *A time for the humanities: futurity and the limits of autonomy*. Bronx, NY: Fordham University Press.

Hayward, D. (2005). *Videogame aesthetics: the future!* Gamasutra. [Online] www.gamasutra.com/features/20051014/hayward_01.shtml (accessed September 2011).

Hazard, C. (2010). *Feedback in games design*. Wolfire Games blog entry posted 2 April 2010. [Online] http://blog.wolfire.com/2010/04/Feedback-In-Game-Design (accessed 20 July 2011).

Herrington, J., Oliver, R., and Reeves, T. C. (2003). Patterns of engagement in authentic online learning environments. *Australian Journal of Educational Technology*, 19/1, 59–71.

HEFCE (2011) *Widening participation*. [Online] www.hefce.ac.uk/widen/ (accessed 30 August 2011).

Hollins, P. and Robbins, S. (2009). The educational affordances of multi-user virtual environments. In D. Heider (ed.) *Living Virtually: Researching New Worlds*. New York: Peter Lang Publishing.

Horton, P. (1999). From romantic to postmodern: imagining the real in the work of Ciaran Carson. *Canadian Journal of Irish Studies*, 25/1–2, 337–351.

Hoyle, M.A. (2011) 'Multiplayer' vs 'multiplayer'. E1n1verse – WoW, learning, and teaching by Michelle A. Hoyle blog entry posted February 24. Available from: http://einiverse.eingang.org/2011/02/24/multiplayer-vs-multiplayer/ (accessed 26 July 2011).

Huizenga, J., Admiraal, W., Akkerman, S., and Dam, G. (2009) Mobile game-based learning in secondary education: engagement, motivation and learning in a mobile city game. *Journal of Computer Assisted Learning*, 25/4, 332–344.

InvisibleBelfast. (2011). *[in]visible belfast*. [Online] www.youtube.com/watch?v=9B9zlB0IK24 (accessed 11 September 2011).

Ivan T. (2009). *Ubisoft: development costs to double next gen.* [Online] www.next-gen.biz/news/ubisoft-development-costs-to-double-next-gen.

JISC (2011a). *Developing digital literacies.* Web page. [Online] www.jisc.ac.uk/developing-digitalliteracies (accessed 24 July 2011).

JISC (2011b). Re-engineering assessment practices in Scottish higher education (REAP). [Online] www.jisc.ac.uk/whatwedo/programmes/elearningsfc/reap.aspx (accessed 20 July 2011).

Johnson, D.W. and Johnson, F. P. 1989. *Cooperation and competition: theory and research.* Edina, MN: Interaction Book Company.

Johnson, L., Smith, R., Willis, H., Levine, A., and Haywood, K., (2011). *The 2011 Horizon Report.* Austin, Texas: The New Media Consortium.

Jonassen, D. and Rohrer-Murphy, L. (2008) activity theory as a framework for designing constructivist learning environments. *Educational Technology Research and Development*, 47/1, 61–79.

Jorgenson, K. (2010). Time for new terminology? Diegetic and non-diegetic sounds in computer games revisited. In M. Grimshaw (ed.) *Game sound and player interaction: concepts and developments.* New York: IGI Global.

Joyes, G., and Chen, Z. (2007) Researching a participatory design for learning process in an intercultural context. *International Journal of Education and Development Using ICT*, 3/3, 78–88.

Kaptelinin, V., and Nardi, B. (2006). *Acting with technology: activity theory and interaction design.* Cambridge: MIT.

Kivetz, R. (2003). The effects of effort and intrinsic motivation on risky choice. *Marketing Science*, 22/4, 477–502.

Kolb, D. A. (1984). *Experiential learning: experience as the source of learning and development.* Englewood Cliffs, NJ: Prentice Hall.

Koschmann, T. (1996). Paradigm shifts and instructional technology: an introduction. In T. Koschmann (ed.) *CSCL: theory and practice of an emerging paradigm*, 1–23. Mahwah, NJ: Erlbaum.

Krawczyk, M. and Novak, J. (2006). *Game development essentials: game story & character development.* Clifton Park, NY: Thompson Delmar Learning.

Kriz, W.C. (2008). Bridging the gap: transforming knowledge into action through gaming and simulation. *Simulation & Gaming*, 40/1, 28–29.

Kuutti, K. (1996). Activity theory as potential framework for human–computer interaction research. In B. Nardi (ed.) *Context and consciousness: activity theory and human-computer interaction*, 17–44. Cambridge, MA: MIT Press.

Laurel, B. (1993) *Computers as theater.* Reading, MA: Addison-Wesley.

Lave, J. and Wenger, E. (1991). *Situated learning: legitimate peripheral participation.* Cambridge: University of Cambridge.

Lupo, K.D. and Schmitt, D.N. (2002). Upper Paleolithic net-hunting, small prey exploitation, and women's work effort: a view from the ethnographic and ethnoarchaeological record of the Congo Basin. *Journal of Archaeological Method and Theory*, 9/2, 147–179.

MacDougall, R. (2011). This is not a game. we play the past blog entry posted 7 May. [Online] www.playthepast.org/?p=1421 (accessed 6 September 2011).

Malone, T. W. (1980). What makes things fun to learn? Heuristics for designing instructional computer games. In *Proceedings of the 3rd ACM SIGSMALL symposium and the first SIGPC symposium on small systems*, 162–169. Palo Alto, CA: ACM.

Malone, T. and Lepper, M. (1987). Making learning fun: a taxonomy of intrinsic motivations for learning. In R. Snow and M. Farr (eds), *Aptitude, Learning, and Instruction*; vol. 3: *Conative and Affective Process Analyses.* Hillsdale, NJ: Lawrence Erlbaum.

Marsh, C. (2009). *Key Concepts for Understanding Curriculum* (4th ed). New York: Taylor & Francis.

Martin, A., Thompson, B., and Chatfield, T. (2006). Alternate Reality Games White Paper – IGDA ARG SIG. [Online] www.igda.org/arg/resources/IGDA-AlternateRealityGames-Whitepaper-2006.pdf (accessed 26 August 2009).

Mayer, R.E. (2001). *Multimedia learning*. New York: Cambridge University Press.

McGonigal, J. (2003). 'This is not a game': immersive aesthetics and collective play. In *Proceedings of Melbourne DAC*. [Online] http://hypertext.rmit.edu.au/dac/papers/McGonigal.pdf (accessed 30 August 2011).

McGonigal, J. (2011) *Reality is broken: why games make us better and how they can change the world*. London: Jonathan Cape.

Meloni W. (2010). M2 research *THE BRIEF – 2009 ups and downs*. [Online] www.m2research.com/the-brief-2009-ups-and-downs.htm.

Miller, D.J. and Robertson, D.P. (2010) Using a games console in the primary classroom: effects of 'brain training' programme on computation and self-esteem. *British Journal of Educational Technology*, 41/2, 242–255.

Mills, E. (2010). Banksy in 'the world's first street-art disaster movie.' *Sunday Times*. [Online] http://entertainment.timesonline.co.uk/tol/arts_and_entertainment/film/article7041167.ece (accessed 11 September 2011).

Montfort, N. (2005). *Twisty little passages: an approach to interactive fiction*. Cambridge, MA: MIT Press.

Moseley, A. (2008). *An alternative reality for higher education? Lessons to be learned from online reality games*. Presented at ALT-C 2008, Leeds, UK, 9–11 September 2008. [Online] http://moerg.wordpress.com/publications/ (accessed 28 August 2011).

Moseley, A. (2009a) A case of high engagement: applying immersive online gaming to History research skills. ALT-C 2009, Manchester, September.

Moseley, A. (2009b). The great history conundrum: solving the problem with research skills. 11th Annual Conference for Learning and Teaching in History, Oxford, 1–3 April. [Online] http://moerg.wordpress.com/publications/ (accessed 28 August 2011).

Moseley, A. (2010). Roll, Move Two Steps Back, and Admire the View: Using Games-Based Activities to Quickly Set Authentic Contexts. In *Proceedings of 4th European Conference on Games Based Learning*. Copenhagen, Denmark: Academic Conferences Ltd.

Moseley, A., Whitton, N., Culver, J., and Piatt, K. (2009). Motivation in alternate reality gaming environments and implications for learning. In *Proceedings of the 3rd European Conference on Games Based Learning*. Graz: Academic Conferences.

Nardi, B. (2010). *My life as a night elf priest*. Ann Arbor: University of Michigan Press.

National Curriculum (2011). Aims for the school curriculum. [Online] http://curriculum.qcda.gov.uk/key-stages-1-and-2/aims-values-and-purposes/aims/index.aspx (accessed 30 August 2011).

Niedenthal, S. (2009) What we talk about when we talk about game aesthetics. In *Proceedings of DiGRA 2009: Breaking New Ground: Innovation in Games, Play, Practice and Theory*. London: Brunel University.

NSS (2011). NSS 2010 shows continued high levels of satisfaction among higher education undergraduate students. Press release, 18 August 2010. [Online] www.hefce.ac.uk/news/hefce/2010/nssresult.htm (accessed 12 May 2011).

O'Donovan, A., Tsvetkova, N., Stoimenova, B., Tsvetanova, S., Connolly, T.M., Stansfield, M.H., Hainey, T., Cousins, I., Josephson, J., O'Donovan, A., and Rodriguez Ortiz, C. (2009). The truth about alternate reality games: ARG's in educational method, ARG's as educational method. In *Proceedings of the 3rd European Conference on Games-based Learning*. Graz, Austria: Academic Conferences Ltd.

Piaget, J. (1977). *The development of thought: equilibrium of cognitive structures*. New York: Viking Press.

Prensky, M. (2001). *Digital game-based learning.* New York: McGraw Hill.

Price, M., Carroll, J., O'Donovan, B., and Rust, C. (2011). If I was going there I wouldn't start from here: a critical commentary on current assessment practice. *Assessment & Evaluation in Higher Education*, 36/4, 479–492.

Ramsden, P. (1992). *Learning to teach in higher education.* London: Routledge.

Reeves, C. (2000). Alternative assessment approaches for online learning environments in higher education. *Journal of Educational Computing Research*, 23/1, 101–111.

Rich, J.M. (1988). Competition in education. *Educational Theory*, 38/2, 183–189.

Rieber, L.P., Davis, J., Matzko, M., and Grant, M. (2001). Children as multimedia critics: Middle School students' motivation for and critical analysis of educational multimedia designed by other children. Paper presented at the annual meeting of the American Educational Research Association, Seattle. [Online] www.nowhereroad.com/kiddesigner/research/aera2001-rieber.pdf (accessed 9 September 2011).

Robertson, M. (2010). Can't play, won't play. Hide & Seek blog entry 6 October 2010. [Online] www.hideandseek.net/2010/10/06/cant-play-wont-play/ (accessed 21 July 2011).

Rose, F. (2007). Secret websites, coded messages: the new world of immersive games. *Wired Magazine*. [Online] www.wired.com/entertainment/music/magazine/16-01/ff_args (accessed 11 September 2011).

Rylands, T. (2011). *ICT to inspire with MYST.* [Online] www.timrylands.com/

Salen, K., and Zimmerman, E. (2004). *Rules of play: game design fundamentals.* Cambridge, MA: The MIT Press.

Savery, J.R. and Duffy, T.M. (1995). Problem-based learning: an instructional model and its constructivist framework. *Educational Technology*, 35, 31–38.

Schell, J. (2008). *The art of game design: a book of lenses.* Burlington, MA: Morgan Kaufmann.

Shaffer, D. (2005) Epistemic games. *Innovate*, 1/6. [Online] www.innovateonline.info/index. php?view=article&id=79 (accessed 1 August 2011).

Sheldon, L. (2011) *Gaming the classroom: syllabus.* [Online] http://gamingtheclassroom.wordpress. com/syllabus/ (accessed 10 August 2011).

Siemens, G. (2008) 'What is the unique idea in connectivism?' *Connectivism* blog entry posted 5 August. [Online] www.connectivism.ca/?p=116 (accessed 26 July 2011).

Spinuzzi, C., Hart-Davidson, W., and Zachry, M. (2006). Chains and ecologies: methodological notes toward a communicative–mediational model of technologically mediated Writing. Paper presented at SIGDOC 2006. Myrtle Beach, SC.

Squire, K. (2005) Changing the game: what happens when video games enter the classroom?. *Innovate*, 1/6. [Online] www.innovateonline.info/index.php?view=article&id=82 (accessed 30 August 2011).

Squire, K. (2011). *Video games and learning: teaching participatory culture in the digital Age.* New York: Teachers' College Press.

Stainer, J. (2005). The possibility of non-sectarian futures: emerging disruptive identities of place in the Belfast of Ciaran Carson's *The Star Factory. Environment and Planning D: Society and Space*, 23/3, 373–394.

Steinkuehler, C. and Duncan, S. (2008). Scientific habits of mind in virtual worlds. *Journal of Science Education and Technology*, 17/6, 530–543.

Steinkuehler, C. and King, E. (2009). Digital literacies for the disengaged: creating after school contexts to support boys' game-based literacy skills. *On the Horizon*, 17/1, 47–59.

Sweller, J. (1999). Instructional design in technical areas. Melbourne: ACER Press.

Syvänen, A., Beale, R., Sharples, M., Ahonen, M., and Lonsdale, P. (2005) Supporting pervasive learning environments: adaptibility and context awareness in mobile learning. In *Proceedings of the 2005 IEEE International Workshop on Wireless and Mobile Technologies in Education.* Tokushima, Japan: IEEE.

Szulborski, D. (2005). *This is not a game. a guide to alternate reality gaming.* Raleigh, NC: LuLu Press.

Thomas, D. and Brown, J.S. (2011) *A new culture of learning: cultivating the imagination for a world of constant change.* Charlston, SC: CreateSpace.

Thompson, J., Berbank-Green, B., and Cusworth, N. (2007). *The computer game design course.* London: Thames & Hudson.

Toth, N. and Schick, K.D. (1986). The first million years: the archaeology of protohuman culture'. *Advances in Archaeological Method and Theory,* 9, 1–96.

Trew K., Scully D., Kremer J., Ogle S. (1999). Sport, leisure and perceived self-competence among male and female adolescents. *European Physical Education Review,* 5/1, 53–74.

Vogler, C. (1998). *The writer's journey: mythic structure for writers.* Studio City, CA: Michael Wiese Productions.

Voida, A., Carpendale, S., and Greenberg, S. (2009). The individual and the group in console gaming. In *2010 ACM Conference on Computer Supported Cooperative Work,* 371–380. Savannah, GA: ACM.

Vygotsky, L. (1978). *Mind in society: the development of higher psychological functions.* Cambridge, MA: Harvard University Press.

Weider, B. (2011). Online game teaches citation skills. *The chronicle of higher education.* [Online] http://chronicle.com/blogs/wiredcampus/online-game-teaches-citation-skills/28837 (accessed 27 July 2011).

White, D. (2007a). Cultural capital and community development in the pursuit of dragon slaying. Presented at Games Learning and Society 3.0, 12–13 July. Madison, WI, United States. [Online] http://tallblog.conted.ox.ac.uk/index.php/2007/07/30/cultural-capital-and-community-development-in-the-pursuit-of-dragon-slaying/ (accessed 26 July 2011).

White, D. (2007b). Dave's top 10 musings on the encouragement of community in multi-user virtual environments, 23 July [Online] http://tallblog.conted.ox.ac.uk/index.php/2007/05/14/daves-top-10-musings-on-the-encouragement-of-community-in-multi-user-virtual-environments/ (accessed 26 July 2011).

White, D. and Le Cornu, A. (2010). Eventedness and disjuncture in virtual worlds. *Educational Research,* 52/2, 183–196.

White, D. and Le Cornu, A. (2011). Visitors and residents: a new typology for online engagement. *First Monday,* 16/9. [Online] www.uic.edu/htbin/cgiwrap/bin/ojs/index.php/fm/article/viewArticle/3171/3049 (accessed 8 September 2011).

Whitton, N. (2007a) An investigation into the potential of collaborative computer game-based learning in higher education. PhD thesis. Edinburgh Napier University.

Whitton, N. (2007b) Motivation and computer game based learning, In *Proceedings of ASCILITE 2007,* 1063–1067. Singapore.

Whitton, N. (2009). *Alternate reality games for orientation, socialisation and induction.* [Online] http://argosi.playthinklearn.net/ (accessed 6 September 2011).

Whitton, N. (2010a). *Learning with digital games.* New York: Routledge.

Whitton, N. (2010b). *Assessment of game-based learning.* Webinar [Online] www.transformingassessment.com/events_27_october_2010.php (accessed 11 September 2011).

Whitton, N. (2011). Encouraging engagement in game-based learning. *International Journal of Game-Based Learning,* 1/1, 75–84.

Whitton, N. and Hynes, N. (2006) Evaluating the effectiveness of an online simulation to teach business skills. *e-Journal of Instructional Science and Technology,* 9/1. [Online] www.ascilite.org.au/ajet/e-jist/docs/vol9_no1/papers/current_practice/whitton_hynes.htm

Wolfe, J. (1993). A history of business teaching games in english-speaking and post-socialist countries. *Simulation & Gaming*, 24/4, 446–463.

Yaneske, E. (2010). Case study 4: red frontier. In N. Whitton (ed.) *Learning with digital games*, 178–183. New York: Routledge.

Yee, N. (2006a). The demographics, motivations, and derived experiences of users of massively multi-user online graphical environments. *Presence: Teleoperators and Virtual Environments*, 15/3, 309–329.

Yee, N. (2006b). The labor of fun: how video games blur the boundaries of work and play. *Games and Culture*, 1/1, 68–71.

Zachry, M., Hart-Davidson, W., and Spinuzzi, C. (2008). Advances in understanding knowledge work: an experience report. Paper presented at SIGDOC 2008. Lisbon.

INDEX

Printed in Great Britain
by Amazon